In My Father's House

In My Father's House

The Journey of One Woman Caught in the Sex Trade

Monica Waters

iUniverse, Inc.
Bloomington

In My Father's House
The Journey of One Woman Caught in the Sex Trade

iUniverse books may be ordered through booksellers or by contacting:

iUniverse
1663 Liberty Drive
Bloomington, IN 47403
www.iuniverse.com
1-800-Authors (1-800-288-4677)

ISBN: 978-1-4620-2533-6 (pbk)
ISBN: 978-1-4620-2532-9 (clth)
ISBN: 978-1-4620-2531-2 (ebk)

Library of Congress Control Number: 2011909594

Printed in the United States of America

iUniverse rev. date:06/17/2011

"In my Father's House are many mansions"
Gospel of John, chapter 14, verse 2

Prologue

I love to walk, particularly in the early morning hours. Nature is still unless there is a storm and then for me it is exciting. The night is coming to an end and the day is not yet ready to waken. It is quiet as I listen to the gentle rustle of the leaves and I am aware of my footfall as I set my sights on the looming hill ahead.

My sleeve snags on a jutting tree branch, I catch my breath and suddenly fear replaces serenity. I stumble as I try to escape the cloying damp terror that has captured my thoughts. The trail recedes into this long dark corridor. I wrestle with the conflict between reality and imaginings.

The trees are all around me, the trail clearly marked by the sentinels that line it. It is still incredibly dark. The sky is starless, with a slim sliver of moon threatening to disappear into the drifting black clouds. The night is still. The branches sprawl over me and at times stretch in ungainly fashion, gnarled and misshapen. The darkness has come alive. My thoughts are jumbled with memory of something ugly and painful—something elusive. I become unhinged and I tell myself to take a deep breath and calm down. I stumble deeper into the forest along the shrouded trail. The treetops sway leaving a rustling sound in their wake. I can taste the fear. I am frozen in this space, yet I know this trail. I can do this. I have no reason to be afraid, but something is different. I sense it shrouded somewhere in the midst of my thoughts and the silhouettes caught in the snare of panic. The branches seem to be reaching out for me with their long outstretched arms, fingers elongated and bent. Ribbons of Spanish moss drape over the branches and leaves hang waiting to ensnare me. Wherever I look I see blackness like ink surrounding me. I struggle to stay calm, but panic claws at my throat. I want to run but I know if I do I will become more alarmed and I will lose all control. I could so easily stumble and get hurt or lost if I get off the path.

It is as if I am in a dream and the only escape is to keep on this course, to emerge into the day and wakefulness.

The horrors of my childhood emerge in front of my eyes. The shadows of a basement fill me with an age-old fear. The stairs leading to the dirt floor and aloneness of that dark cavern materialize out of nowhere. I can hear my mother's shrill voice screaming, 'Molly, get into the basement and stay there until I tell you to come out. I swear your antics will be the death of me.'

I don't want to be that child again and yet she is there clutching at my memory. Her energy is real. I am walking this road to a bitter painful past. Somehow, I know I am going to take that journey again. I am a young girl caught in the throes of war, although the war is on a different continent.

Introduction:

In My Father's House is an unusual story that covers the lifetime of a woman who was entrenched in the sex trade for many years. The time expands 75 years of trauma, abuse, friendships, love and survival.

Molly is a unique woman who was abused from age 3 years until she was 17 years old. She spent thirty more years involved in the sex trade and miraculously made her way out to live a productive and happy life.

I have written In 'My Father's House' as a novel rather than a biography. The events in the story actually happened. The places and names have been changed to protect the innocent and the guilty.

Molly is a pseudonym for a prostitute whose terribly abusive childhood led her into the sex trade; the actual events described in the story include bad dates of two other workers who I know.

I have been involved in a street ministry to sex trade workers over the past twelve years. I have come to know and love many of these women. Their stories are filled with drama and abuse that often led to a life on the streets. In order to survive some of them have turned to drugs and alcohol. Some are addicted to sex and as a result their lives have nosedived into a hopeless dark place filled with despair. Others work inside where dates are screened and conditions are much better than the streets. When you work on the street corners of our cities every date is a toss of the dice and you take your chances.

That is not to say working inside is a viable way to make a living. Both are fraught with danger. I have seen despair, loneliness and hopelessness in both.

I have written the details of her story as she related it to me and I have included other incidents that happened to other women in order to hide Molly's identity. I have changed the backdrop of her young years to ensure her contacts would not be able to connect this story to her.

I continue to work with sex trade workers and witness their ongoing struggle to stay alive. Many of them are very dear friends of mine. Others have disappeared, some have been brutally murdered, some suffered permanent physical trauma due to drug overdose and some have committed suicide.

I am saddened that prostitution is still rampant in our society. We harshly judge the prostitutes without knowing what led them into this way of life.

Things are not always as they seem.

My street ministry takes me to some scary places. At times I get calls to go and rescue women who are caught in an abusive situation. The night that I was assaulted was one of those occasions. Helen had called me to come and get her out of a house where she had gone to buy drugs. I am always hesitant to get involved where there are drugs but she sounded frightened and hysterical. Unfortunately for me I went.

I suffered posttraumatic stress syndrome as a result. I remember how bazaar my own behavior was because of this and have included some of those events.

I used this encounter to launch Molly's story.

PART ONE

MOOSE JAW AND THE WAR YEARS.

Chapter 1

His fist slammed into my face with such force that I fell back and landed hard on the gravel driveway. I tried to crawl away but he grabbed my ankles and pulled me back. I clawed at the stones trying to get a hold of anything to stop my motion. All I got for my effort was skinned knuckles and broken fingernails. I stared into the darkness and tried to see his features. The darkness enveloped us but I could see he was very big, in fact he seemed like a giant from my view sprawled on my back on the driveway.

"Stay away from my woman, bitch." He snarled and yanked me to my feet.

My legs were like rubber and I frantically clutched at his shirt to keep from falling on my knees.

"I was only trying to help Helen." I sobbed.

"She don't need help from you or anybody, stay away from here." He bellowed in my face.

"Okay, okay." I yelped afraid he would hit me again.

He let me go and pulled his hand through his hair and glared at me.

"If you ever come back here I'll do a lot worse than this to ya. Do ya hear?" he grabbed my arm and shook me.

"Yes, I sqeaked.

" Now git outta here!"

He shoved me and I stumbled and fell again. I crawled and scrabbled to get to my car. My legs were like mush and wouldn't hold me.

He turned a walked toward the house and then he turned back to me and made a threatening move toward me.

Terrified I struggled to open my car door, my hands were shaking so hard it took several tries to finally get the key in the lock. I opened the door and flung myself into my car and locked the doors. I sat there and shook so hard I was convinced my car would start to vibrate.

I woke with a start. I couldn't get my bearings right away and fumbled and tried to untangle the covers from my legs. I finally realized I was safe in my bed.

The nightmare was fresh and terrifyingly vivid. I knew I wouldn't get anymore sleep tonight. I slipped out of bed and went to make a cup of tea. I felt as if I was going out of mind reliving that terror over and over again.

I thought back to that night and tried to recall every moment of what happened in an effort to ease the terror I felt.

I had planned a quiet night of reading when the phone interrupted the silence.

"Hello!" I barked into the receiver annoyed I had been disturbed. I glanced at my watch and saw it was 10:30 P.M.

A frantic voice answered.

"Molly? It's Helen, I need your help can you come right now?"

"Where are you?" I felt that familiar feeling of dread.

"I am at Pinkies, I need you to come, please!" she sobbed hysterically.

The nightmares are coming more frequently. I wish I had not gone after Helen that night.

My back top teeth were broken and it felt as if my nose was broken. I had put some cold cloths on my eyes and mouth. I took a couple of aspirin and one of my tranquilizers and lay on my couch until morning. I called my dentist the next day and he saw me right away and we made appointments to get repairs done on my broken teeth.

Others on the street who look after their own ensured that justice was done.

I thought I had everything under control and I was back to my normal self, I didn't recognize that the trauma was buried deep in my subconscious until my life started to unravel.

It wasn't just the memory of that night but other memories started to invade my space.

Chapter 2

I was so ticked that I am sure I had steam coming out of my ears. I was waiting for a woman in a huge black SUV to pull out of a spot in the grocery store parking lot, after driving around endlessly looking for a space. I tried to remain patient but my nerves were jangling. I just needed a couple of things from the store and I wanted to get home before the traffic became heavy. What was taking this woman so long? There she was, sorting her recyclable bags according to their color in the back of the car. How ridiculous is that?

"Just put the bags in the car lady and let's get moving! I don't have all day to wait."

Now what the hell was she doing? Putting her lipstick on! I don't believe this! I blasted the horn and laughed as she nearly jumped through the roof of her car, startled. She looked up and saw me.

"Hello! Can't you see me waiting to pull in?" I yelled. I had to back up to let her out.

"Jeez, woman! Where did you learn to drive, I could back a tank out of there!"

As she pulled out, I am damned if a car didn't zoom in ahead of me.

"Where the hell did you come from, lady?" I screamed, blasting the horn again and again. Then I leaned on it. I gave her the finger, yelled obscenities and shook my fist at her. I was so enraged that all I wanted to do was to grab hold of that long perky ponytail hanging off the back of her head and use it to strangle the life out of her.

"People like her don't deserve to exist on this planet," I mumbled to myself, spewing language not fit for public ears. I stomped into the store after finally finding another spot. I looked around to see if the bitch was there but I didn't see her.

I made my way to the hair products aisle and stared at the endless rows of shampoos and conditioners. There must have been a gazillion brands and sizes.

"Oh my gawd," I started to steam up again.

"These are all freaking plastic squeeze containers. With the arthritis in my hands, it's way too hard to squeeze stuff out of these stupid things and it hurts like spit!"

Now I was royally ticked and I lost it. I yanked all the shampoos off the shelf and dumped them on the floor cursing, ranting and raving.

"Companies should be aware of limitations in the elderly! Not that I feel old in fact I don't feel any older than I did when I was thirty but now it's nearly impossible for me to squeeze containers hard enough to make them work," I babbled to myself.

I emptied one shelf and started on the next, totally oblivious to the crowd gathering around me. I continued to seize containers and toss them on the floor. The manager of the store rushed up to me and grabbed my arm.

"Stop that! What's the matter with you? Are you nuts?" he yelled.

Terror gripped me as I tried to get away from him. I heard a buzzing in my head, and I slipped into a space disconnected from where I stood.

"Take your hands off of me, you jerk!" I snarled, trying to fight him off. But then a too familiar face, a phantom of my memory, superimposed itself on the face of the store manager. I fought like a tigress protecting her young. I struggled to keep my memories hidden in the recesses of my mind. Suddenly, I heard his voice.

"Lady, lady, I don't want to hurt you and I don't want to call the police, but you leave me no choice if you don't settle down!"

I saw him through a miasma of memory and rage. Exhausted, I collapsed in a heap on the floor. He knelt down and quietly asked if he could call someone for me. I looked up through eyes spilling over with tears and, for the first time, I saw the mess of bottles of shampoo strewn over the floor around us and people trying to help by picking them up and putting them on shelves. Some shoppers just stood and gaped. I felt humiliated.

"What's your name?" he asked quietly. He reached out to touch my arm and I cringed.

"Molly. My name is Molly," I responded shakily.

"I don't need you to call anyone. I can drive myself home. I just want to go home. Please, just let me get out of here." I swiped at the tears streaming down my face.

"It's okay, Molly. I understand how you feel but I want you to let me call someone for you please. It would make me feel better," he said in a gentle voice. He offered his hand to help me up, but again I pulled away and struggled unaided to my feet. He held out both hands, palms open and stepped back.

"Please let me call someone for you, you are clearly too distraught to be driving."

"Fine, call my daughter, Carin. I am too tired to argue with you." I told him Carin's phone number and he relayed it to one of the staff members nearby, telling her to call right away. I was still very shaky and felt light-headed. I wanted to disappear. I started to pick up the containers and put them back on the shelf.

"Please, Molly, just leave that. My employees will set them up the way they were. It will be easier for them to do it." He relieved me of the container of shampoo I was clutching and handed it to the clerk who was starting to clean up. He sent another employee for water.

"You people can move on and continue your shopping and give us some space here, please." Most of the people moved away while others picked up containers and placed them on the shelves.

"That's okay, just leave them!" he said as he stepped over the bottles, taking one from a lady's hand.

"We can do this and get them in the right order, but thank you for your help." He gave instructions to an employee to block off the aisle.

"Why don't you come with me, Molly to my office where it is quiet and more private?"

He started to walk away from the destruction and I don't know why, but for some strange reason I followed him to his office where he offered me a chair and sat down across from me.

"What happened to set you off, Molly? Was it one of my employees or another shopper? You are obviously very distressed." His voice reflected his concern.

"It wasn't anything to do with anyone here. I am so sorry for making such a fuss and mess. I just want to go home." I squirmed uneasily in my chair and my hands shook so hard the water spilt as I tried to take a drink.

I felt the anger choking me as I searched for Carin. It was obvious in the way the store manager looked at me that he sensed something was going on with me that had nothing to do with his store or the shampoo. I think he sensed that I didn't want to answer any more of his questions. His kindness made the whole thing more difficult to handle. I could easily have lashed out in frustration if only he had been angry. After all, I had made a complete mess of his store, people were upset and naturally curious, yet he stood there behaving like a saint. I glanced around the small office and noticed how stark and dark the room was. There were no pictures on the wall, the desk was cluttered with paper and the floor had no covering. The slim boards were worn and added to the cold, bare look.

My daughter, Carin finally arrived and was brought to the manager's office. I looked up and felt relief at the sight of her.

She was walking quickly and the expression on her face was not happy. She appeared anxious, agitated and embarrassed.

The store manager took her aside and explained what had happened. Carin was upset by what she heard and apologized for my behavior. She told him that I had been a recent victim of a physical attack. He assured her no further action would be taken and I watched the two of them talking in whispers so I could barely hear their conversation. I ground my teeth in disgust when the manager took Carin's arm and led her to where I was sitting. You would have thought they were fast friends instead of two people who had just met under bizarre circumstances.

"Am I invisible here?" I demanded.

"Mother, please, you are embarrassing me!" Carin said sharply, I hoped she didn't mean to sound that annoyed.

"I'm embarrassing you! You both act as if I'm a child to be chastised and set off in a corner! Really, Carin, I expect more from you. You haven't even given me the courtesy of allowing me to explain my side! You have no idea, nor do you seem to care about my feelings. Take me home right now! Here! Do you want to hold my hand so I don't try to escape or maybe get lost in this great big store?"

Carin's shoulders slumped as she rubbed the side of her head. Visibly upset, she thanked the store manager for calling her and he, in turn, thanked her for her prompt response to his call. Carin lovingly put her hand on my shoulder, which I slapped off and we headed out of the store.

"What about my car?" I asked, between clenched teeth.

"Don't worry about your car. I'll get Bill to come for it when he gets home from work," Carin retorted.

Neither one of us said much in the ride back to my home.

"Can I come in for a cup of tea, Mom?"

"Of course you can. I can use a cup myself and I have some fresh baked cookies."

We both got out of the car and she followed me into the house.

"Sit down, Carin, while I make us a pot of tea." I hurriedly filled the kettle and put out a plate of cookies.

Carin guardedly but firmly asked, "What are we going to do about your erratic behavior, Mom?" She shifted uneasily in her chair and fiddled with her cookie. I could see she was uncomfortable, but her voice grated on me and I snapped back at her.

"Oh, for heaven's sake, I had a little episode, Carin! I was upset, that's all. You know, you might consider I had a reason for getting angry and not be so quick to judge!"

"I am not judging you, Mom, but for the past couple of months your behavior has been quite bizarre. I am concerned for you. Look, I'm not threatening you, but maybe you should give some thought to selling the house and moving into one of those assisted living places."

"What did you say?"

Now Carin started to splutter and her face turned beet red. I saw a vein pop out on her forehead. It always happened when she was mad. In a very quiet voice she hissed.

"You obviously have an apparent disregard for my feelings in all of this."

"Pardon," I asked, "did you say something?"

Carin stumbled over her words as she responded.

"Um—I said – um—it is just a suggestion, that you – um—might want to consider selling this house and going into an assisted living place."

She didn't look at me but stared down at her tea. She pulled her hand through her hair and shifted again in her chair.

I leaped up. My cup smashed on the floor, tea splattering over my shoes and the bottom of my pant legs.

"Why don't you call it what it really is? A home! A place where families dump their parents when they don't want to be bothered by them anymore! How can you even suggest that? Look at me! I am healthy! I'm fit, of sound mind and well able to look after my home and myself. There is nothing going on with me! I am just a little stressed. There is no need for you to fly off the handle and make such an outlandish suggestion." I was breathless as the words spilled out.

"Okay, okay, Mom! Take it easy! Let's not do this right now. We've both had a rough afternoon, but, Mom, if you don't get some help with this, we won't have any choice but to take some drastic action and I don't think I need to spell it out for you. I can't keep coming to get you out of scrapes like this. What if I hadn't been home?

You would be on your way to the hospital or the police station. Think about that! Do me a favor, okay? You know Michael who is a psychiatrist and a friend. Why don't you give him a call and see if he can suggest someone for you to talk to? Just explain to him what's been happening with you and see what he thinks. Okay, Mom?" Carin shrugged into her coat and started for the door, clearly upset.

"Fine! I'll call Michael and see what he suggests. Don't forget to send Bill for my car; I'll need it in the morning. Thanks for the ride home and your loyal support in the store. Oh dear! I hope I didn't get things all confused in my addled, pathetic mind. That was you who took the side of the store manager, was it not? Or am I suffering a 'senior moment' here?"

"You're impossible! There's no point trying to talk to you right now. I'll call you later, Mom, and you can tell me what Michael said and we can discuss our options then. Bill will be home around six and I'll have him pick your car up before dinner."

Chapter 3

A loud knock on the door jarred me awake. I had drifted off while watching the news. I opened the door to Bill, my son-in-law.

"Here are the keys to your car. I parked it in your driveway," he said, handing the keys over.

"Thanks, Bill. Do you want to come in for a cup of tea?"

"No thanks. Carin is waiting in her car. We have to get back for supper with the kids."

"Alright then, thanks again, Bill. Say 'Hi' to the kids for me."

"I will, Molly," he said as he left.

I hung up the keys and went back to my chair, hoping I could get a little more sleep. But my mind started working overtime and thoughts swirled around in my head.

"I hope Michael can help me. I know I am not behaving well these days. It takes so little for me to fly off the handle, I can't settle my thoughts, I am not going to get any rest right now. I can't seem to shut my brain off. This is stupid there is nothing wrong with me. I am just tired and upset by everything. I need to get a grip."

Michael is a gentle person. He had been in our church for a little over two years and I count him as one of my good friends. He has helped a couple of my friends through some very difficult times. I knew he would be discreet and understanding. At least, I could be sure he wouldn't take Carin's side in this. He knew me well enough to know I was quite capable of looking after my home and my personal needs. I felt foolish having to go and bother him with such nonsense. I have been battered before and much more severely than what that punk coward did to me. I decided that I would call him and ask him to be my counselor. I felt much better after consulting with myself and coming to a decision that was going to work for me.

Chapter 4

I was busy cleaning up my kitchen when the phone rang.

"Hi, Mom, it's Carin. Are you busy right now or can you talk for a couple of minutes?"

"Yes, I can talk; I'm just tidying up the kitchen. What's up?"

"Have you been in touch with Michael and have you got the name of a counselor you can go and see?" Carin's voice reflected her trepidation at approaching me on this touchy topic. She added that she hoped I was in a better frame of mind.

I bristled at the innuendo.

"Yes, I have had a talk with Michael and I've set up a time with him for next week."

"Thanks, Mom, that's really good news. Please keep me in the loop. How are things? I haven't heard from you for a couple of days. No more problems, I hope?" Her voice was now hesitant.

"No, I have to go. I will call you after my appointment with Michael. Don't make any arrangements for me to view any homes just yet. Let's wait until I am declared unfit to care for myself."

"Oh, Mom, you know that is not what I want to do! I am glad you are going for help and I hope you find the answer to whatever is troubling you." Carin sounded exasperated at my sarcasm.

"I'll call you next week Carin."

I finished up in the kitchen as tears slipped down my cheeks as I thought about the conversation with my daughter. I felt extremely emotional and frightened at the thought of selling my home. I hoped that Michael would be able to help me come to terms with all of this.

How I wish I had never gone to help Helen that night

That whole episode churned up all kinds of sensations for me: fear, sadness, anger and hurt. Crying wasn't going to help I knew that. I just couldn't believe Carin would have such a negative reaction about a couple of little meltdowns. I knew things would turn out okay, but I was worried about my appointment and what the outcome would be. I wish these feelings would go away. I had a premonition things were going to get harder and harder. The knot in my stomach felt like a rock. I will try with every ounce of my being to get on top of this. I kept talking to myself, hoping to alleviate the fear that roiled around in my stomach. I tried to watch my favorite soap opera but I couldn't concentrate, I closed my eyes and the memories flooded and assaulted my emotions.

Chapter 5

I remember the train trip and the wonderful nun I met on that long journey.

Suddenly, it was November 1939, the world was in the throes of a war that would last for over six years.

I was almost four years old. I was very small for my age and my dark brown hair hung down in my face most of the time. Everyone always remarked on my green eyes and how tiny I was. We were all excited about taking that train ride. The train station had been bustling with people. There were dozens of soldiers in the station waiting to get on trains; their uniforms looked funny to me. They had many things to carry. Each one had a long bag that was stuffed full like Santa's, with another bag on their backs. When it was time for them to move, they slung the long bag over their shoulders and walked toward a different train. I wondered if they were going to fight in the same war as my daddy?

We were vibrating we were that excited. We had never seen so many people in one spot and they were all talking and hugging and crying. The station was big and the voices seemed to resonate around the room. We stepped onto the dimly lit platform. There was a lot of confusion and noise and I couldn't believe we were ever going to get on. Finally, people started walking to their particular train or the train on which their loved one would leave. We stepped into one of the line-ups. I loved the way the man in the uniform yelled from the train steps.

"All Aboard!" and he helped us scamper up the steps on our short little legs. My poor mother was trying to keep us all together and we didn't do much to help. Joseph and I tagged along, clinging to her skirts as she held the baby in her arms and Ross by the hand. Another man in a uniform showed her our seats.

When we were all on board, the train slowly started to pull away from the platform and I watched, mesmerized, as the people who were standing, waving or walking away drifted from my line of sight. The wonder of it all enthralled me.

I watched the world speed by. The train seemed to be riding the wind rather than the rails. Trees, fields and cities flashed by the windows. It was captivating. I couldn't take my eyes from the window and the blur of the outside terrain speeding by. I could hear music being played as one I had heard playing on the radio.

"I Get Along Without You Very Well" was the song playing in the background. And then our favorite song "A Tisket A Tasket" started to play and my brothers, Joseph and Ross and I sang the words. My mother laughingly told us to hush and settle down. When we had arrived at the station that morning, I had no idea what phenomena were in store for me. Six women, all dressed alike, had boarded the train at the same time as we had. I was very curious because I had never before seen the funny clothes these women wore and I asked my mother about them. She bent down and whispered in my ear.

"They are called nuns and the clothes they have on are called habits."

The colors of their clothes were stark black and white with long skirts that went to the ground. I wondered if they were special people. I wasn't too certain they were real. I thought they might be ghosts dressed in unusual clothes so we wouldn't bump into them or walk through them. They smiled and came over as we all settled into our seats. One of them sat down next to my mother and spoke quietly to her. Another one sat down next to me and asked, "What is your name?"

"Molly," I told her. "What's your name?" She smiled at me and put her arm around my shoulder and hugged me.

"My name is Sister Bernadette."

They couldn't be real ghosts after all or else I wouldn't have been able to feel her or hear her. She told me she was going to come and find me every day and take care of me to help my mommy.

I had no way to know that Sister Bernadette would play such a significant role in my life. Her legacy to me was her deep faith and hope for the future. In my darkest moments I would remember her loving words during that trip. I am convinced it was those memories that helped me to survive the years of torture I endured.

Every day I sat nearest the window so she could be sure to find me. My mother was just too busy looking after Ross, my younger brother, and Emma, my new baby sister. The nuns couldn't help but notice the harried state of her at the station before we got on the train. They had watched and seen that she had her hands more than full. In those days, there was a high level of trust for people of the cloth and I hope my mother remained ever mindful of the wonderful way they had stepped in to help. They took Joseph, my older brother, and me every day, sometimes Ross and, even, Emma. I was really lucky to get my favorite nun as my own.

My family and I were on the move from Sudbury, Ontario to Moose Jaw in Saskatchewan. My father had just enlisted in the army and was being trained to fight in the scary Second World War in Europe. We would see him one more time before he shipped out. Each one of us had a special nun as our guardian angel on that train trip.

I loved to snuggle in her habit and be cradled in her generous and soothing arms. I thought she had a halo around her face and head because she always came in full habit. This warm and loving person had encompassed my whole world. Sister Bernadette kept her promise and it was she and she alone who came to me. She would lift me in her arms and carry me off to some magical place on the train, away from my brothers, sister and mother. It was always quiet and we spoke in whispers to each other. The stories she told were delicious and always filled with hope and beauty. My Bernadette was beautiful and loving. My older brother Joseph had a wonderful nun to care for him as well. How happy we were to see our friends come each day. I adored Bernadette. We went on an adventure early in the morning and those adventures were the best. One day, we settled in a quiet, cushioned seat near the back of the train.

"What would you like to be when you grow up, Molly?"

"Maybe I will be a nurse, a doctor, a pilot, a cowgirl, a writer or even a nun. I might grow up to be a famous horseback rider who can do the best rodeo tricks ever." I bounced excitedly on my seat. It didn't matter what I imagined and shared with her.

She always reassured me.

"You can be whatever you want and go wherever you want, if you want it bad enough, Molly"

My dreams were wild and full of impossibilities, but they were mine and I owned them and only shared them with Bernadette and the stars that I wished on every night. The stories were like a magic potion that soothed my hurt whenever my mother was too stressed to listen or, more importantly, took the time to answer any of my many questions.

The wonders of the train itself were an adventure. At night I lay in my bunk and listened to the sound of the wheels as they ran along the tracks. During the day I stared out of the huge window and watched various animals, the sky and the terrain as it flew by. We ate our meals at a beautiful table where everyone sat down to have dinner together. The cloths on the tables were bright white and the silverware shone like the stars. "Over the Rainbow" was playing softly. I was in awe of it all. The nuns were always there to help and make certain everyone ate well and stayed together. It was a joyful noise with all of us children chattering and vying for attention. How I loved that trip! I never thought about how hard it must have been for my mother. Perhaps even our nuns were glad to go to their own berths at the end of each day.

The journey ended all too soon. When we reached our destination, the good-byes were very painful. I clung to Bernadette, crying into her big billowing skirt, wiping my tears and runny nose on the rough-hewn material.

"I want to stay with you and be with you always; take me with you, please. Please!"

Weeping herself, Bernadette said, "That is not possible, Molly. Your mommy will miss you and she will need you to help her."

Over the years, I wondered where Bernadette went that day. Perhaps she became a nursing nun who cared for and nursed the many physical wounds and broken minds of the men and women who fought and claimed victory at such a terrible price?

I wondered if Bernadette had any idea of what horrors lay in the years ahead for me, and would she have found some way to keep me out of harm's way? I wondered too if Bernadette thought of me over the years and remembered me as I remembered her?

I opened my eyes and wiped away the tears that sad memories produce.

I went into the bathroom, took a shower and went to bed.

Chapter 6

I was very nervous about my appointment with Michael. This was the third time I had dusted the coffee table and, if that wasn't ridiculous enough, here I was talking to myself. *Enough is enough. Time for a nice hot cup of tea and I have time to finish reading that magazine article.*

"Brring!" I nearly jumped out of my skin.

"Hello?" I answered the phone, still feeling the pounding in my chest where my heart had vacated its normal resting place and leapt into my throat.

"Hi Mom! It's Carin. Do you want me to drive you to your appointment today? I kept the morning open in case you want some company, and maybe if it is okay with you, I can explain some of my concerns?" Her voice was cheerful.

"I am able to speak for myself and I can manage the drive quite well, thank you! In fact, I am in the middle of getting ready to go out the door, but I will call you later. I will let you know how things go, if I have the time and the energy when I get home." I didn't mean to snap at her.

"Please don't get huffy, I am just trying to help. I hope I hear from your later. Bye Mom."

I was getting a little put off by these incessant phone calls. Now I really did have to hustle and get going if I was going to make my appointment on time.

I rushed to my closet and made an effort to put the negative thoughts from my head. I grabbed my green top and black slacks.

I was tempted to put on my red pumps just for show, but decided to stay business-like. I took my black pumps. I always wear high heels when I go out because I am only five feet tall and I love to look taller. Although I am neither fat nor thin, I wish I still weighed in at one hundred and twenty pounds rather than the one hundred and thirty-five I now weigh. I pulled on my clothes and ran a comb through my hair. It is thick and coarse and has a nice wave. I rarely have to do anything other than wash and comb it. I keep it chin length and streak it to soften the natural steel gray color. I put on some lip-gloss and grabbed my purse and keys and dashed out the door, hoping the traffic was light.

Michael's waiting room was furnished simply but tastefully and I felt comfortable as I waited for him. I liked the soft colors on the walls and the pictures were all of nature. One was a painting of lovely peonies and lilies. One I particularly liked was a dogwood tree in full blossom. It was beautiful. Another painting was very weird. It was a stylized picture of a very overweight person with strange colors of red and brown that made no sense to me. The floors were highly polished, dark hardwood and on it was a delightful scatter rug of soft pinks and greens against a black background. The magazines were the usual inexpensive type one finds in doctors' waiting rooms. His receptionist greeted me in a friendly voice.

"Hello, can I help you?"

"Yes, my name is Molly Smith and I have an appointment to see Michael."

"Please have a seat and I will let Michael know you are here."

"Thank you." I took a seat.

I had no sooner picked up a magazine to read when Michael came out.

"Hi, Molly! I haven't seen you in a long time!" Michael reached out and hugged me. We went into his office and I sat down while he pulled up a chair in front of me with no desk between us.

"Would you like a coffee, tea or water, Molly?"

"No, I'm fine, thanks, Michael."

"What's going on Molly? You seem pretty tense and nervous."

"It's all so silly. There is a complete misunderstanding between my daughter and me. I've had a couple of rather embarrassing public incidences and now she is making noises that I should consider selling my house and moving into one of those assisted living places."

"Wow! That seems a little extreme! Can you fill me in on these 'incidences', as you put it?"

"I have been upset the last little while and I am having trouble holding my temper, but I am not in need of supervision."

I was most uncomfortable and had difficulty explaining my feelings. I saw Michael straighten in his chair and I got the impression he was tuning in to my evasive responses. I unwittingly started to fiddle with the button on my blouse and then wrung my hands as I searched for the words to downplay my real feelings. Michael seemed to understand my hesitancy and eased me into conversation. He leant forward in his chair with his palms open on his lap.

"Can you be a little clearer, Molly?"

I rose from my chair and began nervously to pace about the room.

"It's nothing! I think we are all blowing this way out of proportion."

"Let me be the judge of that Molly. Just tell me what's been happening. Start by telling me in detail about the meltdowns."

"This last major one started with my losing a parking space to some rude broad and it escalated from there."

I told him what happened in the store and how I simply lost my temper. I admitted that I behaved very badly.

"I certainly don't think that warrants the sale of my house and whipping me into a home, do you?"

"Not on its own. But what is causing you to be so anxious? Has something happened to cause such reactions? It's not like you to be volatile."

"I just think it's unfair for Carin to be taking such a stiff-necked attitude. She knows how capable I am. She knows I walk almost every day, I am involved with my church, I am healthy and I have never asked anything of her nor have I needed any financial help. I maintain my own home, work a few hours in the summer. I am involved with my friends with whom I take trips and we have breakfasts together once a month. I get together every week with very good friends to knit and have tea. All in all, I am very happy with my life."

"Can you tell me if something set you off, besides the woman who jumped into your parking spot?"

I didn't want to tell him about being beaten up, but knew I would have to explain why I had been so restless lately. With tears spilling out of my eyes I took my seat again. I reluctantly told him everything.

"A few weeks before, I had gone to try and help Helen, one of the women from the streets to whom I minister. She had called me late one night, very upset, and asked if I could come and take her to a transition house. Her partner was beating her up. I could hear him in the background yelling obscenities at her and I knew she was in danger. I agreed to go and get her. When I arrived at the general area of her location, it was very dark. The street light was broken. The driveway leading to the house was very long and there were no lights other than my own headlights. It was paved with gravel and the only sounds I could hear were the ping of small rocks as they hit the wheel of my car and the scrunch of the tires. The house turned out to be a duplex and I noticed it was sadly in need of work. The outside was dirty and unkempt. Garbage was in evidence, as well as old furniture tossed aside and empty booze bottles of all brands and sizes."

I went on to explain how I had been brutally attacked.

"The next morning, I was really bruised around my right eye and down the side of my face. I felt incredibly embarrassed by the way I looked. I think I somehow blamed myself and I didn't want anyone to stare at me and think I belonged to some abusive man from whom I didn't have the courage to get away."

When I finished relating this to Michael, I was sobbing. I was angry with myself for not keeping my emotions in check.

"That's terrible, Molly. Have the police arrested him? Do you have to go to court?" Michael reached out to take my hand.

"I didn't report it. I can't go to the police because of the kind of ministry I do. I would lose credibility if I went to the police every time something went wrong. Besides, I hate the police! They don't give two hoots about women in the trade.

"What do you mean? Where does this intense hatred of the police come from?" Michael was on the edge of his seat. I realized I had said too much. I have a problem these days letting my mouth spill out words before I think to stop them.

"It doesn't matter Michael, I'm just blowing off steam, and I should go now. Do you think you can convince Carin that I am perfectly fine and not to worry about me?"

"I think it would be a good idea for you to come and see me a few more times so we can work through some of the feelings you are having. Maybe I can help you deal with some of the issues you are facing right now. I don't believe there is an immediate rush to force you into doing anything you don't want to do, Molly. I think your daughter is just concerned by what she is seeing right now. You admit you are overreacting to situations and this is totally out of character for you, so she is bound to pick up on that. Do you want me to talk to her?"

"No, not right now, Michael. I just want things to go back to where they were before all this happened."

Michael didn't seem too happy to end the session on this note and he asked,

"Can you stay a little longer, Molly? I have time right now and I hate to see you leave distressed."

"No, but thanks. I need to go now."

"Why don't we book another appointment for you for next week?"

"Okay, I'll come back next week. Thanks, Michael."

He saw me out and I left after making an appointment for the following week.

I was not happy at the prospect of going back the following week. I was troubled at the thought of going for counseling anyway, just to keep my daughter from harassing and threatening me. How in the world did it ever come to this kind of conflict in such a short span of time? I have always enjoyed a great relationship with my daughter. *What is really going on here?* I wondered as I made my way to my car.

Chapter 7

Memory is a strange thing. It was starting to sneak up on me, invading my thoughts and space, pummeling me with a cacophony of noise and confusion of pictures that were impossible to ignore. So, as memory surfaced, I sank into the turmoil and havoc it wreaked. I was worried as I walked through my home, remembering all the great times we'd had here. The laughter and the tears that are hidden in these walls of time treasured forever. The noise of children playing, growing and finally entering the world prepared for them through the years, fill my thoughts. Then there is a peace that settles over the pain of departure. The gentle rocking of time as it drifts on to envelop me in a new journey, embarked on by the natural progression of life, captivate me. Why couldn't I be left to enjoy these years where I felt most at ease? This house carries my dreams fulfilled and those yet to be realized. It is mine and I will fight to hold on to it and I will prove I am able to end my days exactly the way I want.

We so often convince ourselves that we are the authors of our destiny but life itself makes liars out of us. Simple missteps lead to major upheavals and it is how we tread through the minefield that determines the outcome. The thread that connects us one to the other is tenuous and fragile. At times, life keeps it taught and stretched to the limit of its strength. At other times, it is slack with contentment and peace. But if it snaps, the ends dangle, useless, and shred through time lost to healing. When there is no joining, loneliness eats and destroys the meaning of love, hope and life. It is up to each of us to mend the break before that time. Family is the tie that binds us most intimately. I remembered how dysfunctional my own family was. When Carin was growing up we had several family shows on TV. Each of them told of wonderful well-adjusted children and parents who always solved all problems with little turmoil.

The family I grew up in was very different. The times were different too, most of our fathers were fighting overseas and many mothers were working at jobs formerly held by men. That does not excuse the lack of love and caring my parents gave to me.

I thought back to the day we arrived in Moose Jaw and remembered the deep pain of separating from Bernadette caused.

Chapter 8

The mood in the taxi from the train station in Moose Jaw was subdued as Joseph and I sat staring out the window, watching our dear friends disappear into the crowds we left behind. The trip had started at the end of November and it was now December fourth, less than a week, and yet it seemed a lifetime had passed. The joy and love we shared with those nuns had been timeless to our hearts. Silent tears flowed freely and a wrenching heartache tore me apart. But Joseph and I had already learned the art of not making a noise when we cried. I never saw Bernadette again, but I still carry her memory today tucked in a small corner of my heart.

When we arrived at our new house, the big moving truck was already there and we could see our stuff being carried into what was to become our home.
"Joseph!" I yelled, "We are going to live in a castle!"

To me the house looked like a castle because it was white and had a big verandah with lots of stairs leading to the front door. It had two sections to it. The top one was a cupola that ran the full width of the house with windows all the way to the top. The main part was peaked like a castle as well. Through my young eyes, I believed it to be a castle and a thrill ran through me. The memory of it still overcomes me whenever I stand and stare back to that time and place.

"It isn't a castle. It doesn't have a moat around it, and it is not made of stone. Besides they don't have castles in Canada, don't you know?" Joseph sneered at me.

"Girls are so dumb," he said as he ran up the front stairs.

"I don't care what you think! I know it is some kind of castle. It's too big to be an ordinary house." I sneered back and stuck out my tongue as I followed him up the steps with Ross right behind us.

The whole house was very pretty. It had a white brick front and the black roof barely showed beneath the snow that covered the ground as well.

"Wow!" Joseph said as he ran through the front door and slipped on the wood floors.

"Be careful Joseph," my mother said.

I nearly tripped over Joseph as I came running into the big entranceway.

"Ooh, this is really beautiful! See, I told you it was a castle, Joseph. You don't know everything!"

We just stood and stared with our mouths open. My sadness at leaving Bernadette was overtaken by my sense of the change that was about to take place in my life. We had never lived in such an elegant place, and my brothers and I just gaped at each other.

"Look at the shiny floors!" Ross said, "We can skate on these, only we don't need skates. Our socks will be really slippery and we can slide all over."

"You kids settle down and help me unpack this food," my mother yelled from the back of house. I pretended I didn't hear her and raced up the long staircase that was in the middle of the hall. It was long and curved its way up to the top floor. It had a big banister along it and spindles all the way up and around. It overlooked the front hall and the lounge next to the hall. My brothers were right behind me, pushing and shoving to be first to the top.

"Quit shoving!" I yelled at them.

"Aw don't be such a sissy!" they yelled in unison.

Joseph yanked my braids.

"Ouch!" I cried, "Mommy! Joseph is pulling my hair."

"You kids get down here right now and do as I told you and unpack these boxes!"

"You're such a baby," Joseph hissed.

"Mommy, Joseph is being mean!"

My mother thundered up the steps, grabbed Joseph and me by our ears and pulled us down the stairs. She parked us in the pantry beside of the kitchen. Ross ran behind to keep up and, as usual, managed to stay out of harm's way.

"This house has so many rooms," I whispered to Joseph as we put stuff on the shelves that we could reach.

"I know. We'll have lots of fun finding hiding places."

There were rooms everywhere. I felt overwhelmed by the size of the house, but at the same time I was excited that I was going to live there. We soon lost interest in unpacking and wandered off again, to explore more of the house. We found two bathrooms on one floor, five rooms toward the back, a very big room just off the front hallway and another one next to it. The biggest one would be the lounge. It had a big built-in sideboard with glass in all of the doors.

"Look at the pretty blue walls Joseph! It's like living in the sea," I told him, breathless with excitement.

"We can build a ship with the boxes when they're empty and sail around the world."

Running from room to room, becoming more and more wound up, it was just a matter of time before we landed on our duffs in the kitchen with our mother once again stared down at us. "Damn!" said Joseph.

"What did you say?" my mother demanded.

"Nuthin'," Joseph responded.

"We need to set up your rooms so you kids will have somewhere to sleep tonight."

"Can I have the room with the yellow walls next to the blue room?" I asked.

"No," mom said. "You kids will sleep upstairs."

"Can we pick out our own rooms, please, Mommy?" Ross asked.
"Yes, but you and Joseph will share a room. Molly will share with Emma when Emma is big enough to sleep in a bed."
"Wow! That means I will have my own room for a long time," I squealed.
"That's not fair," Joseph whined, "She should have to share too."
"Don't argue with me. Let's go up and find your beds before Emma wakes and needs to be fed."
"I'm hungry," I whined
"Me too," said Joseph.
"Me three," said Ross.
My mother laughed and said, "Okay, let's fix you each a jam sandwich."

She found the box with the bread and jams and fixed the sandwiches and poured milk for each of us. I missed having butter on my bread. Butter was one of the products rationed because of the war.
We wolfed down the sandwiches and milk and dashed up the stairs to pick out our rooms. We had forgotten the beds were already set up where my mother had directed the movers. The boys' beds were in a room with green walls; my bed was in a room with pink walls.
"I love all the different colors," I said to my mother as she was digging out some bedding and making the beds.
"Grab the end of this sheet, Molly, and help me make up your bed, please."
I helped her make my bed and my brothers' beds. I silently wondered why they couldn't help to make their own beds, but I didn't want to get my mother mad at me so I kept those thoughts to myself.

"There are seven bedrooms up here and two bathrooms. Each of the rooms has different colored walls," my mother told me.
I went in search of the different rooms and saw wondrous shades of yellows, greens, whites, mauve, pink and even gray. It was like living in a rainbow, just waiting for the doors to open and display the vast spectrum of colors. The house was spotless and grand.

"Okay, Molly, Joseph and Ross! Get ready for bed! Remember, tomorrow you are going to be busy helping me unpack boxes. The sooner we get that done, the sooner you can go off and explore outside."

My mother seemed tired too.

"Good night, Mommy," I yawned as she pulled the covers over me. I was really tired and the last thing I remembered before drifting off to sleep was thinking how lucky I was to be living in a castle. The feeling of safety and the blankets over me was delicious. The warmth of the bed, the darkness of the room and the fact that I was worn out overcame me and I fell into a deep sound sleep.

I didn't give any thought to my mother and how tired she must have been. Boxes were everywhere, scattered in different rooms and stacked waiting to be emptied. The movers had unpacked the dishes, set up the beds and put the furniture where my mom had directed. She was the one to put everything in order.

I wonder now at how lonely she must have felt? Her husband had gone to war, and she had left the friends she had and moved to a new city with four young children. She must have been exhausted. Looking back, I am ashamed at how selfish and unhelpful we had been. I wonder if she wept at night for the first few weeks after we had moved into that house?

My mother was very young. She had only been sixteen when Joseph was born. There is eighteen months between each of us. I am amazed at how she endured that move and the following six years that kept her husband captive in a war being waged so many miles from home.

She loved music particularly Frank Sinatra and the radio was always on and I remember her humming along to many of his songs. There were a lot of different songs and performers. One of my favorites was "Little Brown Jug."

Chapter 9

For the next three weeks, our lives remained in flux. Bedlam reigned in our house. We unpacked boxes, shifted furniture and tried to establish a routine.

"We are going to have to decide where we are going to put our Christmas tree when we get it," Mom told us as we ate our breakfast one morning. We finally had some semblance of order in our lives again.

"I hope we put it in the hall and then everyone will see it when they come into our house," Ross said excitedly while munching on his toast.

"We don't have any friends here and no one comes to see us, stupid," I replied.

"Don't talk like that!" my mother snapped.

Later, as we played outside, I asked my big brother.

"Do you think Santa will know where we are Joseph?"

"Of course! He knows where everyone lives all the time."

He always knew the answers to my questions he was my hero.

We built big forts with the empty boxes and played different games with them.

Christmas came and went quietly. It was the first Christmas in our new home. It just seemed to be wrapped up with the newness of everything. We didn't know anyone so no one visited and our dad was away. I remember there was quite a lot happening and we were absorbed with the exciting times of becoming familiar with the house. The boxes and loose packing materials were perfect for building great forts. We had some wild and exciting episodes and that helped me to adjust to the strange transition that was taking place around us. We played nonstop, rushing here and there, fighting warriors, pirates and, of course, monsters. We were kings and queens and we had a large moat with a drawbridge that could only be lowered by us. Our moving boxes were the best toys ever.

My mother concentrated on the details of each of the unused rooms in the house. Colors of curtains and bedding were picked to match the room decor. Furnishings were sparse but tasteful. I resented the time she spent fixing up the house. Most of the rest of her time she spent with the baby.

My mother didn't seem to love me. She was like a stranger in many ways. I don't remember her holding me or reading to me. She loved my brother Ross and was always talking softly to him and holding him. She often cuddled him. My mother was quite pretty, slim and she always kept herself looking attractive. Her hair was jet black and kept in a style that suited her and that was fashionable at the time. She was five feet six. She had flawless skin and hazel eyes, but she rarely smiled. I guess she was weary with the burdens she bore. She didn't talk to me very often. She was kept busy looking after the big house and caring for us. She sewed clothes for all of us. My memory of my mother is sketchy at best.

"Where were you born Mommy?" I asked one day.
"I was born in Sudbury," she answered.
"Where are your mommy and daddy?"
"My mother, your grandmother, lives in Mossbank, a little town not too far from here. My dad lives in the Yukon, the last I heard. He is part French and when my mother met him, he worked in the nickel mines in Sudbury, but he left when I was a very little girl and we never heard from him again."
"Will my daddy never come back too?" I asked, worriedly.
"Yes, he will come home as soon as the war is over."
"Why do you save all the flour and sugar bags?" I asked on another day.

"I use the fabric to make underwear for you and tea towels and wash cloths."

"Is that why you save any elastic we get sometimes?"

"Yes, and I cut off all the buttons when our clothes are too worn out to keep anymore. Rubber is rationed and buttons are hard to get. Lots of things won't be easy to get until after the war, Molly, so we have to keep anything we can reuse."

Those are the conversations I remember most often. I am sure, in her way, she cared about us and I know she was always there. Joseph, Ross and I must have learned from her the things little ones learn from their parents. The skills that allowed us to move from baby to toddler to child were there. After my sister was born she seemed to change and became too busy to stop and talk, play or read to Joseph or me.

I don't remember very much about Sudbury and what life was like with my parents. My memory is sharp and painful of the times with her in Moose Jaw and Mossbank, until she left when I was twelve. She had a wicked temper and most often it was vented on me and at times on Joseph. She loved the attention of men and dressed accordingly. She never went anywhere unless she was well attired and highly made up. I don't remember if things like make-up were rationed but she always had lots of lipstick, powder and paint for her face. Nylons were impossible to get so she would use leg paint and a black pen to paint a straight line up the back of her legs to make it look as if she had nylons on. In those days there was a heavy seam at the back of the nylon that always had to be straight.

I don't think she was mean. She simply could not love me. I can still hear her words whenever she left the house to go to town.

"How do I look, Molly? Does my hat look nice and are my 'nylons' straight?"

I always answered, "Yes, Mommy, you look very pretty."

She would respond, "Don't ever lie and say I do if I don't look real nice when I ask you, Molly."

"I won't. I whispered.

She loved to sing and had a sweet voice.

One day when I came into the house she was singing along with the radio as Frank Sinatra sang "I'll Never Smile Again" and it sounded lonely and sad.

Chapter 10

Early that January, women started to come to talk with my mother. I came running into the house one day and there was a really attractive woman sitting in the kitchen with her.

"Molly, this is Sadie. Sadie, this is my eldest daughter, Molly."

"Hello, Molly! It is nice to meet you."

"Hi," I said back. "Your hair is pretty, what color is it?"

"It is auburn."

I remember just staring at her. Her hair had a million little curls and hugged her face. Her eyes were a radiant blue. Her skin was smooth and white and shone like a pearl. These were the first thoughts I remember about Sadie.

"Sadie is going to come and live with us, Molly," my mother said as she poured cups of tea for her and Sadie.

"Why?" I asked.

"She is going to help us look after this big house."

And so Sadie was the first to move into one of the spare rooms.

I was far too busy with my adventures to think about why we needed help.

My mother continued to have what I thought were visits from women. We saw a number of them come and go and then we noticed something disturbing. One day, soon after we saw taxis coming and going. Joseph and I were outside trying to make a snowman. Ross was off searching for eyes, nose and mouth.

"Why are those women coming here with their suitcases?" I asked Joseph.

"I dunno."

Two more women came along and walked up the front steps of our house with suitcases in hand. My Mother opened the door to them and invited them inside. I ran up the steps and rushed through the door into the front hall where four women were standing with my mother and Sadie.

"Goodness, Molly, you are in such a rush! Do you have to go the bathroom?" my mother asked.

"No, I was wondering why everyone has a suitcase Mommy?" I was nervous, thinking maybe we were going to have to move out so these women could move in.

"Please excuse my daughter's rudeness," my mother said to the women as she gave me her evil eye.

"She is not even four yet and is already such a little busybody. Molly, these women are going to live with us from now on. They will help with all the work. Now go outside and finish building your snowman. I will introduce these ladies to you children at lunch. Right now they will want to unpack and freshen up."

"Okay." I yelled and ran out the door, feeling relieved that we would still be living in the home I had come to love. I knew my mother was tired and often cranky with my brothers and me, and I believed these women would be her friends and they would be like the nuns on the train. I was excited about that.

At lunch my mother introduced the newcomers.

"Susie, I want you to meet my children, Joseph, Molly and Ross. Children, this is Susie, Mindy, Rachelle and Sissy." She lightly touched each one on their arm and showed them where to sit at the table.

Susie was attractive with jet-black hair that was short and perky. It suited her dark complexion and pale gray eyes. She was of medium height and quite slim. She had a soft mouth that was colored with a neutral lipstick.

Mindy, seated next to Susie, was Asian with striking dark brown eyes and straight black long hair . She was small in stature and her skin was flawless. She wore a vibrant red sweater and bright red lipstick colored her wide generous mouth. Rachelle had short-cropped hair that looked to me like curly wool. She was gorgeous and her skin was the color of ebony. She was tall and slim and had those brown eyes that seemed fathomless. Her lipstick was scarlet on a mouth that seemed to pout.

Sissy was tall as well. She had striking blue eyes and wore lots of makeup. I remember always wanting to look at her. She looked like an angel without wings. Her blond hair shone like gold and was long and straight. She wore a pale blue sweater. She had a pink complexion, complemented by a light colored lipstick. She was sweet and kind and I don't ever remember her getting mad or impatient with me.

One day, my brothers and I were outside playing in the snow and all of a sudden I had to go to the bathroom. I went running into the house, lunged through the door, and yelled for my mother. Sissy came rushing down the stairs.
"Goodness, Molly, where is the fire? What is your problem?"
"I have to go to the bathroom!"
If you have ever lived on the freezing, winter prairies, you know how many clothes you have to wear to go outside to play.
"Quick, Molly, sit down and I'll get your boots off while you take your hat and mitts off. Stand up now, while I get your snowsuit off. Keep still, Molly! I can't undo the buttons with you bouncing around like that."
"I can't help it, Sissy, I'm going to pee my pants if you don't hurry and then my mommy will yell at me and I won't be able to go outside anymore till she washes my snow pants." I hopped from foot to foot, trying to keep my bladder closed up tight.
"Calm down, Molly, we're just about there. Here, let me help you into the bathroom and I'll help you get your bloomers down and get you up onto the toilet. Come on, run."

No sooner was I done and she was helping me to get back into my clothes, when Ross came screaming through the door.

"I have to go pee!"

"Land sakes, why do you kids wait until the last minute to come in to go to the bathroom?" she said, starting to work on getting his outer clothes off.

But she never seemed to be cross, no matter how invasive we were.

Chapter 11

Each of the women had a private room, and they quickly adjusted to the living arrangements. Soon after they moved in, I began to notice men visitors coming to our home at night and sometimes in the day.

Sadie and I were fast becoming friends and I loved being with her. One day, while sitting on her bed, watching her prepare for a "guest" (to use her term) to arrive, I gave her a compliment.

"You look real pretty today, Sadie."

Her radio was on and she was singing along with it "All Or Nothing at All"

"Why, thank you Molly!" she said in her strange accent.

"Why do you always wear nice dresses and shoes that have such tall heels?" I asked, lolling back on the bed.

"I'm not very tall, and I like the way they make me look. Don't you like the way I dress?" She patted her hair and peered into the mirror. She touched the corner of her mouth with the tip of her finger and smoothed her dress.

"Oh yes!" I exclaimed as I sat straight up on the bed.

"It's just that you look nice all the time. Sometimes, my mommy doesn't look very pretty when she is working or feeding Emma, but you always look pretty. Is that why so many men come to visit with you? Why do you bring them up to your bedroom?" I asked as I jumped off the bed and fingered her beads that were lying on the dressing table where she sat.

Sadie stroked my hair.

"It is always good to dress nicely for any friends, Molly. One day soon you will understand. We have a surprise for you and I am going to be your teacher in learning about the surprise. Won't that be fun?"

"Oh, thank you, Sadie! My friend Bernadette taught me about lots of things and she always had surprises for me. When can we start?" I hopped from one foot to the other.

"Soon, sweetie. Run along now while I finish getting ready for my guest."

One morning, while at breakfast with the women, I watched horrified as Sissy put two spoonfuls of sugar and a lot of milk into her tea. I looked at her asked.

"Are you going to have a baby?"

Astonished, she replied, "No, why, do I look like I am?"

"No, but my mommy says only ladies who are going to have a baby can have extra milk, and no one should use what little milk we get in their tea. Don't you know milk is rationed and so is sugar? We can only have a little bit on our porridge and only a little bit of milk. My mommy uses lots for making us supper, so everyone gets the same, she told us. You took more than your share." I said all this with somber authority. I sat up very straight and tall in my chair so she could see I was very knowledgeable and I was quoting my mother.

"I'm sorry," Sissy said. "I didn't think about all that because I have lived by myself and I am not used to sharing. I will be more careful and I will try and do without milk and sugar in my tea.

Joseph piped up.

"Tea is rationed, too. We keep our left over tea and just warm it up with hot water and it lasts longer that way."

Rachelle chimed in, "My goodness, you are all so smart. We will all have to do our part to make sure our rations last so we don't run out of food before our new ration book is issued."

They all looked at one another and I thought I saw them smile at each other.

"As the war in Europe progresses, more and more staples are rationed here in Canada. Women work at jobs that were previously considered men's jobs. Life is changing because of the conflict. The war is raging on a different continent but it is affecting the whole world." My mother explained to all of us.

Joseph and I cleared up the dishes so we could go outside and play. It seemed to me we were doing more chores than when the women weren't living with us. I failed to see how they were 'helping my mother around the house' as she had put it. But I knew I couldn't say anything to her about how they didn't do much to help, because she always got mad at me whenever I pointed out obvious things to her. Instead, Joseph and I snagged Ross and dashed out of the house before we had to do more chores.

Chapter 12

Our house was on Ninth Avenue SW, which was a busy street, but there was a little park nearby where we often played. That day we went to the park, making sure there were not too many people around.

It was nice out, so we decided to play pirates. Joseph was the boss pirate and Ross was a prisoner and I was a helper pirate. The wharf would be our famous pirate ship. Some small tree branches were our swords. Joseph made all the decisions and Ross and I went along with him most of the time. We made our way onto the little wharf that was at the edge of a large pond. Ducks and geese swam around and seemed to be the only other inhabitants of the park. We yelled and swung our swords, running back and forth on our "ship". We were murdering our enemies as we fought to take over their ship after we had boarded it. We took Ross prisoner. Joseph kept our ship on course after pillaging the enemy ship and sinking it.

"Tie up the prisoner!" Joseph ordered.

"Put your hands behind your back!" I yelled at Ross as I pretended to tie them.

"What are you going to do to me?" Ross whined.

"You will walk the plank," Joseph determined.

"Oh please no!" Ross wailed.

"I will do any work for you. I will scrub your decks, cook your meals—anything, but don't make me walk the plank!" He was most convincing.

"I have decided," Joseph answered strutting back and forth on the small wharf.

"Bring him to the plank."

"Come with me, Ross!" I ordered and grabbed him by his arm to pull him to the edge of the wharf.

"Walk now and turn yourself over to the deep waters forever," Joseph said in a loud, but kind voice. He pushed his sword against Ross's back.

"Please don't make me do it," cried Ross.

"Move!" Both Joseph and I yelled together. We nudged Ross a little and as he pretended to struggle against us, he lost his balance and fell into the pond.

None of us knew how to swim.

Ross flailed in the water and screamed for us to help him. I was frozen with fear and cried and yelled for Joseph to do something. Joseph jumped into the water and grabbed Ross and tried to pull him to the wharf. Now both of them were thrashing around in the water.

"Help him! Grab him Joseph!" I yelled, running back and forth on the wharf. I looked around, trying to find something to throw into the water to help.

"Catch this!" I threw a board that was lying on the wharf. It sailed over their heads, falling uselessly into the water.

Ross was struggling and flaying the water as Joseph tried to keep his grip on him.

Finally Joseph got him to the wharf and told him to grab hold of the edge. Ross clung to the wharf gulping in air, laying his head on the edge. I seized his hair and tried to pull him up.

"Ouch!" he cried and let go of the wharf.

Joseph grabbed him and screamed at me.

"Don't be stupid!

He yelled at Ross.

"Take my hand!" Ross was too afraid to let go of the wharf and sniffled.

"I can't! I don't want to sink!"

We finally hauled Ross out of the water. We were all shaking and shivering with fear and the cold.

"We have to get home fast," Joseph moaned, "before we freeze to death."

We high-tailed it home and dashed through the door screaming, crying and bawling, while dripping smelly, muddy water on the floor.

"What's going on?" my mother shouted as she ran to investigate. At the same time Sadie, Sissy, Mindy, Susie and Rachelle came running down the stairs to see what the commotion was.

"Ross nearly drowned, but Joseph saved him!" I squealed, trembling and sobbing.

"We fell in the water!" Both Ross and Joseph wailed, shivering uncontrollably.

We were all scared and very cold. My mother grabbed Ross and hugged him to her and screamed at the women to take Joseph and me and put us in a warm tub of water. She took charge of Ross. Once we were all warm and dressed and sitting down at the kitchen table with warm milk, my mother started her tirade.

"What is the matter with you two, taking Ross on the wharf and then pushing him off?"

"We were just playing pirates. We didn't mean to push him off; he fell off. It was an accident." Joseph wheezed out his words.

I sat there quaking, afraid to say anything.

That was when we were introduced to the most frightening punishment ever. "The basement" was dark and there were lots of stairs leading down to it. She yanked open the basement door and screamed at Joseph and me to get down the stairs and stay there for ten minutes.

"Maybe next time you won't be so stupid!" she said as she pushed me through the door. I was petrified as I grabbed onto the back of Joseph's shirt and clung to it as we crept to the bottom of the stairs. She shut the door and turned out the light.

"Joseph," I murmured, "I'm scared. Do you think there are ghosts down here?"

"No, silly," he said, his voice quavering. I could feel him shaking as hard as I was.

From that day forward, I knew Joseph would be brave even if he were scared. He would make sure he would keep Ross and me safe. There would be many times when he would rescue us or help us to be brave. Where he found the courage to dive into that pond was a mystery to me. He never did learn to swim. He was always afraid of water after that. Both Ross and I looked up to him and leeched strong emotions from him until he left to join the Air Force years later.

That was the first time I was sent to the basement, and from that day forward I have been afraid of the dark. It was the punishment I feared most of all. After what seemed like forever, my mother opened the door, turned on the light and let us out. Ross was wrapped in a blanket and she cuddled him, while Joseph and I stood in front of her shivering from the cold. We were still badly shaken.

"You and Molly should know better. Sit at the table and drink up your warm milk and go to bed and stay there and think about what you have done. You could have killed Ross with your shenanigans." She was visibly shaken, her hair in disarray and her dress wet from where she held Ross.

"Come on Joseph, I will take you up to your room, "Sissy said as she put her arm on his shoulder and led him out of the kitchen.

"But it was an accident and I saved Ross. Why am I being punished and he's not?" Joseph complained as he left.

"What about food, don't we get to eat?"

"Just come with me," Sissy said, hushing Joseph.

Sadie said, "Molly, you come with me." She took my hand and led me up the stairs to my room.

"Why does my mommy hate me?"

"She doesn't hate you, Molly, she is scared and upset. She'll be okay in the morning.

"But I'm hungry."

"I know, Molly, but you will have to wait until breakfast now."

"It's not fair! Ross gets to stay up and eat and everything." I started crying again.

"I know, but things are not always fair and we can't do anything about it now. You and Joseph won't starve before morning, sweetheart. It just feels like you will."

"My mommy is mean and I hate her!" I climbed into my bed.

"Good night, Molly."

"Can you read me a story?"

"Not today, honey, I have to get dressed. I'm expecting company. Good night!" And with that, she left the room.

Chapter 13

When I look back on that night, I remember how isolated and sad I felt. I was going to be four years old in a month and already learning what aloneness really meant. Although I was very young, everything about that near drowning and the aftermath lodged itself in my memory bank where it is as clear today as the day it happened.

Things changed a lot in our house as time moved along. Sadie was paying more attention to me. She spent more and more of her time with me. She started to take me aside and teach me how to keep myself neat and clean to make me attractive to men.

"Why do I have to be different from Ross and Joseph and be cute for men?" I asked one day when she was showing me how to iron pretty ribbons for my hair.

"You will understand as you learn more, Molly. Just be patient right now," she answered.

"Why do I have to iron my stupid hair ribbons?" I asked, bored with the job.

"They look so much nicer when they don't have wrinkles where they were tied before, Molly. It is the little things like that that people notice about us."

"I don't care, Sadie, I want to go and play."

"Let's just finish this, she said, shaking her head in obvious disappointment at my reluctance to be a part of this lesson, and then you can go and play."

"Why don't Joseph and Ross have to do dumb things too? It's not fair that I have to do stuff and they don't." I swished the iron back and forth haphazardly.

"Just finish what you are doing, please, Molly." She turned and walked away.

My mother seemed to abandon me to Sadie, and most of the time I was happy to get the attention. When I wasn't off playing with my brothers, I was with Sadie. She always made time to talk to me. One day when we were together, she asked.

"How would you like to have a nice room all to yourself and never have to share it with your sister?"

"I would really like to always be by myself and have my own room,"

She took me up to a lovely room decorated in pink, frilly curtains and a bedspread with pink and white lace edges on the pillow and spread. The pictures on the creamy white walls were of little girls hugging or sitting with little bunnies, lambs, puppies and kittens. There was one with a baby wrapped in a pink blanket nursing at its mother's breast.

"Oh! I love this room! It is really pretty. Does my mommy say I can have this room?" I asked, twirling around and dancing.

"Yes, she wants me to show you some things and you will be able to use this room sometimes, Molly. It is just for special times, but only you can use it. Not your brothers or sister."

"Sadie, I love you!" I reached out and hugged her. I was really excited.

"When can we come here? What special stuff? And will you come with me?" I asked in rapid fire.

"Slow down, Molly, you will need to learn first. We will start our lessons tomorrow. For now, come with me while I change for my company."

I followed her to her room. Sadie took off her dress and I was enthralled with her lacy underwear.

"Why do you wear such pretty underpants, Sadie? No one else sees them and I can see right through them and they are pretty little. My underpants are bigger than yours and not so pretty."

"I love frilly things, Molly, and you will have nice underpants like these in your special room. They will be soft just like mine." She held up a beautiful red dress.

"Do you like this color, Molly?"

"Oh yes, it is really pretty and bright." I answered, grinning. I felt very grown up.

Sissy walked in just as Sadie was doing up the buttons on her dress.

"I have company coming in ten minutes, Sadie. Do you think this blue suits me?" she asked.

"Why are you wearing that nightgown?" I asked, shocked.

"I can see right through it."

"I will explain that to you one day soon Molly," Sadie said.

"It looks lovely, Sissy, it looks nice with your blond hair.

"Should I wear my hair up or down Sadie?"

"Wear it up to begin with. He will enjoy taking it down for you as your evening progresses."

"Thanks, Sadie. I have to dash, he should be here any minute," Sadie held her curls up away from her cute face.

"What do you think, Molly, should I wear my hair up or down? It's so curly, but it's fun to pin it up."

"It looks pretty up."

"Okay, I'll put it up. And now, young lady, you have to go, because my company will be here soon."

I scurried out of her room in search of Joseph.

That night, Joseph and I snuck out of our rooms and sat on the landing so we could peak through the railing into the big lounge just off the entrance hall. We were mesmerized, watching the men and women dancing and laughing, kissing and hugging. The Andrews Sisters were belting out a recording of "Boogie Woogie Bugle Boy" and everyone was having such fun dancing.

There were many nights when we sat huddled at the top of the stairs and peeked through the railing down into the lounge watching and listening. The music was loud and everyone seemed to enjoy it all. Joseph and I learned the words to many of them. "Mares Eat Oats" by the Merry Macs and "Drinking Rum and Coca Cola," were two of the most popular and most of the women would jive to the beat.

Vera Lynn songs, like "We'll Meet Again", "Lili Marlene" and Gracie Fields' "White Cliffs of Dover," were very popular and they were often played. We knew them all and would sing them in whispers, giggle, and watch the players' downstairs dance and sway and disappear when the atmosphere got so charged with the music, cigarettes and drink. Sometimes their sexual desires took over and they would act out their fantasies in the lounge. Joseph and I began to realize what the women were there for, but we still didn't understand the full ramification of what it meant.

Sadie and I started to spend even more time together. She always took my hand whenever we went anywhere, whether it was just a journey to the pink room, her room, or to the store. One day we snuck off to the pink room for more lessons.

Chapter 14

"Why do you wear see-through nightgowns when you dance with the men who come to visit you?" I asked, as I lay sprawled on the bed.

"They are called negligees, Molly, and the men like to be able to peek at us. It makes them feel good."

"Why do you want them to see you?"

"Because that is what we do. The men pay to come and play with us and we make sure we do things that make them happy. I am going to show you how to do some of those things so you can play with some men too. You will make money, so your mommy won't have to worry about feeding your brothers and sister while your daddy is away fighting in the war. Isn't that exciting?"

"Will I have pretty see-through negligees too? And will the men tickle me and make me laugh?"

"You won't wear negligees, Molly. You will wear these pretty clothes." She took some very white lacy panties, a white petticoat and a frilly pink and white dress out of the dresser drawer and laid them on the bed for me to see and touch.

"Can I try them on now?"

"Yes, let's do that and see if they look as nice as I think they will look. Take off those clothes and I will help you into these."

I was shy about taking off all of my clothes. I hunched my shoulders and stared into my lap with my hands clasped tightly between my knees. Sadie put her arms around my shoulders and leaned her head against mine and spoke into my ear.

"Come on, Molly, don't be shy. You will be taking off your clothes for the men; remember what I told you. They won't bring you nice presents and give money to your mommy if you don't let them see you naked and let them touch you. You have seen us take off our clothes and dance with the men and we all laugh and have fun. I've watched you and Joseph hide in the shadows in the upstairs hall. Come on, sweetheart, you will get used to it. Here, let me help you."

She stood up and lifted my dress over my head. I sat there, frozen, wondering what was going to happen. She tried to pull me off the bed.

"Come, stand up next to me, Molly." She coaxed

I climbed off the bed and stood next to her in my underpants. She gently slipped them down and I nervously stepped out of them.

She proceeded to do things to me and introduce me to sensations I had never experienced before. She was kind and gentle and explained how others explored each other in this way. I don't remember how long I was there but I remember the intensity of the emotions and feelings. I felt like the blood was rushing through my veins and my lightheaded thoughts swarmed dizzily through my mind. I didn't know what had happened but I knew I liked the sensations she made me feel.

My pounding heart began to slow down and I was dazed with the intense feelings that thrummed through my body. I looked into her eyes and felt a sense of shame, but at the same time I wanted more. I didn't understand the emotion, but I knew it was the best feeling I had ever felt in my life. It was like looking at a rainbow. The colors burst brilliantly against the back of my eyes and I shamelessly wanted more.

"Just remember the men will do things that will make you feel like this. It will hurt a little at first, but you will want even more once that is over."

I didn't care about the hurt. I just knew I could hardly wait to experience that explosive sensation again. I was still breathless with the wonder of those feelings.

"Come on, let's see these pretty clothes on you."

She helped me off the bed on to my rubbery legs. I was still shaken up from the dizzying effects of those feelings. She helped me into the panties, the white slip and then the dress that had pink and white checks on the top and a very full pink skirt with a row of white lace on the bottom. The tie belt was wide and Sadie made a big bow at the back.

"Put these white socks on." Then she pulled out from under the bed some beautiful black buckled shoes. I put them on and we twirled around the room together.

"Don't you feel special, Molly? You look very sweet. We will French braid your hair with pink satin ribbons in it."

"Will I get to wear lipstick and blue stuff on my eyes like Sissy, or green like Rachelle, and that black stuff on my eyelashes like Mindy?" I gasped with excitement.

"No, you don't need any of that stuff on your face. Your company will want you to look like a pretty little girl, not like a painted woman. Always remember, Molly, the men are paying for you because you are a little girl. They like to play with little girls and not grown up women."

"Okay, Sadie, I will remember. Can I start soon to come here with a man? How many men will come to see me? Will I have to share my presents with my brothers and sister? I don't mind if I get lots of candies. I will share. Will my mommy start to like me more do you think?" I fired questions at her, barely pausing to breathe.

"Your mommy loves you Molly, she just needs help. Try to remember you are the only one who can help her like this. How special is that? You have to run along now while I get changed and ready for my guest." Sadie shooed me out of the room.

I ran downstairs, excited by what I had felt and had learned, knowing that soon I would be helping my mother. What was even better was that I was going to be getting lots of presents.

I rushed into the front room where my mother was sitting with Emma.

"Mommy, I love these new clothes! Do you think I look really pretty? Sadie helped me get dressed and she said I look lovely and she showed me some stuff that made me feel all excited and I can hardly wait to play with the men like Sadie does." I blithely chattered on like some record set to fast forward speed.

She looked at me like she was ready to explode with rage.

"What are doing wearing those clothes down here? You get right back upstairs and change and don't you ever wear them outside of that room again! I don't ever want to hear you talk about what you and Sadie are doing. You sound like a wanton little tart! Get out of my sight right now and get out of those clothes. Fold them up neatly and Sadie will put them away. Now get out of here!" Her voice was shaking with fury.

I walked away confused and hurt, wondering what I had done to make her so mad. I cried as I trudged out of the room and slogged up the stairs and met Sadie coming down.

"Molly, what are you doing wearing your new clothes down here and why are you crying? What happened?" She knelt down and hugged me to her.

"My mommy yelled at me and got really mad because I wore them downstairs. Why doesn't she ever like me Sadie? I wish she would hold me like she does Emma! She loves Emma and she's a girl."

"Oh, Molly, it's my fault, I thought you understood these clothes are just for the men in that room. You must never wear them anywhere else, sweetheart. Come, I'll help you get into your other things. We need to hurry, though. My company will be here any minute."

We went into the room and Sadie helped me change.

"What is a wanton tart, Sadie?"

"Why on earth do you want to know that, Molly?" Sadie looked at me with brows furrowed and seemed clearly mystified as she picked up the dress to put it back in the drawer.

"Because my mommy called me that."

"You know what, honey, I really have to hurry downstairs. I'll tell you later when I have more time. Let's get the rest of these clothes put back in the dresser. I'll help you back into your regular clothes."

She wiped my face and made me blow my nose and gave me a little hug. She brushed the side of my face pensively with her hand.

"Thanks, Sadie, I won't ever wear my special clothes again."

As we entered the upstairs hallway, I looked around to make sure my mother was nowhere in sight.

"Okay now, Molly, let's go downstairs and you can go off with Joseph and play. I saw him in the back yard from my bedroom window." Sadie headed out the door and down the stairs with me right behind her.

"I'll see you at dinner, Sadie, "I murmured and I snuck past the front room door and out the back door.

"Okay, Molly." She turned and waved at me as she tripped along in her high heels.

Chapter 15

A couple of days later, my mother said I would be needed one night soon to help serve some refreshments to the guests.

"What will I be doing?" I asked.

"You will help Rachelle and me in the kitchen get food ready for the guests."

"Will I be having a guest too, Mommy?"

"No, you are going to help and maybe meet one or two of them, but you won't be helping in that way yet," my mother said as she fed Emma. Her eyes never met mine.

"How will I know what to do?"

"Don't worry about that, Molly. Rachelle will help. Now you run along and play while I tend to Emma. She's tired and needs her nap."

"Okay. Do you know where Joseph and Ross are?"

"They're outside playing in the backyard."

"Joseph!" I yelled as I ran into the backyard, "Guess what!"

"What are you so impatient about?" Joseph asked as he ran over to where I was standing.

"I am going to get to stay up late one night and help Mommy and Rachelle serve food to guests who come to visit. Too bad you're a boy and can't."

"That's a stupid rule. I'm older than you," he snapped.

"I should be able to stay up later than you." He dismissed me, turned away and ran into the yard to play with Ross.

"Wait for me, Joseph, I want to play too!" I noticed the big fort they had built with the boxes we had kept from the move.

"Too bad, you can't. This game is just for boys."

"You're mean, Joseph! I was going to ask Mommy to let you help me too, but now I won't!" I shouted and stomped off into the house and up to my room.

What seemed like an eternity to me was only four days.
At breakfast, my mother announced,
"Tonight I want you to help Rachelle and me, Molly. You need to take a nap this afternoon so you won't be tired." She was mixing up food for Emma.
"Why does she get to stay up and I don't? I'm the oldest," Joseph whined as he fidgeted in his chair.
"Because only girls can do it. Boys would just mess things up," I said in my most haughty voice.
My mother glowered at me and snapped.
"Don't talk like that to your brother, Molly!"
"I don't care! Who wants to wait on a bunch of old people anyway?" Joseph snarled and walked away.
It took forever for that night to come. I was full of enthusiasm just thinking about it. Sadie came up to help me get ready.
"Wear your cute little pink pajamas with the teddy bears, Molly."
"I want to wear my pink and white dress."
"No, that is for when you are going to entertain a guest in the pink and white room. Remember, you can't wear that dress any place else, unless we tell you it is okay. Tonight you are only going to be helping and you might meet some men and we want you to look cute like a little girl."
"All right," I said, slouching with disappointment as I got my pajamas out of the drawer.
"Won't everyone think I'm just waiting to go to bed if I wear my pajamas, Sadie?" I looked at her with my hands on my hips and my eyebrows raised as high as I could, to convince her I was not a little child.
"Come, Molly, let me braid your hair in one long braid," Sadie said smiling to herself. Her eyes seemed to be laughing.
"Can't I wear my hair long and loose like Mindy?"

"Not tonight. You are going to be near food and we want your hair out of the way. Now come on. I need to hurry and get downstairs. I have someone waiting for me. Rachelle will come for you and you won't be ready."

"You wait here for Rachelle." Sadie left to go downstairs after braiding my hair with the pink ribbon she had weaved through it. Finally Rachelle came to take me downstairs to where all the guests had arrived.

"You look pretty, Rachelle," I said eagerly.

"Thank you, Molly. I will be helping you and your mommy tonight." We walked into the lounge and sat down on the big comfy couch. I looked at Rachelle's beautiful brown hair and eyes.

"I like touching your hair, Rachelle."

"I know, so does Emma," she said chuckling to herself.

"It looks like wool but it is so soft and the curls wrap tight around my fingers. I wish my hair was curly like that."

"We always want what we can't have, Molly," Rachelle replied, "I wish I could have straight long hair."

Just then, a kind-looking man came over and sat next to me. Rachelle moved over.

"Hi. My name is Roger and I've been told that your name is Molly."

"Hi. Yes, I am Molly and I'm going to help my mommy and Rachelle serve lots of food that they got ready this afternoon for tonight. I'm going to give it to you." I laughed and wriggled with delight.

"That's very sweet of you, Molly. Maybe one day you and I can get to know each other better, would you like that?"

"Yes. Are you in the army, like my daddy?" I asked, looking at his uniform. I reached out to touch the shiny buttons and he took my hand in his.

"No, I am in the air force, Molly. I fly planes and I teach other men how to become pilots so they can fly planes too. Army uniforms are brown. Ours are blue." He tweaked my nose.

"My daddy drives tanks in the war."

I liked his voice and the nice way he touched my hair. He was handsome with dark blond hair that was slicked back. He had nice green-gray eyes that had crinkles in the corners. His voice was very deep, but his words sounded muted. He seemed old to me but now, as I look back, he was probably very young. He was slight of build, but he had an uncompromising strength about him. When his leg touched mine, I felt funny in the pit of my stomach and remembered my special time with Sadie. He smelled like rain.

Since that night I have loved the smell of rain when the sun comes out and dries the earth.

"That's a very brave thing to do. I hear your mother calling me, so I will talk with you again, Molly." He kissed the back of my hand and laid it on my lap and went to find my mother.

Just then another very nice looking man came over and sat down next to me.

"Hi, Molly. My name is Duncan. Your mommy has told me lots of nice things about you, but she forgot to tell me how pretty you are. I love your pajamas!" He fingered the fabric in my top.

"Thank you, I love pink so I have lots of pink things. Do you like pink?"

"It is my favorite color for little girls." He spoke in a subdued manner as he hugged me to him.

"Your uniform is scratchy, just like Roger's and it is the same color as his. Are you in the Air Force too and do you know Roger?" I asked my questions in quick succession.

"Yes, I know Roger. He is stationed at our air base just south of Moose Jaw. Do you know that we train student pilots for wartime service and that we have one of the best aircrew training programs right here where you live?"

"Where is it?"

"It's a military base called 15 Wing and it's just a little ways away from here, so I can come and visit you quite often if you would like." He never took his eyes off mine when he spoke to me. He had a kind face and smiled a lot.

"That would be fun! Maybe I could wear my pretty clothes and you could come into my special room where just men who like to play with little girls can come. Would you like to do that?" I asked, animatedly wriggling in my seat and turning to snuggle my face into his chest. He smelled like peppermint as he leaned down and brushed his lips across my forehead.

I felt immediately comfortable with Duncan. He was handsome with black hair. His eyes were blue and caring. He reminded me of my brother, Joseph, except Joseph had blond hair. He was quite big, but not fat. He felt very strong when he squeezed me and nuzzled the top of my head. I wanted him to take me up to my special room so he could make me feel warm and excited. I felt funny and a little afraid because my thoughts seemed wrong. It was because I knew I couldn't have any clothes on when I felt that really nice feeling Sadie had made me feel. I knew it was a bad thing to be bare-naked in front of people other than my mommy and Sadie. I was very confused.

"I look forward to that, Molly. I think Roger likes to do that too. I have a surprise for you, Molly, would you like to see it?"
"Oh yes what is it?" I asked breathlessly.
He reached into his pocket and pulled out a piece of chocolate and handed it to me.
"Thank you!" I squealed with delight.
"Chocolate is rationed and we never get it. My mommy gets a little bit of cocoa instead so we can cook with it and have hot cocoa as a treat. I love chocolate, do you, Duncan? Will you bring me some more when you come and visit again? Will you come into my special room and play with me next time you come?" I pleaded with him.
"I think I would like that Molly."
"First I have to ask Sadie some stuff, Duncan. I will find out fast and tell you."

The ringing phone jangled me out of my daydream. "Hello!" I snapped, still shaken by the abrupt interuption.

"Hi, Mom, it's me, Carin. How did things go today?"

"Gracious Carin! The phone startled me. Give me a minute to get my thoughts together."

"Oh, were you asleep? I'm sorry; you never take a nap in the middle of the day. Are you all right?" she sounded concerned.

"I'm fine. I was just drifting and caught up in daydreams. I wasn't really asleep. My session went well today and I have another appointment next week. Michael feels the same as I do, Carin; there is nothing to be concerned about. I am just a little tense and still recovering emotionally from the incident downtown, so please don't worry any more. I promise to keep you up to date as my sessions move along. Right now I am starved so I would like to grab myself something to eat. Have you had dinner? Why don't we meet at that little coffee shop on the corner and have a coffee and sandwich? I'm sure Bill and the kids could manage without you."

"I'd love to, Mom, but Bill and I are going to see "The Titanic." The reviews are spectacular. Let's take a rain check and one night this week, you and I can go out for a burger or something."

"No problem, it was just a thought. I'll catch up with you later in the week. Good night, dear."

"Good night, Mom. I'm really glad you are getting some help; it makes me feel a lot better knowing that."

"Thank you, Carin. Enjoy the movie." I hung up the phone. I opened the fridge and paused at how little food there was. I found some cheese and made myself a sandwich, poured a glass of vegetable juice and settled down to watch some TV. I wrote a note to myself and stuck it on the door of the fridge.

"Get some groceries in!"

I was soon too tired to stay awake, so I put my dishes in the sink, rinsed them off, turned off the kitchen light, grabbed a book and prepared myself for bed. I fell asleep before I had read more than a couple of pages.

Chapter 16

I woke up feeling more refreshed than I had for a long time. It was my knitting day. We are a group of five women, all of us in our sixties and seventies, who have known each another for over ten years. We met in our church and have remained close friends. Our purpose is to knit toques, scarves and shawls for women and children in Afghanistan and the women in my ministry. I spent a relaxing morning tidying up the kitchen.

"C'mon you two," I called to my dogs as I grabbed the leashes, "Let's go for a walk before I have to leave."
I have two sweet dogs. One is a beautiful red Rhodesian ridgeback, who stands about two feet tall. She loves to walk. Her name is Christine. The other is a little female named Pippa. She is a sleeve shiatsu, almost totally white with a brown splotch on her shoulder. I never have to leash them, except when I cross the one busy road that intersects the trail and even then, I only have to restrain Pippa, because Christine stays right with me. Christine is eight years old and Pippa is just four. I walk them on a trail that is about a mile long and very near our house. It is a challenging, hour-long brisk walk. On this particular day, the weather was nice and sunny, but still cold, as winter was making itself known with the odd snowfall, cool days and cold nights. The trail crackled with each footfall. The ground was a little frozen and had the odd patch of ice. The dogs skittered and slipped on it, but it didn't deter them. They ran, barked and chased each other, oblivious to the cold. We enjoyed our walk and when I returned, I made a quick lunch of hot soup, crackers and a cup of tea.

There was no need to have any dessert, as I knew Maggie would have some sweet treat to serve with our tea later.

I locked the dogs in the kitchen and changed out of my tracksuit. I pulled on a pair of jeans and a pink sweater. I quickly ran a brush through my hair, threw on a jacket and picked up my knitting bag, then drove over to Maggie's.

We all arrived within minutes of each other.
"Hi everyone," I cheerfully said as I sat down in my favorite spot.
"Hi, Molly, how is everything with you these days? Still as busy as always I guess?" Maggie asked me.
"Yes, too busy for my liking, but I am working at reducing my workload to allow for more time to paint and spend with my family," I responded, settling in. I pulled my knitting out and started to knit on a blue and white shawl.

Maggie is a lovely and dear friend who hosts our group in her home each week. Her home is always immaculate and is quite modern. Her furnishings are mostly neutral in color and her walls are adorned with her husband's paintings. They are very beautiful, some colorful, some stark. They are paintings of trees and landscapes of the Canadian prairies. We usually do our knitting in the front room just off the entrance. It is a large bright room with a good size gas fireplace against the main wall. Sometimes when there are only two or three of us, we go into her den that is off the back of the house. It is a light and cheerful room with a small sunroom off it. It is mostly glass with some brickwork halfway up the walls and it is full of beautiful plants. She always has pretty pastel towels in her bathroom and nice smelling hand soap. It is a pleasure to come here every week. Maggie is tall and slim and knits grand shawls, toques and scarves. She is a fast knitter and makes four times as many things as the rest of us. We are all gray haired and have our share of wrinkles. Maggie lost her husband to cancer as well as one of her two sons. She is a retired nurse and is very active in her church, singing in the choir and is deeply involved with her surviving son and his family.

"Well, girls, I did it again!" Amy said. "I got Henry so riled up today with another stupid thing I did. Honestly, I don't know what is the matter with me these days; I am certainly forgetful and disorganized." She held up her knitting and puzzled over a mistake and how to fix it.

Amy is a delight, always expounding on her shortcomings and seemingly hectic life. Her husband is a sweet and loving guy and they both get along famously. She, like the rest of us, plugs along with her projects, knitting and ripping out row after row because she drops stitches while she is talking. She is fairly tall and well built. She is well dressed and is as active as a forty year old.
"What did you do to upset Henry this time?" Betsy asked.
"Well you know how Henry loves his desserts," she snickered.
"That we do know!" We all laughed and answered together as we listened to Maggie's long commentary.
"This morning, I started to bake some lemon loaves and I was doing great, measuring and mixing and singing to myself. But when I poured the milk into the ingredients, I was horrified to see how much milk floated around the bowl; it obviously was way too much. I picked up my recipe and noticed side-by-side ingredients; one side was for one cake, the other side was for four cakes. I guess I had baked some for a church bake sale or something. Obviously, I had altered the recipe to accommodate the changes and never erased them. Well, I didn't know how much of anything I had put in the bowl, so I had to toss the whole mixture away, and wouldn't you know, at that precise time, Henry came into the kitchen and asked what I was doing and not in those specific words, let me tell you! He was a little miffed! I explained to him what had happened and he went off on a tangent telling me how pathetic I was and wasteful to boot. Well, anyway, I stood there and stared at him while he railed on at me and then I rinsed the bowl and set it down, not too gently and suggested in fairly strong language that he bake his own lemon loaf and stormed out of the kitchen. I picked up a magazine, stomped off to our bedroom where I stayed until it was time to come here. Be warned I have only had a banana and a cookie that I

snagged as I left the house, so I hope we have lots of desserts to eat today." There was mischief in her eyes.

We all laughed, including Amy. It wouldn't have been normal if Amy didn't have some long soliloquy to tell us about her and Henry. We laughed and giggled about how forgetful we all are so much of the time. We are like schoolgirls when we get together and talk about our lives and the crazy things we do as we age.

"I had to rip out most of my scarf the other night," Betsy lamented good-naturedly.

"I was watching this TV documentary and I didn't notice I had dropped a stitch until I went to put it away. I looked at it, very impressed with how much I had knit, when I noticed this gap in one of the rows and when I checked it, I saw the dropped stitch. I really don't know why I bother to try and knit and watch TV at the same time. It's the same here when I talk and try to knit. I'm just not good at concentrating enough on what I am doing so I keep making mistakes." Betsy is so well organized in everything she does and she gets upset when she messes up her knitting. She is an attractive woman who is a wonderful and loyal friend. She is like the rest of us. She recently legally became a senior and enjoys the benefits associated with that. She, too, has a husband, Raymond, who tends to criticize her excessively. She loves to get away and talk about her own shortcomings in a fun way. She and Raymond enjoy traveling a lot so we don't see her sometimes for a couple of months at a time.

"I know what you mean," added Annabelle as she shifted in her seat next to me on the couch. "I do the same thing when I'm here and talking while I am knitting. I'm glad it happens here, though, because Maggie can pick up my stitches when I have to unpick. I can't do that without going right back to nothing. I don't have time during the week to do any knitting. I don't know why, but the time just seems to fly by and it's time to come here again and I haven't done anything on my project. We just seem to have so much company, with kids dropping by and spending the night or a couple of days. I'm glad when they come to visit. I don't get to see them that much and the ferry is very expensive, particularly for families who want to come to the Island. And gas is not cheap, even where they live in the United States." She smiled and shook her head as she explained her week to us.

Annabelle is the wise one. I love her dearly. She is level-headed all of the time, even in a crisis. She has traveled extensively to many foreign lands and is well grounded in the Bible. It is wonderful to listen to her perception of Scripture. She is a couple of years older than I. She has handsome features and always wears co-ordinated colors. She is a little taller than I, but not by much. Her husband, Alf, is not too well and she has an adult daughter who lives with them. She is very close to Amy and I believe it is a blessing for them to have each other.

"Have you girls thought anymore about our calendar?" I asked.

We all roared with laughter. It is a standing joke that we are all going to pose for a calendar wearing nothing but a feather or a huge fan in front of us. We joke we are going to sell them to the public starting with the church congregation to raise funds for my ministry and to buy more wool for our projects.

"It will take a really big fan to cover my body," Amy declared.

"I would love to see Andy's face when I come home with a picture of me wearing nothing but a huge fluffy red feather," Betsy laughingly added.

"Well, Alf would not want to see my knobby knees tucked behind a feather with nothing on but the skin I was born in," Annabelle exclaimed, laughing.

"I know I am short, but I will need a long and bushy feather to cover my breasts that hang down nearly to my waist. I would love to hear my Carin's remarks," I squealed, holding my side from laughing so hard.

By this time, we were laughing hysterically and gasping for breath, while at the same time throwing in outrageous remarks on how each of us would look and the reaction of those we know.

We carried on with mundane chatter about what was happening, each of us interested in what the others had to say.

"I'll put the kettle and the coffee pot on. Betsy brought pumpkin pie for dessert today so you can have a couple of pieces, Amy, seeing as how you didn't have much lunch," Maggie joked as she went into the kitchen.

It seemed that the afternoon had just flown, and on my way home I realized what a breath of fresh air these gatherings are and how grateful I am to have such dear friends at this stage of my life. Without my weekly meetings with my friends I would surely sink into a deep depression. These dear friends keep me grounded.

Chapter 17

"I wonder what I am going to be talking about today in my meeting with Michael?" I mused as I entered his reception area.

"Hi Molly, how are you doing?" Beth, his receptionist, greeted me with a friendly smile when I walked in.

"I'm okay, Beth; I wonder why I am here? I don't feel like I belong. I feel just fine."

"You would be surprised at how many people who walk through these doors say the same thing. I don't think Michael would insist on more sessions if he thought it wasn't necessary"

Beth is an older, pleasantly plump woman. She appears to be very kind and dresses like a model. Both times I have come here she has worn a smart dark suit with a pretty scarf. Today it was a red scarf with a navy suit. Last week it was a white scarf and black suit. I have only seen her wear skirts and I will be interested to see if she wears slacks. Many women of my generation still believe women should wear skirts in public. She seems like a no-nonsense woman who is comfortable with whom she is.

"Have a seat, Molly. Michael will be out in a minute. Can I get you a coffee or anything?" she asked, as she took an incoming phone call.

"No thanks." I mouthed the words back at her and took a seat.

I appreciated the fact there was no one else in the waiting room; I didn't want to know anyone else who comes here nor did I want anyone else to see me here.

"Hi, Molly, won't you come on in?" Michael said, greeting me as he came into the reception area from his office.

He handed a slip of paper with instructions to Beth.

"Would you give this person a call and cancel my appointment next week, Beth? Something of an emergency has come up and I must attend to it."

"Yes, of course." She took the slip of paper from him and picked up the phone.

I followed Michael into his office and he and I took our usual seats.

"How have things been going for you, Molly?"

"Good, I'm doing good," I answered, fidgeting in my chair.

"Can you tell me how you've been feeling? Any anxiety? Are you sleeping well?"

"I feel a little anxious right now," I responded, fiddling with my shirt buttons. I do not want to be here. I just don't feel like I need to do this. There is nothing wrong with me and I haven't had any more problems since I saw you last week." I twirled a section of my hair and gazed at a picture on the wall.

"You seemed upset when you left last week when I asked if you could tell me why you didn't call the police. What has you so angry with them?" He took his pad of paper and wrote something on it. I started to feel very hot and my heart was pounding like a drum in a rock band.

"I have seen what they do and how they behave and I am not about to put myself in that position again, only to be humiliated and verbally abused. Have you seen a hooker arrested or hassled by the cops?"

"Just the other night when I was meeting with the women on the stroll Marsha told me how she had been arrested in front of her children at her home. Someone had reported an argument she had with her live in boyfriend. The police responded. They knew her because she has been arrested several times for soliciting. They called her crude names and treated her roughly in front of her children. She was hauled off to jail in a police car, her children were crying out to her and she couldn't do anything to help them. A neighbor gathered them and took them to her home. I was full of rage at the memory of my own arrests.

Michael leaned forward and asked, "Molly, something is going on here that has little to do with my question." He reached over and clasped my shaking hands.

"You haven't answered my question, Michael. Have you ever been arrested?"

"Yes, as a matter of fact I have, many years ago, and I agree I wasn't handled very gently. But I understand now it had a lot to do with my own belligerent attitude and not a lot to do with the police who were just doing their job. Surely, you can see that now, as a mature adult? I wouldn't hesitate to call on the police today for help in any type of real emergency. Why would you think they would not treat you with kindness and respect in a situation where you were the victim?" His eyes were full of concern.

"Tell me about it, Molly. Maybe I can help."

"What's the point, Michael? It all happened so long ago. It doesn't matter anymore." I still slouched in my chair.

"I think it does, Molly. I think when you got beaten up it caused memories to come back. Any memory that causes your extreme reaction needs to be confronted. Talk to me, Molly. Trust me and let me help."

"I don't understand! Why am I having such vivid recollections of my childhood? It scares me and I don't know what to do to stop them from flooding my mind." I sat up straight in my chair and I had taken charge of my feelings. I was determined to trust Michael but I was hesitant to share my past. I drifted off into silent thoughts.

"Share your thoughts, Molly," he whispered, almost inaudibly.

"I was thinking back to one day last week when I lost myself completely in reliving my family's move to Moose Jaw from Sudbury. It was such an exciting time and yet sad, I think, for my mother to leave all her friends behind. My father had joined the Army and she had just had my sister. That meant she had to travel with three young children and a newborn on the train with no help."

I shared the memory of the move with Michael, leaving out the times I was being groomed by Sadie. I was much too embarrassed to share such secrets at this time. I took a quick glance at my watch and was relieved to see our time was up.

I stood and started to put on my coat.

"Okay, Molly, have you made some appointments with Beth?"

"No, I just made this one last week. How many should I book?" I hoped it will only be another one or two.

"Why don't we do six now and see how that works?" he said, walking out of his office.

"Six!" I sqeaked. "Do you really think I need to come back that many more times?"

"Yes, definitely six for now."

"Beth, will you book Molly in for the next six weeks please?" Turning to me he reiterated, "You can call me anytime, remember, if things start to get too much for you."

"Thanks, Michael, I know and I promise I will call if I need to. I'll see you next week." Taking the appointment card from Beth, I walked out the door feeling a little overwhelmed and relieved at being out from under what seemed like an interrogation.

Chapter 18

"Hi Carin, I thought I would stop by for a quick cup of coffee if you are not too busy," I said as she answered the door.

"Sure, Mom, come on in! I'm in the middle of making some buns for supper, but I'd love to stop for a coffee with you. I'll put the coffee pot on. Come on into the kitchen. Where have you been? You look all flushed, is everything okay?" She wiped her hands on her apron.

"I just left a session with Michael and I find I get a little anxious with all the questions and always trying to answer in a way that doesn't appear that I am sparring with him. I'm okay, I can handle it. I haven't seen you for awhile and just thought I would stop by on my way home. Please don't let me take you away from what you are doing, dear. I can come back another time."

"No, no, Mom it's okay. I can do what I have to with you here. I feel a little grungy, though. I haven't done a lot to tidy up the house or myself yet." Carin glanced around, a little breathless after rushing to put the coffee on and trying to straighten up the kitchen table so we have a clear spot to put our cups. She is small just a little over 5 feet, her hair is full of curls and a little unruly right now. The pretty blue T-shirt she wore highlighted her blue eyes. Carin appeared uncomfortable as she fluffed her hair a little and straightened her T-shirt. She tried to cover the stains on it by pushing it under her apron. She looked down at her dirty slippers and shuffled from foot to foot, trying to hide the scuffmarks.

"Don't be foolish dear, I came to see you and I don't give a damn what you have on or if your house is a little untidy. How are the kids and Bill?"

"We're all fine, Mom. Tell me what's happening with your sessions, are they helping you to handle stress a little better? I am still concerned for you and hope you will keep going to see Michael. It's important that we get to the bottom of what these flare-ups you have are about. We need to know that you're okay and that you can deal with everyday circumstances without overreacting."

"There you go again, Carin, making me sound like I rant and rave over every little bump in the road. What is your problem? Can't we just have a normal conversation without you bringing up your 'concerns' as you put it? Don't bother pouring me a coffee. I'm leaving. I don't know why I try to do this, knowing you are convinced I am too old and too senile to look after myself or my house." I pulled my coat off the back of the chair, shoved my arms into the sleeves, turned and walked out of the kitchen.

"Aw, Mom, I didn't mean to upset you again. I just want you to know that I care and that I love you. I want to help. I'm not trying to take away your independence. I need to know you are okay on your own, that's all. I'm glad you are seeing Michael and working things through with him. I want to help, too, any way I can. Please stay and have a cup of coffee and a nice fresh bun. They should be ready in about five minutes." Carin stood up and reached for me.

"I'm too upset right now and coffee will just make me more agitated than I already am. I'll call you later, Carin. I'm sorry I've upset your day. Say 'Hi' to Bill and the kids for me."

I let myself out of the house and hurried down the walkway to my car. I didn't look back as I slid into the car and drove away.

"I can't deal with this crap," I mumbled to myself as I drove home. "I can't handle all this stress. Damn! Bloody Hell!" I screamed with rage and pounded on the seat beside me.

"What the hell is the matter with everyone in my life? Are they all convinced I am nuts and can't look after myself anymore?" I ranted and raved, slammed the car door and stomped into my house. With shaking hands I unlocked the door. Pippa and Christine rushed to greet me.

"Hello you two! Give me a minute to change my shoes and we'll go for a short walk." I started to breathe easier.

"You know what, Pippa and Christine? We're going to have to skip our walk today. I'm too upset to do anything. I'm going to take a hot bath, get into my PJ's, grab a sandwich and hot chocolate and go to bed and read. Sorry guys, but that's life. Some days life sucks." I turned with tears clouding my vision. I took what I needed and headed to my room. I banged the door to shut the dogs out. I lay down and wished I could climb out of my skin and start over again.

I drifted off into a dreamless but restless night.

Chapter 19

I put on the coffee the next morning, dropped a slice of bread into the toaster, let the dogs out while I waited for my toast and coffee. "We are going for a walk right after we all have something to eat, I promise," I told my dogs as I let them in and poured some dog food in their dishes. I was desperate for my coffee fix and felt it kick in as the hot liquid soothed my nerves and throat. I enjoyed it and my toast and thought about the day ahead.

I cleaned up the kitchen and put my dirty dishes in the dishwasher. I looked around and felt such a sense of belonging. I had recently remodeled it. I painted three of the walls a lime green and the other a pale yellow. The east wall has a sliding door that opens on to a large ground level sun deck. My studio is on the left side of the deck. I have a lovely flower garden surrounding it. My deck has built-in benches so I can have my family and friends over for barbeques and evening snacks. I realized with a catch in my heart, just how much I love my home and how furiously I intended to fight for it. I don't care who gets in the line of fire.

"C'mon girls let's go. We'll do the flats today," I said to the dogs, reaching for my coat, scarf, leashes and gloves.

"I love it out here, it's a great day for a walk, cold and a little overcast but we'll do the whole trail today."

I chatted to them as we hiked along together. The scrub brush was thick and dark, having had to endure the cold, snow and little sunlight that we had experienced over the past couple of months. The flats were covered with water from melted snow and rain. Mallards, drakes, swans, Canada geese, snow geese and grebes came in great numbers, gently floating along the water's surface. When the dogs disturbed them, the water birds scolded them in their throaty voices. They made it clear that they were upset with the rudeness of these two hooligan dogs that seemed to think they can trespass on the birds' territory.

"They certainly gave you guys a piece of their mind," I laughingly told the dogs. I walked vigorously to keep warm and gave myself a good workout. I passed a few others who were walking, some with dogs, and they gave a friendly nod or a quiet 'Hi!' None of us stopped to chat. Each of us seemed absorbed in our own thoughts.

I had hardly slept that night. I had been so upset by the turmoil of the day.
"Man, I wonder if the end result is worth the chaos all this is causing me right now? What with Carin prattling on about my 'moods,' as she puts it, and Michael giving me the third degree on things that happened so long ago that can't possibly be causing havoc now. What do you think, Christine? Do you believe we should keep going and dredge up things long past? You do? Okay then, you're a wise old girl." I continued to shoot the breeze with the dogs until we arrived back home.

Walks are a blessing for me these days.

Chapter 20

"Brr, I'm cold! I'm going to make some hot coffee," I muttered to myself.

While I waited for the coffee to brew, I went to fetch my down quilt out of the hall cupboard. I picked up a small book tucked in the corner of the cupboard with other books I had read to Carin when she was a little girl. These stories are so sweet and each has a charming message that even small children grasp. Feeling nostalgic, I leafed through the pages and longed for those innocent times. I wondered why we were fighting over the smallest things these days? I found it hard to cope, worrying about what she might do if I made many more slip-ups with my temper, but I found it darn frustrating, walking on eggshells around her. Carin and I have always been able to sort through our differences, but this time it was different. She had never interfered in my life before now and I have steered clear of her personal life, except in times when she has invited my opinion.

Here I was again, getting myself into another tizzy. I started to put the books back on the shelf, when I remembered the coffee, noticing the wonderful aroma wafting through the house. I headed down the hall to the kitchen and poured myself a cup. I sweetened it a little and made a mental note to quit worrying about things over which I had no control. I love my home and I resolved to hang onto it, regardless of what Carin, Michael or anyone else might think of my ability to do so.

I settled down with my coffee and a romance book to read but I couldn't concentrate. I put the book down and let the memories in to remember.

***

"I love your yellow negligee, Mindy," I had said. I bent my knees up under me on her bed in her room.

"Thank you, Molly. How did you know it's called a negligee? That's a pretty big word for you to remember." She pulled her hair back and put a lovely yellow ribbon through it.

"Sadie taught me. She is teaching me lots of things so I can play like you do. How do you keep the ribbon in your hair, Mindy?" I rolled onto my tummy with my knees bent and my ankles crossed.

"I weave it through my hair. Come here and I will show you how." She held out her hand, inviting me to move near her.

"You have beautiful long dark hair, Molly, and it shines with red highlights. See how lovely the ribbon looks woven into your braids? You are a little small to do this on your own, get Sadie to do that for you when it is time for you to meet your men. Hand me those panties. I am getting a little behind here and I need to be downstairs very soon."

"Wow, they are really small but kind of lacy. You look really nice, Mindy. I bet you will be the first to get to dance tonight."

"Run along now Molly, I have to finish getting ready." She turned back to her mirror and finished with her make-up.

I ran out and found Joseph.

"Let's sneak out and peek again tonight, Joseph." I encouraged him to do my bidding. "Everyone looks so good."

"Molly, come with me," Sadie called.

"Where are we going Sadie?" I asked, running along the hall to her room and leaving Joseph behind.

"I want you to go and get into your little white long nightgown, the one with the white ruffles and the pink ribbon running through the cuffs and neck. You know the one I mean?" she asked as she slipped into her red bra and panties.

"Why do you wear the garter belt outside your panties, Sadie? They look funny with the garters hooked on your black stockings where I can see them. Aren't they supposed to be hidden? And why have you got on such high heels?"

"I'll explain later, Molly. Right now, just do as I ask and come back here. Don't put on any underpants, just wear the nightgown." She sat at her dressing table putting on her makeup as she gave me directions.

"When you are old enough to wear make-up Molly remember less is better. You don't want to overdo it and make yourself look garish. I hope you don't start too young, natural beauty is the best. If you eat right and take care of yourself you won't need make-up. Maybe a little lipstick but not bright red or orange just a soft pink.

"Why do you wear so much make-up Sadie? Rachelle wears really red lipstick."

"We have to because the men we entertain like to see us all painted up. I think it makes them feel better knowing we take so much time to look pretty for them. I started wearing my make-up too young and that is why I don't want you to make the same mistake Molly." She heaved a deep sigh and smiled hesitantly at me.

"Run along now and get into the nightgown and come back to me."

I ran to my room tore off my clothes and pulled the nightgown out of drawer. I was excited that I was included in the night party. I wondered why I had to wear my nightgown though as it seemed wrong to me but then I remembered some of the men liked me to look like a little girl.

I pulled the nightgown over my head, but felt bare and uncomfortable without my panties. I shrugged off my concerns and quickly rushed back to Sadie's room.

"Why do I get to wear my pretty night gown? I think my mommy will be mad at me if she finds out I am wearing it out of my special room."

Her room was amber with beige trim. The furnishings blended well. They were dark mahogany with brass fittings. Her dresser lamp had an orange shade on a burnished base. Her bed quilt was chocolate brown with yellow daisies scattered throughout. She had a cream-colored wicker chair that I often sat on.

"No, she won't. You are coming to our very special party tonight. There are going to be some very important people there, including Roger and Duncan. Now come over here and I will weave a pink ribbon through your braids like Mindy did."

"Will you teach me how to do that one day, Sadie? I like it better this way than with just ordinary braids and ribbons tied at the end."

"Yes, but maybe we should get Mindy to teach you. She is much better at it than I am. You are only four and it is pretty tricky for small hands." She wove the ribbon into my hair, and then glanced at me in the mirror and our eyes locked briefly. I could sense some hesitation in her, but I was too excited about the night to ask if I had done something bad.

"Okay, we are ready. Now, take my hand and we'll go downstairs. Are you ready to do this, Molly?"

"Am I going to get to go to my special room tonight, Sadie? Will I get two presents, one from Roger and one from Duncan? Maybe Duncan will bring some more chocolate. I like Duncan the very best. He is really nice to me. He talks in a small voice. I promised to give some of my candies to Joseph and Ross. Maybe Joseph will peek and see us playing," I snuck a look at Sadie and covered the giggle that was erupting in my chest.

"Not tonight, kitten, to both questions. Duncan, Roger and you will stay downstairs, but they will be with you and maybe will dance with you. Joseph has been given strict instructions to stay in his room with threats that I am sure will keep him there. Now c'mon, let's do it!" She slipped into a long red flimsy robe.

We walked down the stairs. At least I walked down the stairs. Sadie seemed to drift down with her robe billowing behind her. I looked up at her and she looked really pretty. When we walked into the

84

lounge all eyes turned to her. I felt embarrassed because I only had on my night-gown even my feet were bare. But Sadie kept hold of my hand as we went into the room.

"Hi, Molly, you look very sweet tonight," said Roger. He came over and took my hand. "Come and sit with me for awhile. Sadie has someone who wants to dance with her."

"Where are you taking me?" I asked as we walked toward the back of the room where it was dark with just a few lamps lit.

"Just over here on the divan. Duncan is here too. We want to talk to you a little bit and maybe we can teach you a short dance. Would you like that, Molly?" He lifted me onto the divan.

"I guess so. I'm not good at dancing, though. I've never tried to dance with a man, just my brother Joseph when we hear fast music on the radio."

"Hi, Molly, you look very pretty, who did your hair up so nice?" Duncan asked as he reached for me and stroked my hair.

"Sadie. But Mindy showed her how to weave the ribbon in. It is very hard to make sure the ribbon doesn't come out. Roger's going to show me how to do a little dance." I snuggled between the two of them.

"Maybe in a short while. It's a little busy on the floor right now. All the ladies are dancing. Your mother is a very good dancer. I love the way she uses those clinging scarves, very beautiful, don't you think?"

"Sadie says men like women to look like that, but I am supposed to look like a little girl. Do you like to play with little girls?" I asked, looking up into his face.

"Yes, we do Molly," he said, pulling me closer to him. I found his jacket scratchy and I pulled away.

"Will you make me feel like Sadie did?" I was shy but I wanted them to understand it was okay.

"What did she do, Molly?" Duncan asked, touching my knee as he moved closer.

"She played with me like you are going to she told me."

Do you want us to play with you like that Molly?

"Oh yes, I would love you to do that again. Sadie says it is not a bad thing to do as long as it is only in my special room or with her, so maybe we shouldn't do it here."

Just then Sadie came over to the divan and knelt on the floor in front of me.

"We're going to do some nice things to you, Molly, and I am going to stay with you and help make you feel all warm and funny again, just like we did before?" She put both of her hands on my knees and squeezed them softly.

"It will be all right. It is dark here and no one else will come in here for quite a while. Most of the ladies are upstairs now or dancing. They will soon go upstairs too," Sadie reassured me as I looked around, scared that my mother would come in and catch me downstairs with my special nightie on.

"Is that okay?" I whispered.

"Of course its okay." He fondled my face and tweaked my nose.

"I guess so." I squirmed and felt nervous that someone would come in and see us, but I was getting excited too.

They reignited that powerful force that took over all thought and feelings. I was lost in the emotion and frightened as it all seemed too much and very wrong but I was pulled into the vortex and felt like an electric coil that was fully charged. I wanted more, but I was spent of all energy. I laid my head back against Roger's lap. I was so sleepy.

"Did you like that, Molly?" Duncan's eyes were shiny and he too seemed excited.

"Oh yes. Will you do it again in a little while? I am too sleepy right now." I felt my bones turn to rubber and my eyelids seemed heavy as lead.

"Next time, you will be with just one of us up in your special room. Have a little nap right now and then we are going to show you some things and teach you how you can make each of us feel good like you. We'll stay here until it's time for the next part of your lesson and after that we will play with you until you feel like you are on fire. Have a little sleep now." Duncan's words sounded muffled to me as I drifted off into a sound sleep.

Caught in deep slumber, I didn't stir as Roger carried me up the stairs to my room, all thought of further lessons on this night lost to sleep. The next part of the lesson would take place much too soon. I was draped in the arms of the man who was so perverted that he paid whatever price was asked to rob a little girl of her innocence.

And so the night of exquisite sensation was over for me. I slept, lost in the throes of awakened sexual awareness in the body of a very young girl. I could not imagine the pain and feelings of betrayal looming in the shadows of days and nights to come.

Chapter 21

Whoa! Maybe I shouldn't try and remember such disturbing times. Wandering off into my past wasn't going to help keep calm and anchored. I felt squeamish and unsettled with the memories still fresh in my mind. I yawned and looked at my watch and with disdain, I realized I had lost the whole morning. I needed to go out and buy a birthday gift for Meagan, my granddaughter. She would soon be fifteen and I knew she loved pretty panties and bras and, of course, she loved those music videos. The last time she was here, she had confided in me that she loved thong panties and that they were the best under tight jeans. She had told me bras come in a variety of bright colors and they looked sweet under her low T-shirts. I changed in a hurry and headed over to the mall.

As I walked into the mall, I decided to get her some lingerie, so I made my way to the big lingerie store situated in the middle. I love this mall. It is only a twenty-minute drive from my house. It is brightly lit, has a nice variety of outlets and the prices are reasonable in all of the stores. The colors of the walls, the window displays and the cheerful greeting of most of the employees, encourage shoppers and make it a very pleasant place to spend an afternoon.

I had to pass the chocolate shop and I was tempted to buy a box of caramels and a butter pecan ice cream cone. I hesitated outside the shop but denied my craving and momentary weakness and continued to the lingerie shop.

"Hello, can I help you?" a clerk asked as I glanced around for a nice gift.

"Thank you, but right now I would just like to look awhile until I can make up my mind. I'm not sure what it is I want."

"No problem. Let me know if I can help." The clerk left me to browse.

Meagan loves bright colors, so I searched through a variety of multicolored bras and panties. I picked up a lovely delicate thong and chuckled to myself, remembering some of the G-strings I used to wear. They are the same brief, unmentionables, only now they call them "thongs" and anyone uses them, including many young girls because they don't leave a panty line when you wear tight pants. How things change over the years! What was considered naughty but nice in my day, is used every day now. Too bad! It's these little extras that add spice to relationships. Somehow, the spice gets lost when you know your young daughter is wearing the same thing and calling them "panties." Oh well, I again smirked at the thought of all the spice I remembered. I continued to rummage through the panties, holding them up and trying to decide whether to go bright or a soft pastel, when a woman beside me grunted her disapproval at the scantiness of the thong I was looking at.

"Don't you think it is fun for the kids to have such bright and pretty colors? I remember when we had black, navy blue and white only and black was not the color nice girls wore, unless they were bloomers in the winter on the prairie," I laughingly told her.

"It is no wonder our children are so inundated with sexual thoughts with this kind of trashy underwear," the woman retorted, "and we all know what is on television and the movies. They are like 'how to' movies on violence and sex. I get so angry about the things to which our kids are exposed." The woman spewed her feelings in such a derogatory manner, that my dander rose.

"Oh come on, surely you don't believe scanty underwear is going to make sex trade workers out of our kids? These are pretty and with the kind of pants our girls wear, there is no panty line to worry about when one wears a thong." I was trying not to show my disparagement for her tirade.

She persisted. "You are like so many unsuspecting grandparents out there, living in your little bubble of innocence, going along, apathetic to the real world and its trappings under the heading of entertainment." She was so indignant that she was almost frothing at the mouth!

"Really? I can probably singe your ears pretty good with some of my adventures! You are unbelievable! You shouldn't judge others by your ridiculous narrow thoughts." I tried not to giggle at the prospect of filling her with my supposed innocence of the real world, but at the same time, I was starting to get annoyed with her.

"I get a pretty good picture of you, just by seeing the kind of trashy panties, if you can call that thing with no crotch a panty, you are thinking of buying," she retorted, flinging her hair back with her hand. Her nose was so far in the air, I was surprised she didn't wrench her neck!

"How dare you judge me? Who do you think you are talking to? Do you think you are some kind of saint with your high and mighty attitude? People like you, with your prim, narrow outlook on everything, go around looking down your nose at the rest of us. You, and others like you, are the ones that label everyone. You don't even know me for heavens sake!" I yelled into her face and by now I am out of control. I am furious at her stupidity and warped outlook.

She backed up as I continued with my diatribe. By this time, people were gathering and, once again, a store clerk came over and tried to diffuse the situation. But I was not having any of it! I was livid and my fury was directed at this judgmental prig, and I continued to let her have it with both barrels. The woman walked away with her head up and spine so stiff I wondered it didn't snap in two! Somewhere in the back of my mind, I was aware that I needed to get control of my emotions, despite being provoked by that female. The clerk tried to calm me down, but I was too damned upset.

"Just back off," I raged. "I will be fine. I still need to buy my granddaughter a birthday present and I don't need you to hover over me like some guardian angel. I am sorry for that little drama but it has nothing to do with you. People like her behave in such a self-righteous way, they need to be pulled down off their high horses. I am just the one to do it, so you carry on and look after your business and I will carry on with mine." All the while my stomach was churning with indignation. I was, once again, the center of attention because of my angry outburst.

Sadly for me, someone in the mall recognized me and called Carin who arrived on the scene just as I was paying for the items I had picked for Meagan.

"Mom, Mary phoned me to tell me you were screaming at some woman in the store. She thought you were going to hit the woman you were so mad. She said you were yelling right in her face. For crying out loud, Mom, I don't know what has gotten into you lately. You flare at the least provocation. I am going to call Michael and tell him about this latest eruption, you can be sure of that. Your sessions with him don't seem to be doing much to help you do they?" She spouted off near tears.

I am not certain if her scarlet face was from being embarrassed, rage or indignation.

"Of course he is helping me! Once again, Carin, you were not here to hear what that stupid woman was spouting on about, so don't be so quick with your remarks. You are very willing to conclude and assume that I was the one in the wrong. I am going home and I would appreciate it if you would let me get on with my life with a lot less interference from you. I will call you when I have something to say that I believe to be important for you to know. By all means call Michael. I feel quite confident he won't recommend you confine me to a Senior's Home just yet! As a matter of fact, I have to hurry to keep my appointment with him today. I have to be there within the next two hours. If you hurry, you may get lucky and reach him before our session, so he can be fully apprised of my appalling behavior!"

Carin made no response, but walked away, shoulders slumped, head down, deeply hurt by my unkind sarcastic words.

The truth was, I didn't have an appointment with Michael that day, but I had to get Carin out of my hair. The thoughts bouncing around in my head were so troubling that I didn't feel the least bit guilty for lying to her. I hastily paid for my merchandise and hurried to my car, hoping I wouldn't run into anyone I knew.

"Hello, Mr. Hopkins," I shouted to my neighbor as I drove into my driveway and got out of the car. I fought to stay in control of my still-churning stomach.

"Hi, Molly! Nice day today; a little on the cool side, but nice to see the rain gone for awhile," he called back.

"You bet! I look forward to getting my garden cleaned up and ready for planting which should be very soon now," I answered as I unlocked my front door and let myself into the house, glad to be where I felt safe and knew I wouldn't be disturbed by anyone.

Just to be sure I would be left alone, I turned off the phones and put the kettle on for a cup of tea to enjoy while I thought about what to prepare for my supper.

I marveled at the serenity of my home while I waited for the kettle to boil. I have a small back yard where I grow tomatoes, lettuce and carrots. I love blueberries and have two bushes that I hope will give me a good crop this year. I grow daffodils, hyacinths and tulips in the spring. I love dahlias and have a large selection in a separate plot of ground. My front yard is largely lawn with some iris, daffodils, tulips and gladiolas. I have some flowering bushes like roses, lilac, and rhododendron along the front windows and side of the house. My house is white with gray trim. I spend most of my time in the front room when I am home. I enjoy the dark green of my feature wall and the soft white of the rest of the room. My pictures are of flowers and people. I laid my head back in my favorite beat-up chair and reminisced. It reminded me of my days when I sat in this same chair rocking, singing and reading to my sweet little girl. My musings reignited my anger at Carin. I wondered what had happened to the sweetness of her young years? From my perspective, she had now taken on the role of my enemy, challenging and threatening everything I cherished. My daughter, my grandchildren, my home and garden were all at risk. I had this feeling that clawed and tore at my mind. I was no longer in control of my destiny and yet I knew I could not let anyone take my life over no matter what they thought. I still had power over my own fate. Let the chips fall where they may . . . hot tears of anger spilled over my face and I shut my mind to the here and now . . .

Chapter 22

My thoughts wafted back to that amazing house in Moose Jaw that holds so many memories . . . I was overwhelmed as I watched the recollections unfold and felt the emotions connected to each as I opened my mind to those years of turmoil . . .

The house was large and such fun, with so many places to play and hide. Joseph, Ross and I were busy playing hide and seek. We all ran, helter-skelter over the house and found the best hiding places. Joseph came running into the room where both

Ross and I were hiding. I hunkered down as Joseph found Ross and I squealed as Ross pointed to where I was hiding. Busted and found.

"That's not fair!" I shouted at Joseph, my hands on my hips and my feet planted firmly on the floor.

"You little spy!" I yelled at Ross. "You're such a baby you can't stand to lose any games can you? You spoil it for everyone else." I shrieked into his face.

"Aw c'mon Molly, he just gets really excited and wants to help," Joseph said, putting his arms around Ross who had started to cry.

"He's a creep who won't play any game fair." I started to cry too.

"You never would have found me if it hadn't been for him squealing on me."

"It's only a game, Molly, let's go ask Mom if we can have some cocoa and a cookie." Joseph led both of us into the kitchen where she was busy with Emma our little sister.

"Can we have some cocoa, Mom?" we all asked in unison.

"No, not today. We only have a little sugar left and we can't get any more for two weeks when we get our new rations book. We have to use what we have sparingly."

"I hate the war," I whined. "We always have to wait for good things to eat and drink."

"Be grateful, young lady, that we are fighting that monster in Germany. Hitler is where you should be directing your anger to, not at the rationing of goods that you can and will do without." She looked stern.

I again wondered why she hated me and not my brothers or sister. It couldn't be the war. I wished I knew what I could do to make her love me too. I did lots of chores for her and I was learning how to make money like her and the other ladies. I hoped when I started to make some money she would begin to love me.

I stomped out of the room and up the stairs into my bedroom. I knew she would never understand me, but I hoped she would want to care for me like she did for my siblings. I had a surprise for her though, and I knew she would be really happy with me when she saw what I had been doing. I reached into my dresser drawer and pulled out a small ball of string I had been saving. We saved string, rubber bands, elastic and ribbons because they were hard to get too.

Just then my mother came into my room.

"I'm tired of your constant tantrums, Molly, whenever things don't go your way. You and I are going to have a talk and you are going to listen and do as I tell you. What is that you are holding behind your back?" She yanked my arm around and saw the ball of string.

"You selfish little bitch! You are hoarding string when you know how much we need to reuse so many of these things!" She tried to take the ball away from me.

"I was saving it for you, Mommy. I was going to surprise you when I had more. Honest, Mommy, I only hid it because I wanted it to be a surprise for you." I was whimpering as I handed her the ball of string.

"Don't lie to me! Come with me!" She grabbed my arm and dragged me down the stairs and opened the basement door.

"Please don't put me in the basement, Mommy. I am scared down there!" I wailed, clinging to her. "Please Mommy, I didn't do anything bad."

"Get down the stairs and stay there until I tell you to come out. I don't know what I am going to do about you and your rebellious ways, Molly. Why can't you be more like your brothers?" she demanded.

"I hate them! You always like them best. I don't ever want to be like them. They are boys and they can't help you make money like me. Ross always tells my hiding places. He is such a baby. He always cries when he doesn't get his own way and then you are always good to him and not to me. Why don't you like me, Mommy? Please send me to my room and I will stay there all day, but please don't shut me down those stairs and into the dark basement." I sobbed and moaned with terror. I clung to her legs and clutched at her ankles.

"Get down there! I am sick of looking at you!" She slapped my face and shoved me through the door and I slunk down the stairs clutching the railing. I hoped she would call me back but when I reached the bottom, she turned out the light and shut the door.

"Oh, mommy, you are supposed to love me. What is so bad about me that you don't care and you just always hurt me so bad?" I wept curling up on myself, too afraid to move off of the bottom step. It was way too dark and scary.

I laid on the bottom step and keened to myself. I was greatly relieved when, what seemed like hours later, Sadie came down the stairs and took me up to the brightly lit kitchen.

"Why is she so mean to me, Sadie?" I whimpered, limply leaning on her.

"I can't answer that, Molly. You just get her into such a fury, she can't seem to help herself when you do and say things that upset her. You do get mad and say some very stupid things when you know she is upset with you. Why don't you try and just keep your mouth buttoned and take your punishment and then maybe you wouldn't end up in the basement?"

"I don't mean to make her mad. She just always seems to be mad at me. I just wanted a cup of cocoa." I moaned into her skirts.

"Yes, but Molly, it's what you said when you were told you couldn't have any. Come, go and wash up for supper and try to stay out of your mother's way until bedtime."

Chapter 23

It was later that same week when my mother sent Sadie to talk with me.

"Molly, tonight Roger is going to come for you," she said as she took my hand and sat me down next to her. She looked sad when she told me about Roger.

"Oh, goody! Will he play with me again, Sadie?" I asked.

"Yes, but you will have to play with him too, Molly. I am going to explain some things to you, so you won't be so surprised."

"I know how to let them undress me and do good things to me, Sadie. I will play with them and make them feel good too."

She looked right at me and smiled but she still looked sad.

"Yes, lots of times and I have peeked at the men in the lounge when you and the other ladies let them touch you and make you wiggle over them and dance with them. They get so big and then you take them up to your rooms. Sometimes you hold on to their weenies while you walk up the stairs. Joseph and I ran back to our rooms and giggled in our pillows, because it looked so funny. Should I hold onto Roger like that?"

"Molly what is going to happen with Roger will be different than anything you have done before. I want you to be good and brave. You know I wouldn't ask you to do anything that would be harmful to you, if there was any other way we could help your mommy we would. Please remember that and think of really good things in your mind and it will end much faster.

It might hurt a little, Molly, but I want you to be brave and remember you are doing this to help your mommy pay for all the things she needs to look after you and your brothers and sister. Do you think you can do that for me?" She lovingly ran her hand over the side of my face.

"I will, Sadie. Will you come in and play too?"

"Not this time, Molly. It will be up to you to make Roger happy enough to pay for you. You have to be good, and then he will want to come back again."

"I'll be really good and he will only want to play with me, you'll see, and maybe my mommy will be really happy with me. Will I get to use a different name like my mommy?"

"No, you will be called 'Molly'."

"Why does my she call herself 'Rose'? She never uses her own name when she is playing with the men and when they come to the door, all the men call her 'Rose'."

"She does that so we all know she is working and not being a mom. One day, you may use a different name for the same reason. Now I need to go and help Sissy get ready for a date she and I are going on together."

"Will you and I get to go on a date together sometime, Sadie?" I asked.

"I don't know; we will have to wait and see," she answered. I took her hand and followed her into Sissy's room.

"Hi, you two," Sissy said as we knocked and went into her room. Sissy's room was light and airy. One wall was cream, the other three were lilac. Her furnishings were maple except for her makeup table; it was antique cream with gold embossed along the legs and edges. Her quilt was a pastel yellow with small purple rosebuds scattered on it. Her room was always neat and tidy. She had an old rocking chair that had an oversized seat with large armrests. I could almost get lost on it; it could easily hold two of me. Her floors were a light-colored oak with two lovely scatter rugs. Both rugs were mottled purple with large cream-colored flowers.

"Hi, Sissy. I am going to get to play in my special room with my special clothes later," I told her excitedly as I jumped onto her bed.

"That's wonderful, Molly," she said as she took off her robe. I was surprised that she had nothing on underneath it.

"Molly, you must not talk about what you or what anyone of us do, except to us girls. It is very important that no one else knows about us. Can you promise me you will never tell anyone outside of your mommy, Sissy, Rachelle, Mindy Susie and me, no matter what? You must never tell." Sadie skewered me with her eyes and I was momentarily scared speechless.

"Sadie, I won't ever tell, I promise! We aren't doing bad things, so why can't I tell how much fun I have playing? I would like to tell Joseph that I am going to help our mom by getting money for letting the men play with me. Maybe we could teach Joseph how to get really happy and excited too, and then he could help our mom too."

"What we do here is a secret, Molly If everyone knew, we would not make much money because so many other people would do it. What you do is the very best secret so we must make sure no one ever finds out. Even when you are older, you must never tell, Molly, or we will all be in very big trouble. Please don't ask me anymore about this. Just never break your promise to me." Sadie looked so fearful, I knew I must always keep this promise.

"I promise, Sadie. Cross my heart and hope to die. I will never tell anyone." I mumbled.

"Sadie, you have to help me get ready. We need to leave in an hour and you still aren't ready," Sissy stated. She was clearly stressed.

"Okay. Have you got your tassels ready?" Sadie asked Sissy.

"Yes, here they are. These are my favorites. They have a lovely red in them and they will go with my sheer red lacy bra." Sissy gave the tassels to Sadie and Sadie attached them to Sissy's breast just around the nipples.

"Oh those are so fun!" I exclaimed, "Can I have some for when I go with Roger?" I pleaded.

"No, silly. You have to have breasts to wiggle so the tassels will twirl," Sissy laughingly told me and she twirled them.

"When you have breasts like us we will see if we can find some nice pink ones for you to use, Molly. Until then, remember I told you to be like a little girl for the men who come to see you. They don't want anyone who is built like me or Sissy or any other adult woman. Don't be in such a hurry to grow up, sweetie," Sadie cautioned and snuggled me against her thigh.

"Run along now, Molly, while Sissy and I continue to get ready. I will see you later. If I am not back before Roger comes, be sure you get Rachelle or Mindy to help you. Have a nice bath and they will help you put on your pretty dress and stuff. Put on your fancy shoes and socks too, Molly, and remember Roger will want to undress you himself, so don't be too anxious for him to play. Make sure you do as he asks you and don't try to act like a grown up." Sadie breathlessly gave me all of my instructions while she took off her own blouse and bra so Sissy could put some tassels on her.

"Okay, Sadie," I said and ran out of her room and down the stairs. I was burning with anticipation. I could hardly wait for tonight to come.

"Mommy, what time will Roger come to see me tonight?" I asked as I sat and drank my glass of milk in the kitchen.

"Why does *she* get to stay up late again tonight when I am the oldest and who is Roger and why is he coming to see Molly?" Joseph asked and made a face at me.

"It's none of your business, Joseph. It is a very important secret that I am not allowed to talk about and neither are you supposed to," I admonished him in my most haughty voice.

"Joseph, what Molly is learning is essential and you cannot be concerned with it. Molly, asking questions like that in front of others will not be tolerated. You know the rules and if you can't abide by them then I will find someone else who can. Rachelle will come and take you upstairs to get ready after supper.

In future if you have any questions like this you will ask me in private not in front of anyone."

My mother glared at me like I was some kind of bug. She sternly reprimanded me. She seemed a little jittery to me and I wondered if she was worried I would tell or maybe she was worried for me.

"Not even in front of my brothers?" I asked, not understanding.

"What did I just tell you? Do you ever listen to me, Molly, or do you just not understand English?" My mother again chastised me in front of my brothers.

"She just likes to think she is better than us," Joseph said. He smirked at me and that made me angry. I wanted to lash out at him, but I knew I would be the one to get into trouble.

"That's enough! Both of you, go on outside to play until supper. I will call you when it is ready and, Molly, keep your thoughts and questions to yourself!"

"I will, Mommy," I sighed and went out the door after Joseph.

"Pretty soon it will be hot and we can go to the pond and swim, Joseph. Won't that be fun?" I cheerfully chattered on as I skipped along the path to the park.

"I'm not ever going swimming. I hate the deep water. It is nice out now, so let's go and find a trail that leads to one of the small caves and play pirates," Joseph hollered back. He ran ahead away from the pond.

"Okay, but I don't want to be a prisoner like last time. I want to be a pirate too," I yelled running to keep up to him.

"You can't be a pirate too, silly, otherwise we couldn't have a robbery if we are both pirates. I am in charge, Molly, and I know how to play this game. Don't I always show you the best way for us to have fun and laugh and play?"

"Yes, Joseph You always look after me real good."

"Are you afraid of what's going to happen tonight, Molly?" Joseph asked.

"I don't like the way the men touch mom and the rest of our friends, do you?" He didn't look at me when he asked.

"It's okay, Joseph. I'm not allowed to tell you things, but they are really nice to me and they don't hurt me and they are going to give me candies that I can share with you and Ross."

"I don't know, Molly. How can they get so much more chocolate and sweets when the rest of us have to use our ration coupons? Once ours are used up, we have to wait for the next booklet. I don't think it's right but I don't know what we can do about it. I hope you are not being tricked into things that will hurt you and make you sad. Please be careful, Molly. I can't look after you at home the way I can out here. You can tell me if they do anything to hurt you and I promise I will help you get away from them." Joseph shuffled from foot to foot. He appeared embarrassed by what he was saying to me.

"I can't tell you things, Joseph, or mommy will punish me. We have watched Sadie, Rachelle and the others and they laugh and have lots of fun, so I think I will have fun too. It's too bad you are a boy or you could do what I do and make money too."

"What do you mean, Molly? How do you make money?"

"I can't tell you anymore, Joseph. Please don't ask me ever again, promise! Okay?"

"All right, Molly. We're here at the cave so you have to find a place to hide your treasure. I will try and find you and take away your loot and take you prisoner. I will count to fifty and then I will come and search for you."

We played until we were hungry and then we went home in time for supper.

Chapter 24

I love the memory of those days. I remember how much Joseph wanted me to talk to him so he could look out for me like he always did when we were outside being carefree and full of adventure.

We were both so young, he was just in grade one but he seemed grown up to me. I longed to go to school and be a big kid like him.

Looking back, I am convinced he knew that something bad was going to happen to me and he wanted to stop it. He tried to protect me but he was neither big enough nor strong enough to make a difference back then. The memory of that day and that conversation still haunt me.

My Mother told me to eat up my supper so I could go upstairs with Rachelle and get ready for the evening.

"You boys can listen to the radio until eight o'clock and then you have to go to bed," she instructed Joseph and Ross.

"Oh, boy! The 'Green Hornet' is on tonight!" Ross said enthusiastically with a broad smile.

"Yeah! He's great! His car is the best," Joseph remarked.

"Let's go and listen to 'Fibber McGee and Molly' until the 'Green Hornet' comes on," Joseph said and gulped down the last mouthful of his dinner.

"Don't you want some desert? I have a nice surprise for all of you," mom beamed as she got up from the table. You boys gather the dishes and put them in the sink."

"What, Mommy?" we all asked together.

"We have some corn syrup, and tonight I can put some butter in it because tomorrow we get our ration books for the month and we still have some butter left." She smiled at us and seemed pleased she was able to give us that treat.

"Thank you, thank you!" we all yelled together. We bounced excitedly in our chairs.

"Once you finish your desserts, go and listen to your radio show until bedtime."

Bedtime for the boys came and Rachelle came to take me up to the bath. She ran a nice warm bath that overflowed with bubbles. I could hardly contain my excitement.

"Climb in Molly and just let the water relax you and the bubbles will leave a nice scent on your skin." She swished her hand through the bubbles and dropped a handful on my nose.

"What's a scent?" I asked.

"It's a word for smell like perfume Molly. We don't want to use perfume on you. It is too strong."

"Rachelle, will Roger play with me in my special room tonight?" I giggled and rubbed the bubbles off of my nose.

"Yes, Molly, and you must do what he tells you to do. Don't forget! He is paying a lot of money to be with you tonight," Rachelle explained.

"I will, Rachelle, and I will make him feel good like he does to me, I promise," I answered. I was all flushed from the warm water. Every part of me was a rosy pink.

"Climb out now, Molly, and I will scrub you dry with this fluffy towel. She wrapped me in it and scrubbed and tickled me dry, I squirmed and wriggled in her arms, I giggled and kissed her cheek. C'mon down to your special room and we'll get you all dressed in your pretty dress, petticoat and panties." Rachelle led me back to my special room.

"Get your clothes out, Molly, and come on over here while I help you to dress. Do you want me to play with you before we dress you, so you feel nice and excited for Roger?" she asked.

"Why are your nipples purple, Rachelle?" I had been dying to ask her about that for a long time.

"I put coloring on them, Molly. The men I have like to rub the color off with their tongues and I like the way that feels,"

"You are going to be very good for this business, Molly. I know the men are going to enjoy being with you. Remember it may hurt a little to begin with because they are big, but they will be gentle with you. Now let's get these clothes on you and take you downstairs. How do you want your hair done tonight?" she asked as she flipped my hair through her fingers. "Do you want one long braid or do you want French braids?"

"One long braid, Rachelle, and a white ribbon weaved through it, please." I looked up at her and I squirmed with anticipation.

"Okay, Molly. We are ready. Let's go downstairs and wait for Roger to come." She took my hand and led me down the stairs.

I was very happy to see Roger when he came in the door. My brothers were in bed and Rachelle and Mindy made certain they stayed there with threats of doom if they showed their faces at the railings in the upstairs hall.

Joseph told me about that night when we were much older. Both he and Ross seemed to sense that that night was different and decided that if they tried to peek through the railings and got caught, the result would be a very bad time for them, probably a long time in the basement as well as a good tanning on their backsides, so they made a pact not to sneak out.

"Hi, Molly," Roger said as he came into the lounge where I was sitting with Rachelle.

"My, but don't you look pretty as a picture!" He put his hand beneath my chin and lifted my face and planted a delicate kiss on my forehead.

I giggled and squirmed.

"You smell real nice, Roger!" I sniffed his hand and kissed his palm.

"Roger, I am dressed pretty for you. We're going to my special room tonight where we can play together." I coyly smiled at his compliments.

"Why don't you and I go up to your special room now, Molly? Would you like that?' he asked as he reached for my hand.

"Sure, Roger," I replied, and went with him. I skipped along, anxious to do well and make money so my mommy would be happy. I wanted to feel that fuzzy sensation in my tummy again. It was so good!

The room looked really nice with just a small bedside lamp that threw off a soft glow. Roger's shadow flickered on the wall and the picture of the mother and baby seemed to be alive. The dark and light played tricks with my sight. The mother seemed to move when the shadow moved with Roger. I felt warm and velvety. I was barely able to keep still.

"I have a little drink for you to try, Molly. You may find it tickles a bit going down your throat, but it will make your tummy feel warm and it will help to relax you for me," he said and poured a drink from a bottle he took from the bedside table. He mixed some soda pop with it.

"Yuk! I don't like that Roger!" I turned up my nose and shivered at the ugly taste. "What is it? I like soda, it's fuzzy and sweet. That's a horrible taste! What is in the big bottle?"

"It's a special drink just for you, Molly. I know it tastes a little strong, but drink it up, babe! It will please me if you do that. You want to please me don't you?" He chucked me under my chin and rubbed his nose on mine.

"Okay, but it burns my tummy when I swallow it," I said. I finished the drink, but shuddered with the taste.

"Now come over here, my little princess and let's have a good look at you." He nestled me between his legs and sat on the edge of the bed.

"I want to take the ribbons out of your hair to start with, Molly. Is that okay?"

"Yes, I know Sadie told me you would want to take my hair down and let it hang loose," I whispered. I began to feel that warmth in the pit of my stomach again. I felt a little woozy. In thinking back, it was probably the liquor that contributed to both of those sensations.

"Ssh! Let's not talk about what Sadie said. I want you to listen to me and let me teach you what I like. Okay, sweetie?"

"Okay, Roger."

Are you feeling comfortable with me, Molly? You don't look embarrassed." He groaned and leisurely removed my sock and sucked on my toes.

"That tickles," I giggled and he yanked off my other shoe and sock.

"I'm not embarrassed, Roger. Rachelle and Sadie told me you would like to look at me bare naked," I sighed. He stood me up and stroked his hand over my shoulders.

"Remember our pact, Molly. Let me teach you my way. No more talk of anyone else." His voice was a little harsh when he spoke.

"I'm sorry Roger, I forgot."

"It's okay. I'll keep reminding you if you forget."

"Holy cow! You are covered in hair!" I exclaimed.

He stopped and looked at me. His eyes had become very shiny, and there was sheen over his top lip.

"I don't think I like this, Roger," I told him. "Can we get dressed and go downstairs, please?" I asked, trying to get away from the feel of his skin. The hair on his chest was thick and prickly and made me itchy.

"No, not yet, Molly!"

"I don't want to play with you, Roger. I'm scared," I whimpered.

"I don't feel very good in my tummy. Please can I go to my other room?"

"No, damn it! I paid good money for you! You will do as I tell you to do! Stand there and play with me like I showed you," he snarled. Then he grabbed my hand but I pulled away and started to protest loudly. He yanked me roughly to him and moved me closer. He forced my legs apart to straddle him, and I struggled to get down. He lay down but hung onto me and we both ended up together on the bed. I was still straddled over him. Then he pushed me down onto his lap and started to move and grunt. He clung to me, rocking me up and down.

"Please stop, Roger! You're hurting me real bad!" I fought him and yelled out as he got rougher each time he moved against me.

His pubic hair was stiff and harsh and with each of his thrusts my skin was grazed.

"Mommy! Mommy!" I screamed. I was frantic to get away from him.

"Shut up! You little vixen!" he growled.

"I want to go to my mommy . . . Mommy! . . . Mommy!" I wailed at the top of my voice.

"What's all the commotion about, Molly? What is the matter with you?" my mother roared as she rushed through the door.

"Roger, you were told to be easy with her. What in the world is wrong with you?"

"Mommy, please take me out of here. I don't want to do this with Roger and he won't let me go." I was extremely relieved when my mother had finally come to my rescue.

"Just be still, Molly. This is what you are being paid to do. Now stop your wailing and do like you've been taught," she snapped.

"Roger is hurting me and won't let me go," I howled. It was only then that he released me. I quickly rolled away from him.

"Shut up!" she banged the door shut and came into the room. She grabbed my arm and hauled me off of the bed.

"You will do as you are told, Molly, unless you want to spend the night in the basement. You have been bragging about how good this stuff feels! Now get on with it!" she snarled.

"And you, Roger, go easy with her. This is her first time with a man," she derided him.

"Sadie should have told me it would hurt this bad and she didn't. It isn't my fault, Mommy. Please don't make me do this. It hurts too badly. I want to come with you." My pleas were wracked with hysterical sobs.

"Stop it right now! You are behaving like a baby, Molly. I am sick of trying to deal with all your histrionics. Roger has paid good money for you. I better not hear any more noise out of you or you will be put downstairs for the night after he is finished. Do you understand?" She knocked the glass of booze onto the floor. Her face and my face were almost nose-to-nose.

"Yes, but why are you so mean to me, Mommy? He is too big for me and he hurts me too bad. Please make him stop." I made my last desperate appeal to her. I was still weeping uncontrollably.

"Don't say another word, Molly, or it's in the basement for you!" she snapped She turned and left me there alone, with Roger. I was bereft because I knew there was no way out for me. I was more afraid of the basement than of anything more Roger could do.

"Come here, Molly." He pulled me to him and lay me on the bed. He lay down beside me and lifted me up to straddle him. He moved me on him and I felt him getting hard and his breathing became more ragged. He moved me up and down faster as his own needs surfaced. My tears were unrepressed. I was completely bewildered and terrified by what was happening.

"Oh, Molly, my sweet thing!"

"You're hurting me! Please stop!" I moaned. I tried again to get away from him, but I couldn't even shift a little. He laid me down beside him while he caught his breath. He was utterly spent because of his brutal struggle to control me and his own final release.

"Lie still, Molly, and let me rest a minute and then I'll clean you," he sighed deeply. "That was a lot of work! Next time it will go easier for both of us. You'll be a little sore for awhile, but you will be fine in a couple of days."

We lay there for what seemed a very long time to me but I was afraid to move in case he wanted me to do some more things. I was beyond enduring any more, and I started to shiver with shock and shame.

"I won't come with you ever again, Roger! You're mean and I hate you!" I choked, taking great gulps of air between sobs.

I was stunned by what had happened. I was dazed and I wondered why it happened to me. I curled up into myself and hoped he would go away; instead he pulled me to him.

"Come on, Molly! You don't mean that. I will be coming back again and you will get so you are very happy to see me. I will bring you a present next time. What would you like, a doll? A book? What? You tell me and I will try and get it for you, I promise," he said, holding me forcefully while I again struggled to escape.

"Let me go! I want to go out of here right now and I don't want your presents! I don't want anything from you and I won't do this again ever! Never! Never!" I screamed at him. I wrenched out of his arms and ran to the door.

"Mommy! Mommy! Can I come out now . . . please . . . please Mommy?" I folded in a heap onto the floor and lay there moaning.

"It's okay my little princess. It will be okay I promise," Roger cooed from the bed.

Finally, the door opened and I looked up through red swollen eyes and saw Sadie standing in the doorway.

"Molly, baby! Come here!" Sadie crouched and enfolded me in her arms.

"Oh! Sadie! Why did you lie to me? He hurt me so bad. I want to come out of here! Please take me away from him now," I begged. I continued to weep grief stricken by all that had taken place.

"Alright, Molly. Let's go and run a nice warm bath and you will feel a lot better. You go on down to the bathroom and I'll come right away. You can get dressed, Roger. I will look after things now. You should settle with Rose and then do whatever pleases you. Have a drink, dancing, whatever. I'm sorry this was so hard for her. She'll come around in time."

I stood and felt utterly betrayed as I listened to what she told Roger. I left and slunk down the hall to the bathroom. I had to cling to the wall. I was completely bewildered. I was barely able to walk because I was in severe pain.

"Here you are, Molly. Let me help you into the tub. Just sit in it. Don't try and wash or anything. Just let the warm water soothe away the pain." Sadie fussed and stroked my hair.
"You're a fine looking mess! All red faced and red-rimmed eyes, snotty nose and disheveled hair! Goodness, Molly! You really need to try and do better than this!"
"He was mean. I'm not ever going in my special room again," I bawled.
"Hush now! We will have your mother down on us. You know you have to, Molly. Your mother will be angry if you don't."
"She's always mad at me anyway, so I don't care! Why, Sadie? Why do I have to do this? It's horrible and I'm just a little girl. I shouldn't have to do this stuff. It's bad, I know it is and that's why I can't tell, isn't it? Will I be punished if anyone finds out? Why did you call my mommy 'Rose'? That's not her name. You know what her real name is." I fired my questions breathlessly.
"That's her special name she uses when she is playing with the men. I told you that before and, yes, you and all us of will be punished if anyone finds out what we do. Your mommy and all of us will go to jail and you, Joseph, Ross and Emma will go to a place where they put children who have no mother to look after them. It's called an orphanage. Do you want that to happen, Molly? Do you?" Sadie was getting cross with me now. I was confused by everything she said and by everything that had happened with Roger. I sat trembling in the tub. I cried and sniveled unable to cope with it all.

"None of you care about me! I don't think I like you anymore either, Sadie. I thought you loved me but if you did, you wouldn't make me do stuff that is bad. What makes me a bad person that no one cares? I want everyone to love me and take care of me, Sadie. Why can't I be liked like Joseph and Ross and Emma? I do stuff to help and they don't. What can I do that will make you all care about me too?" I shouted, kicking my legs and flailing my arms in a tantrum. I splashed water in all directions. I was unable to control my feelings anymore. Sadie looked astonished at my behavior and was soaked with the splashing water.

There was a soft knock on the door.
"May I come in?" Duncan stood behind the door and peered in with just his head showing.
"No!" I shrieked. "You want to be mean to me too! You can't see me! I won't let you touch me anymore and you can't come in!"
"It's okay, Molly," Sadie murmured and caressed my hair. She attempted to calm me.
"No, it's not Sadie," I wailed, hiccoughing in my sobs, "he will do bad stuff like Roger."
"No, I won't Molly. I just want to hold you and let you know how sorry I am that you are so upset. I promise I won't do anything but hold you. Let me help Sadie get you into your pajamas and I'll carry you to your own bedroom, not your special room." Duncan spoke in a hushed voice.
"It's okay, Molly, I will stay with you and Duncan until you fall asleep. He won't hurt you he just wants to love you and cuddle you, I promise," Sadie assured me.

I was too exhausted to argue any more. Duncan came in and helped me out of the tub. He wrapped me in a towel and carried me to my room. He and Sadie helped me into my pajamas. I burbled and fought to break away from him, terrified he would do what Roger had done.

113

"Just relax, Molly. I won't hurt you. I just want to hold you until you fall asleep. I love you and I know Roger did not mean to be so rough." He held my wrists to keep me from running from him.

"Please let me go, Duncan," I begged, squirming. I desperately tried to get free of him.

"Alright, but let me lie down beside you and hold you until you fall asleep. Okay baby girl?" he sighed.

"I'm not a baby!" I retorted.

"I know, Molly. That's just a term of endearment." He dried my eyes with his handkerchief. He released my wrists and put his arms around me. I stood rigid in front of him.

"What's a dearment?" I hiccoughed and wept crocodile tears of a grief more deep than anything I had ever felt.

"It just means I love you sweetie." He tucked a straggled piece of my wet hair behind my ear.

I wished with all my might that I had more power to control my life. Those were my thoughts as I choked and gasped, but the tears kept falling and I kept swiping at them. I noticed then that Duncan was not in his uniform but was wearing the clothes he wore when he took me on long walks. We always held hands and talked freely. Somehow, seeing him in those comfortable clothes started to ease my plight.

He had on a scratchy sweater and nice pants. The pants and the sweater were shades of brown and he smelled nice like rain. His hair was wet and I reached up to touch it and wondered how it got wet. He seemed to care and looked saddened by my rejection of him. I tried to squish the fear down into that dark place I sometimes go to hide myself. I kept my arms in front of me tight against my body so he couldn't get too close. But he was near enough that I could smell his clean smell. I let my thoughts go to our quiet walks. I began to visualize the park he sometimes took me when he was pretending to be like a daddy to me. We sometimes made believe I was his little girl. I tried to slip away in my head, but I was too traumatized. I worked at stifling my sobs and finally I was too tired to argue any more. I lay down under the blankets and Duncan lay down on top of the covers and snuggled me to him.

"I love you, baby girl! " he said in my ear.

I fell into an exhausted sleep with his quiet words lodged in my heart. I desperately wanted to believe him.

Chapter 25

The next morning, I came downstairs for breakfast. It was a hard and fast rule in our household that everyone appeared at the breakfast table on time unless we were sick. I sat but I could not eat. I felt pain, despair and loneliness.

"What happened to you, Molly?" Joseph leaned over and quietly asked.

I didn't say anything. I stared at my porridge. The tears trickled down my face. I quickly brushed them away.

"Molly, sit up and eat your breakfast or if you're going to sit there and feel sorry for yourself, go back up to your room," my mother barked. She had not looked me in the eye yet.

"Please, may I be excused?" I vaguely asked.

"Yes, go!"

I gingerly stood up and made my way up to my room. I could hardly walk. I was very sore.

"Can I come in Molly?" Joseph enquired. He had come upstairs a few minutes after me and knocked on my bedroom door.

"Go away, Joseph!"

"C'mon, Molly! Let me in! I have to go to school in twenty minutes. Please let me in."

"Oh, Joseph! Yes, please come in. I am really sad and I hurt bad." I wanted someone to understand my grief, so I opened the door a little and he came in.

"What happened to you, Molly? I couldn't come out last night when I heard you screaming, because mom told us if we came out to peek at the top of the stairs or if we came out of room at all, we would spend the night in the basement. I'm sorry, Molly, but I am too scared to go down there. I couldn't come and help you." He took hold of my hand. "I'm really sorry, Molly. I should have come anyway."

"It's okay, Joseph. You couldn't do anything to stop him. It doesn't matter. It's not your fault." I started to cry openly. "Please don't ask me anymore questions, Joseph. I can't tell you anything and if you say anything to anybody, bad things will happen to all of us. Promise me you will never tell, no matter what you see or think you see. Promise me!" I choked on my sobs. I was terrified that he might tell someone something and I knew we would all be put in jail or an orphanage.

"I promise, Molly. But you gotta tell me what happened. Okay?"

"No! Don't you get it? No! I can't ever tell you or anyone! Please go away and just leave me alone!" I pushed him away.

"Joseph it's time for you to go to school," Mother yelled up the stairs.

"I gotta go, Molly. I'll come see you after school."

"You're going to get to stay home all this week, Molly," Sadie said when she came into my room a short time later. Won't that be fun having a whole week off of school? May I sit on your bed with you?"

"I want to be by myself, Sadie." I turned my face away from her.

"I know how you feel, Molly, but you can't lie around and feel sorry for yourself. You have to work your way through problems, not ignore them. Now tell me what went so wrong last night? I told you it would hurt the first time you were with a man. I should have prepared you better and I'm sorry for that. You seemed to enjoy everything before, so I didn't think it would be so traumatic for you. Will you please forgive me?" She put her arms around my waist and pulled me to her.

"It's not your fault." I leaned into her. "I am not doing that ever again, Sadie. It's ugly and horrible and I hate him." I cried and threw myself face down on my pillow.

"You feel that way right now, Molly, but you know you will have to go with Roger and others too. That is what is expected of you now. You know what the consequences will be if you disobey your mother. Get up now and stop that blubbering. Let's you and I go for a walk and talk this out some more. You need to get out of this room." She jerked the covers off of me.

"I can hardly walk! Dontchaknow?" I shouted and buried my face into the pillow. I was trying to muffle my sobs.
"Okay, Molly. I'll be downstairs if you change your mind." She shut the door and I was relieved to hear the click of her heels on the hall floor.

I roared great shrieks deep into my pillow. I was frustrated and frightened. I wanted someone to pity me. I felt alone and at the same time, I couldn't cope with anyone trying to tell me everything was okay. It wasn't okay and it would never be okay again. I was lost totally lost. I knew it would happen again and I was powerless to stop any of it!

The days that followed were hazy to me. I remember I had this lump between my legs. It was excruciating every time I took a step. I had no one to turn to who would help me. I knew that my life had changed and that I was now very different from my siblings and any other child my age.
I broke away from the memories and thought to myself.

What breaks the bond between mother and child? I wonder if in fact there ever was a bond between my mother and me? That night, I knew beyond a shadow of a doubt that she had no love for me. It felt as though a new birth had taken place and once the umbilical cord had been cut, I began my free-fall in to the depths of a hell no words could describe.
And yet that bond between my mother and me was still held by a thread called 'hope.' I never stopped hoping that one day she would embrace me to her heart as her child and not as a "wanton slut" to use her words.

I existed in a kind of madness. I had found a safe space of darkness within myself where I could escape. I embraced the demons that inhabited that place. In them I saw the evil in me as it grew and took on the personality of who I had become. It allowed me to live in that place and do the things I was paid to do.

I shut off my thoughts and slumped in my chair saddened by my memories. I was too weary to think anymore. I got up and let my dogs out and waited for them to do their business. I let them in, turned out the lights and shuffled down to my bedroom. Without changing into my pajamas or brushing my teeth I collapsed onto my bed and fell immediately asleep.

Chapter 26

"Good morning, girls! Time for you to go out and take care of business," I said to Pippa and Christine, letting them out.
"I hope today is going to be a good one." I peered at the nice blue sky, put my coffee on to brew and put a slice of bread in the toaster.
"As soon as we all have had breakfast, we'll go for a short walk. We have to do it early today as it's my knitting day." I chatted away, expecting my dogs to understand my prattle. I put their food and water down for them. I munched my toast and enjoyed my caffeine fix and skimmed over the morning paper.

I nearly jumped out of my skin when once again the ringing phone jerked me away from my concentration.
"I do hate the intrusive phone." I sighed getting up to answer it.
"Yes?" I answered. I wiped the front of my shirt where I had spilled my coffee when I reacted to the ringing phone.
"Mom, it's Carin! Can you come over for coffee? I really need to talk with you."
"I can't today, Carin. I have my knitting group. You know I go there every Thursday afternoon."
"Can you come this morning, say in half an hour?"
"I need to take the dogs for a walk."
"Mom, please! We need to do this today."
"Oh, alright. I'll be there as soon as I can get changed." I hung up the phone.
"Sorry, you two. I promise I'll take you out for a walk tonight right after supper," I said as I put them in the kitchen and shut the door.

When I arrived at Carin's, she poured out coffee for the two of us and for a brief moment, I thought that maybe I could smooth over our differences. I mistakenly believed she could understand some of what was happening with me. She sat down across the table from me and ran her fingers through her hair. Then she started to play the same game she had been playing since all of this had started. I vowed to myself that I would listen to what she had to say with patience.

"What is causing your temper to flare so quickly these days, Mom?"

"I am on edge a lot with memories that I am trying to decipher and face. I need you to understand and back off, Carin, and I need you to give me some time to work my way through it with Michael. It makes it too difficult for me if I have this continuing threat over my head. I worry all the time, thinking I might be forced out of my home and into a care facility because you don't get it."

"Okay, Mom. Let's make a pact. I won't interfere and make threats anymore and you will keep me apprised of what is happening."

"Don't expect me to be at your beck and call and give you a blow by blow description while I work through all of this, Carin."

"What am I supposed to do when these bizarre things take place in public, Mom?" Carin stood up, with hands on her hips waiting for me to respond.

"I hope there won't be any more outbursts. Let's just leave it that for now, Carin. We can declare a temporary truce for now." I was concerned for her as I watched her nervously pace in front of me.

"Okay, that's fair enough, but you still need to keep in touch so I know what's going on. Promise?" She sat back down and took a drink of coffee. She seemed calm but I noticed her hands were shaking.

"I promise to do what I can, but now I have to run and get some lunch and go for my afternoon gab fest with the girls." I drank the last dregs of my coffee and placed my cup in her sink.

"You can have lunch here, Mom, and then go directly to Maggie's." Carin appeared a little more at ease.

She put the rest of the dishes in the sink.

"I can put a sandwich together for both of us. It's no problem." She smiled and, leant against the sink.

"No, thank you, dear. I need to get my knitting." I took my sweater off the back of the chair and left.

"See you soon, Mom!" Carin called out as I pulled out of her driveway and headed home.

I felt good as I reflected on the main part of our visit. I made my lunch and packed up my knitting bag. As usual, I hadn't even taken it out all week. Oh well! I hoped I was right in assuming Carin was more able to handle and understand my little problems. Above all, I hoped she'd keep her promise not to threaten me anymore. Time would tell. I was scared to think of what might happen if things didn't go the way she apparently expected.

Chapter 27

"Hi, everybody!" I acknowledged my friends as I entered Maggie's home. "I'm a bit late. I was held up in heavy traffic driving through the park."

We shot the breeze for a while, oohing and aahing over all the shawls and toques Maggie had made.

"Have you all been watching and listening to Obama's take on the America's summit?" Betsy asked, shuffling through her knitting bag, searching for her needle.

"Yes!" we chorused.

"He certainly is looking after his borders," I added as I settled in and started to knit..

"I worry about his safety. It would be horrible if someone assassinates him too," Maggie said, leaning forward in her chair.

"What makes an individual take the life of another with no thought to those left behind?" Annabelle asked, shaking her head.

"Cultural differences for one thing," Betsy offered.

"Religious beliefs. Sometimes people become so fanatical they lose sight of the real things that are important and focus on their own agendas," Maggie replied, her brow furrowed. She nipped at her bottom lip and seemed to be pondering as though she wanted to say more, but then settled back in her chair.

"Amen to that!" we all declared.

Amy, with glistening eyes, then added an animated contribution to the discussion. "I certainly hope we don't have a repeat of the '60s again. That was a terrible time in our history. I, too, wonder how a person can snuff out the life of another. Oh, I can see in a fit of rage

or unending cruelty, when one is caught in an abusive situation. Mind you, I still don't think it's right, but I understand how these things can happen. I know I could never kill anyone, no matter what the circumstances. I think one has to be pretty off balance to do that. Killing for religious reasons is just wrong and we can't condone that kind of fanaticism, because our culture is different. We value life above all else as a society."
Her face was animated as she spoke.

I was becoming uncomfortable with the direction of this discussion. I didn't understand why I felt defensive. I scrunched back into my seat and tried to settle the anger that was building up in me.
"I don't believe any of us can make judgment calls on what others do! We can't always know what motivates people's actions. None of us can say we wouldn't do this or that until we are face to face with insurmountable rage or overwhelming sadness." I spoke more forcibly than I had intended. My voice seemed sharper to my ears and a little impatient.

Amy quickly responded. "Oh, come on, Molly! We should be able to deal with rage and sadness without killing someone, unless we are unbalanced or fighting for our lives. I can't believe you condone that kind of stuff?" She gave me a sardonic sneer.
"I didn't say I condone it," I retorted, feeling my control slipping. I didn't want to lash out at Amy's harsh response.
"I simply said there are always mitigating circumstances that drive each of us to act in ways not in accordance with what society expects."

"Are we ready for tea, coffee and cookies? Maggie jumped in to diffuse the confrontation that was starting to heat up.
"I know I am! I have only knit a couple of rows. I keep losing my concentration and have to rip out what I have knit because of mistakes," Betsy chortled. She laid her knitting on her lap. She glanced at me and quickly looked down. She seemed uncomfortable with the conversation.

Annabelle, ever the peacemaker chuckled.

"Whoa, things are getting a bit tense. Let's have our refreshments. I don't think any of us have done much knitting again today. But we are lucky we can say what we think without fear, because we are such good friends. You seem a little on edge today Molly. Is there anything you want to share with us?" She turned to face me with a friendly smile and set down her knitting.

"No, I'm fine. I am having trouble with Carin, but we declared a kind of truce today just before I came here. I admit I tend to fly off the handle these days, but I can't seem to relax. Keeping my home and independence is riding on my ability to maintain peace with her." I stuffed my knitting beside me and bit nervously on my bottom lip.

The room took on a funereal quiet. The gas fireplace spilt its blue flames with a soft hiss giving a sense of warmth and comfort. We all sat sipping on our coffee or tea and munching on a savory. The calm and warm room created a buffer against the harsh conversation that, moments before, was rattling around. The abrasive words seemed to have lain down and nestled into the sculptured cream carpet. Peace had settled.

Suddenly, Betsy broke the mood and her voice was like an echo bouncing around and off the walls.

"Kids! No matter how old they get we still see them as our children, needing our guidance. I know I have the same problems with Laura, my daughter." She paused to take a sip of her tea. "She constantly rejects my advice and then comes crying to me when exactly what I tried to tell her would happen, happens. But do you think she remembers what I said? Not on your life! And she still doesn't want to hear what I have to say, so I just throw up my arms! Be the listener and the comforter and wait for her to ask for my advice. But I know that she will ignore anything I have to say, anyway. It really sucks, but we are just mothers and can't possibly understand what they are experiencing." Betsy breathlessly rattled on hands, flaying in front of her as she became more and more wound up.

We all laughed, and agreed with her. We put away our knitting and ate and drank our refreshments, then carried on with womanly small talk, reverting back to our girlish laughter.

As I drove home, I was upset with myself and had an unsettled feeling in my stomach at the way I had lost my temper and snapped at my friends.

I unlocked my front door and was lavishly greeted by my dogs. They jumped, wagged their tails and tried to lick my face in their exuberance.

"Hello, you two! I'm home! Let's have some supper. It is later than I hoped to get back, but it will be fun to go for a walk in the evening." I smiled and patted their heads.

We ate our supper and I put the dishes in the dishwasher, slipped on my jacket, picked up the leashes, locked the door and started on our walk.

The trail was dry, but there were puddles of muddy water on the side and in some places on the track. It was a fairly warm evening. Spring was making itself known more and more each day. My dogs and I stepped along at a good pace. The Canada Geese scolded Christine and she heeded the warning and kept a safe distance between them. She walked parallel to the pond that was overflowing its banks, thanks to the recent steady rain. The bulrushes were dried and white with no indication of the beautiful fuzzy brown spike that is so pretty in the summer. The blackberry bushes were ragged, ravished by the winter storms. They lined the trail in a haphazard way, waiting for the warm sun to dress them in their summer finery. Grass was dried to straw and was lying crushed in some places, failing in its attempt to stand tall. In other spots, it was too flayed by the dark winter days to stand at all, but, drooped and bent, it bowed to the muddy terrain beneath its roots. Hawthorne trees bared their long, razor-sharp thorns, showing off tiny buds that promised to cover their nasty barbs with their beautiful green leaves that will shimmer in the rays of the summer sun. The creek was filled to capacity and the grasses along its edges showed the beginning of green and yellow that will dress up the meadow when the warm season emerged. Daffodils were poking their heads through the dark earth, promising to challenge the yellows of nature to better their bright yellow petals. They were volunteers from plants long ago forgotten by farmers and previous owners of this bountiful glen, nurtured now by nature in its wild state. Crocuses and snowdrops displayed their colors of purple, white and yellow. Redwing blackbirds sang their haunting songs as we disrupted their nesting places, high in the branches of the Garry Oak and Poplar trees as we walked along. Our footfall noisily crunched the gravel path. This is one of my favorite places to wander and waste away the hours. I enjoy what God has created.

Darkness had descended more rapidly than I had anticipated and we were in a heavily wooded area, still an hour from home. The hoarse cry of a crow unnerved me. I called out to my dogs to stay close. The wind had started to blow, rustling the branches; a chill crawled up my spine. I don't like the dark. I stayed close to the edge of the trail. I focused on the gentle gurgling of a small brook that wanders through the darkened glade.

I tripped and nearly fell! My heart was racing!

"Christine! Pippa! Come!" I reached out for their collars but they darted past me, running ahead. "Christine! Pippa! Come back here!" I shouted.

This time I snapped their leashes on before they could dash past me.

"You stay with me, both of you!" I snarled. My irrational fear was taking over.

A rabbit ran in front of them and they darted after it, jerking the leashes out of my hands. I was propelled forward, tripped and fell.

My momentum carried me down a small incline and I came to a stop at the edge of the brook. I lay there terrified! I was unable to get my bearings right away.

"Please don't leave me here!" I whimpered, as memory pulled and fed the fear in my gut. Suddenly, the stairs to the basement of long ago were in front of me. I gasped and wheezed, trying to breathe. I lay in a grip of terror.

"No, no this can't be happening. Sadie! Where are you?" I called out.

Silence and darkness were my answer.

I curled up on myself and groaned, lost in the moment.

I heard a voice.

"Get up off the floor, Molly, and come here!" the voice hissed. The voice of my mother assaulted my thoughts.

"No, I can't go in there again, ever, please don't make me!" I sobbed and squeezed my eyes shut.

Memory of a room in the basement swirled just out of reach. I couldn't quite connect it, and it lingered on the peripheral of my petrified thoughts.

"No! Mommy! Please take me back up the stairs! Why won't you turn on the light? Please turn on the light," I begged.

Then a voice I couldn't distinguish teased, "No, the light is in the room. See? It is just ahead. You have to stand up and walk toward the light under the door. Do you see it, Molly?"

"Yes, I see it," I whimpered. "But I can't go there again. Mommy, where are you? Please don't make me—puleese!" I wailed.

"You're such a baby! Get up or do I have to come and drag you?" she sneered and this time I recognized the voice of my mother.

"Please turn on the light," I whined.

"Never! Molly. The only light is in the room. Come and walk toward it. You can see it under the door. I know you can."

I felt a cold nose nuzzle my face; it was like a bolt of lightning and it jolted me back to the present.

"Thank heaven you came back!" I quaked and clung to my dogs. I struggled to get my thoughts in order.

"Let's get out of here!" I shrieked. I thrashed my way up the incline to the path, instead of going back along the trail I had started on. I followed a track that led me out to the other side and onto the road where there was a steady stream of traffic. I held the leashes in a death grip until I finally reached home.

I put some water down for the dogs and I made myself a cup of hot chocolate and settled down with a chocolate chip cookie. I tried to make sense of what had happened on that trail. My heart was still plowing itself against my ribs but I knew I was safe here. I picked up my book and attempted to read, but I was too shaken to concentrate. I turned off all the lights in my front room and put on a CD. I sank back in my chair and let Perry Como lull me to sleep singing "And I Love You So."

Chapter 28

I searched frantically through my closet to find something to wear to my next appointment with Michael. I spent so much time trying on and rejecting different clothes, that I was pushed to get there on time. I finally decided on my good old standby. A red sweater and brown skirt. I quickly shoved my feet into my knee-high boots, snatched up my purse and keys and locked the door. I dashed to my car and prayed I wouldn't hit anyone in my rush to get there on time.

"Hi, Beth! Sorry I'm a little late. I started out late, and then had a dickens of a time finding a parking spot. Why does your office have to be downtown? I never come down here because of the parking problem." I prattled on as I rushed into the reception area.

"No problem, Molly. He's just finishing up some letters. He'll be right out." Beth looked up from her computer and smiled.

"Beth, the daffodils are lovely! Where on earth did you get such a perfect color vase to put them in?" I gushed over the flower arrangement she had on the corner of her desk.

"I found it in a little second hand store out in Sidney last fall. It is perfect, isn't it? The soft green of it goes with most of the cut flowers and particularly spring flowers. I love having fresh flowers in my office." She laughed and stood to shift the vase a little.

"I love second hand stores, Beth. There's one called 'Second Time Around' just a few blocks from here, and it has some dynamite bargains. I used to go there when I worked and still do when I am going to a one-time special event. They are great places to shop when I don't want to pay a lot for a dress."

I gently touched the petals of the daffodils.

"I know what you mean, Molly."

Michael greeted me when he came out of his office.

"Hi, Molly! It's nice to see you again. Come on in. Can we get you something to drink, tea, coffee, water?"

"No. thanks, Michael. I'm good. I had a coffee at home before I left. Thanks, though."

I slipped off my jacket and took my usual chair. Suddenly I began to feel most uncomfortable.

"How has your week been, Molly? Are you still dealing with flashbacks?"

"Not of getting beat up, but I am having some heavy duty flashbacks of the years in the house in Moose Jaw." I was looking down at my folded hands lying on my lap as I spoke.

"Can you explain?" He looked up from his notepad.

"For example, I took my dogs out last night and it was later and darker than I expected and I got really unnerved and so did the dogs."

I went on to explain the whole episode. My voice seemed hollow, like that of a stranger to my ears, as I related the previous night's happening.

"What about the room is so frightening for you, Molly?" He leaned forward in his chair. "I don't want to remember that room. Terrible things took place there and they are best forgotten, believe me! I don't know what prompted me to even go there in my head. I had just about forgotten it was even there. I carry the fear of being sent down into the basement as punishment. I was taken into that room when I was a bit older." I started to experience anxiety and the need to get out of there. I stood up and started to pace. I fiddled with my hair and suddenly I started to hyperventilate.

"What's happening, Molly? What has you so spooked?" His voice was soothing and he reached out to touch me in his attempt to make me feel safe.

"Jeepers, Michael! Can't we just leave this stuff alone?" My fear was palpable. I pulled back from him and sat down again. I leaned forward with my head in my hands. I tried to catch my breath.

"Can I get you some water, Molly?" Michael asked.

"No, I'm okay. I just need a minute, I need a little breathing space here."

We sat waiting for me to settle down so we could resume our session. I was too anxious to leap right back in to the memory of that room. A few moments passed, then Michael spoke to me.

"Can you tell me about it, Molly? I believe it will help you and it will definitely help me to understand what is happening here." His voice was like a warm balm, pouring over my fright.

"Yes, okay, okay! You asked and I will answer," I replied and I fiddled with my hands, checking my fingernails. I wished I were anywhere but here.

"The basement was a terrifying place for me as a child. My mother would lock me down there, turn out the lights and make me stay until she said I could come out. I would stay on the bottom step and not move until she turned the lights back on. One day when Sadie, Susie, Sissy, Rachelle, Mindy and my mother were sitting in the kitchen having a cup of tea with my little sister Emma, they all decided it was a good time to show me 'the room.' My mother put Emma down for a nap and returned to join the women and me for a trip into the basement. I had no desire to go down there with them but when I held back, Sadie assured me they would all stay with me. She said there was a very nice little room down there that I would find quite interesting.

The room was at the bottom of the stairs and to the left. It was a delightful room, with different colored pillows lying in various positions on the floor. Sadie explained that it was a room where they and some of the men would come down to practice their worship rituals. I remember being confused, but once we had walked around the room we went back upstairs. It was about a month later that I was to go back down to see some strange and eerie things taking place. I can't talk about all this right now, Michael. I can hardly breathe, just thinking about it." My voice was weak, my mouth dry and I was perspiring and fidgety. My heart was pounding against my ribs. I thought it would jump right out of my chest if I didn't calm myself. I could feel my blood thundering through my veins.

"Okay, I think I understand what happens in that room, maybe we can go there again sometime, when it is not so difficult for you to talk about it." He quickly jotted some notes on his writing pad.

"How is everything else, Molly? Any other difficulties?" he asked, changing the topic and tone of voice.

"You might say that," I answered in a sarcastic tone.

"Oh? Why don't you tell me?"

"I confess I am a little concerned about my lack of control these days. I seem to lose my temper more quickly than seems normal to me. Not only with my daughter, but now also with my friends." My tone was more solicitous.

"It's good you recognize that, Molly. That's really why Carin has been concerned, isn't it? What do you think is behind the outbursts?"

"It is memories, dreams, flashbacks—all of which make no sense to me. I am really scared of saying and doing things that upset others. I have never had problems like this before and I sure don't want to put myself in a situation where my back is to the wall. Do you think I am going crazy, Michael?" I twisted my hands together and yanked at the bottom of my sweater, afraid of what his answer might be.

"No, definitely not, Molly, but I do think we need to keep on top of this. You need to call me when you can't handle things. I don't mean to alarm you, but this is not a good way to handle stress and we all know it is not the way you usually behave."

"I know. That's why I am so scared," I mumbled, and gazed at my lap.

"Don't be frightened, Molly. We'll work through this. Just keep track of strange episodes and try to remember the dreams and flashbacks. Write them down as you recall them and bring your notes with you when you come. Our time is up for today. I'll walk you out." He took my hand as he stood up, and helped me out of my chair.

"See you next week!" he said as I walked into the reception area and out the door.

The drive home was uneventful and yet I felt uneasy about the way the session had gone. I tried to understand what was going on. Why was I remembering that room when I hadn't thought of it for years? I was confused by what was happening. I know that I was going to have to get a hold on my thoughts and try to control my temper a lot more or I would be heading for deep trouble.

My house was dark when I entered the driveway and I wondered at that. My appointment with Michael was early afternoon and I know I didn't stop anywhere on my way home. I glanced at my watch and saw it was nearly seven o'clock.
There had to be a mistake, my watch must be wrong. This is crazy making, it can't be dark yet. Rapid thoughts raced through my brain.
"Where in the world did I go?" I wondered.
I wrestled with my thoughts, trying to get them in order. I must be able to remember where I went after my appointment. I truly started to believe I was losing it. I didn't dare phone Carin and ask if I stopped off there. I opened my car door and slowly walked to the front door. I unlocked it with trembling hands. I knew I didn't have Alzheimer's, but why couldn't I remember where the previous four hours went? I felt cold and disconnected. My emotions were flat and confused. I tossed my coat on the chair and plugged the kettle in to make myself a cup of tea. Both my dogs barked, whined, wiggled and wagged their tails in greeting.

"I know you have been locked up in the house all day. I am sorry I was gone so long. Go on out and take care of business while I get your supper out for you." I let them out the back. I put their food in their dishes and made a cup of tea for myself. I went through the motions like a robot.
"I know you want to go for a walk," I told them when I let them in.

"It is too dark now, maybe in the morning we can go. Eat up your supper while I get something to eat." I reached into the fridge for something with which I could make a sandwich.

I wonder if everyone who owns dogs talks to them as if they are people? Oh well, I had more serious things to worry about than that. I munched on a sandwich and tried to recall every step I took after I left Michael's office. For the life of me, I could not remember anything between the time I left there and the time I arrived home. How bizarre is that? I pondered.

I opened my purse to check and see if there were any receipts from anyplace where I might have been shopping. Maybe I had stopped off for a coffee? There was nothing there to indicate I went anywhere other than to his office that afternoon. My stomach was churning as I wondered if I should call Michael and tell him. I decided it was a good idea to at least let him know, in case it happened again and I got lost. I picked up the phone and dialed his number at home. As the phone rang and rang, I became concerned that he wouldn't be home. I knew I wouldn't have the courage to call him again.

"Hello!" The voice on the other end of the phone was not Michael.
"Hello, is Michael there please?" I asked on the verge of losing my nerve.
"Yes, may I say who is calling?" a very polite young man replied.
'Please tell him it is Molly," I responded hesitantly.
"Please hold on while I get him." I listened as the voice on the other end shouted. "Dad! Telephone for you!" I heard the rustle of the phone being set down on something and then silence.
"Hello, Molly! Are you alright?" Michael asked, concern reflected in his voice.
"Michael, I don't know if I should be worried or not but something very strange happened to me after I left your office." I struggled to stay focused and not think about how nervous I was that I called him at his home.
"Tell me about it, Molly, and let me be the one to decide if there is any need to be alarmed." He was very gracious and reassuring.

I related the whole sequence of events as best I could remember. I informed him that I had tried to retrace my steps, but could not recall what happened between the time I left his office and the time I arrived home.

"That is very strange, Molly, and yes, we need to be concerned. I want you to do me a favor. Put my name and phone number on your cell phone under the heading of "Ice" and be sure and carry your cell phone at all times. As well, I want you to carry my business card in the jackets and the coats you wear most often. That way, if you should wander into some sort of trouble and you are not fully aware of where you are, or how you got there, the authorities will be able to contact me."

"Why can't I remember, Michael? I am so scared!" I moaned, leaning the phone against my forehead.

"It's alright. This is probably some form of hysteria associated with the memory you had to deal with in our session. Let's not get too apprehensive at this point. I am glad you called me, Molly. Do you want to come in in the morning to talk this over with me?"

"No, I don't think so, Michael. I have an appointment to see you next week. I just wanted to make sure you knew what happened, so you could help me if it happens again. Heaven only knows! I could get lost or do something stupid. Thanks for talking with me, Michael. I will see you next week."

"You're welcome, Molly. Please promise to call me right away if this happens again or if you need to speak with me for whatever reason. I'll see you next week. Bye for now."

"Bye, Michael."

I still felt very uncomfortable with this, but I knew I couldn't do much about it. Once again, I had doubts about my mental stability. Was I so stressed that it was overwhelming me to the point where I would simply check out for a period of time? It scared the heck out of me. I put frozen pasta in the microwave and settled down with my tea. Turning on the T.V., I switched on the news and decided on a night of television to take my mind off of myself before I went to bed. The news was the same old stuff, murder, mayhem and a dash of promise of things to change for the better.

I switched it off and read my book. I managed to escape into the pages and became lost in the story for a couple of hours. I yawned and put it down and got the dogs settled for the night. It felt good to lose myself in a good mystery and let my body relax. I took a long hot shower and slipped into my nightgown and crawl between the sheets and sink into the warmth and a soft sleep.

Chapter 29

Darkness as black as tar is everywhere. She searches for any kind of light and sees a sliver of light shining beneath what looks like a door. She gingerly walks toward it, trying to keep her footsteps silent. That's when she notices she is barefoot. What in the world has she done with her shoes? Oh well, that can't be a concern right now. She needs to focus on where she is and why it is so dark. She reaches the sliver of light and realizes it is a door. She clutches the doorknob and releases it, jerking her hand away. It is too cold to touch. She tentatively takes hold of it and slowly turns it, praying there is no one on the other side who might want to harm her. She very slowly opens the door. Suddenly a cacophony of noise assaults her senses. The bright light blinds her and she staggers back, trying to move away from the opening. She is too late and a hand grabs her arm pulling her further into the room. She gasps at the sight before her. There are so many people here. She tries to see anyone that she might recognize, but the faces are all in the shadows.

She can feel her heart. The beats thunder in her head. They bounce against her ribs, their rhythm, racing and irregular. She sees the table to which the hand is pulling her and she tries to get away, but the grip is too strong and she is unable to break the hold. The hand pulls her closer and then two arms lift her onto the table. She is sobbing, but she can't hear any sound coming from herself. She tries desperately to scramble off the table and flee. More hands and arms push her down, pulling at her clothes, ripping and tearing them off her. She tries to scream, but no sound escapes her. All of her attempts seem futile. She is naked and feels someone trying to push her down flat on table as he lies atop of her. She struggles to get free. The noise around her is getting louder and more frenzied. She can feel her own hysteria suffocating her. She fights and wrestles against the body on top of her, pummeling him with her fists. He tries to kiss her lips. She rolls her head from side to side, sickened that he might succeed. His lips seem huge, wet and disgusting. His eyes are enormous. His face is grotesque and it comes nearer and nearer. He is still trying to capture her mouth. Hands now clutch her hair, pulling at it from both sides and virtually anchoring her head to the table. His lips are pulled back in a grin showing uneven teeth. Spittle clings to the side of his mouth and his breath is foul and he finally connects himself to her. She can't breathe and she is certain she is going to die. Her thoughts and actions are chaotic. The noise of the others is deafening now and she makes one last attempt to escape from this maniac. Freeing her mouth from his, she opens it to scream out. It is then I see her face clearly and am thunderstruck when I recognize myself staring back at me.

I woke up startled, searching for light in the darkness that was surrounding me. I clung to the blanket over me, struggling to find calm to settle my terror-filled thoughts. My scream was still locked in my throat. Confused, I thrashed about the bed, trying to orient myself to where I was. I sought air for my oxygen-starved lungs. I was trapped in my blankets, the smell of my own fear was rank in my nostrils. I untangled myself from the sheets and blankets and climbed out of my bed on unsteady legs, reaching for the light switch. I finally felt a quiet come over me as I bathed in the light and realized I was in my own bedroom. It was only a dream. Uh-uh! More like a nightmare! I knew I would not get any more sleep that night, so I slipped on my bathrobe, went downstairs and put the kettle on. I wondered what other memories were locked in my subconscious, waiting to attack me in my most vulnerable state? Sleep takes away all barriers and leaves me open to my mind's vivid imagination, mixed with real thoughts and memories. I picked up my book and went into the front room to sit down and read until morning. Within a few pages I felt myself drifting off. I shifted my position, trying to remain awake and alert, knowing I could not face another nightmare like that. I went back to the kitchen, filled my cup with tea and poured lots of sugar into it. I hoped it would give me the zing I need to keep awake. This time, I turned on the television and found one of those disgusting talk shows that belittle people by pitting one against the other.

The next morning I decided to call Michael and set a time to meet with him later in the day. I was disturbed by everything that was happening.

I arrived a little early for my appointment. I thanked Beth for moving times and appointments around to fit me in.

"That's okay Molly." She kindly smiled and went on with her work.

Michael came out and ushered me into his office.

"Do you want anything to drink Molly?"

"No, I'm fine, thanks Michael."

"Why don't you fill me in on what happened after that first night alone with Roger Molly? It must have been devastating for you to realize what everyone was asking you to do."

"Oh Gawd Michael it was beyond my comprehension. I remember I wanted to die, run away or find someone to protect me and rescue me from the nightmare of my life."

"Tell me what happened after things settled down." He crossed his legs, sat back in his chair and prepared to listen."

Chapter 30

I started to hesitantly tell him and it was as if I was back in that house those many years past.

"Time had passed quickly since that horrible night with Roger. I sat at the kitchen table enjoying supper with everyone. My mother told Joseph to take Ross and Emma upstairs and read a story to them until it was time for "The Shadow" to come on the radio.

"Aw, do I have to?" Joseph whined, "I want to read my comic book by myself."

"Just do it now! Your program will be on in fifteen minutes. Don't argue with me!" My mother seemed anxious.

"C'mon, Ross and Emma, but we're reading what I want and not what you guys want," Joseph insisted. He took Emma by the hand and the three of them went upstairs.

Sissy asked, "Molly, do you know who was here last night and wanted to visit with you?" She pulled her long blond hair back from her face as she started to clear the table.

"No, who?" I asked, getting up to help.

"Duncan and Roger. They were very disappointed you had gone to sleep so quickly and we didn't want to waken you," Sissy absently responded, running water in the sink.

I spat back.

"I don't want to see them ever again!"

"Don't talk like that, Molly! You know what is expected of you and you will do as I say and not as you please." My mother jumped into the conversation. She picked up a dishtowel to help with the clean-up.

I replied angrily, "I won't go with them again. I don't care what you do to me and if you make me go I will run away and you will never find me. I might even get dead."

"That's enough! You run away and you will end up living with other people away from all of us. That, my dear, is your choice." She seemed to be sad.

Visions of the place Sadie had described to me of what would happen to my brothers, sister and me, if I didn't do as my mother wanted, floated in front of me.

"Why do you be so mean to me, Mommy? It hurts too bad, I don't like what Roger did to me." I was horrified at the prospect of going back into that room. I stood helpless in front of her. My arms hung limply at my side, my shoulders hunched and tears started to spill down my cheeks.

"Sadie's going to take you upstairs and she, Mindy and Susie are going to show you how to relax so it won't hurt so much. The more you let them play the easier it will get, Molly. Now go on upstairs and get ready. Both Roger and Duncan are coming tonight.

Tomorrow night there is another man who would like to meet you. You won't have to do anything tomorrow. Just meet this new client and get to know him a little until next week." She seemed distressed and she turned away from me and finished drying the dishes.

"Let's go, Molly. I promise it won't be so bad. In fact, you might enjoy it again. You know how gentle and loving Duncan is? Remember how sweet he was the last time you saw him?" Sadie led me and the other ladies upstairs and into her bedroom.

Sadie said, "Sit on the bed, Molly," and she, Susie and Mindy sat around me.

I scrunched my legs underneath me and pouted, waiting for them to say something.

Susie continued, "You have to learn how to relax, Molly. Otherwise, you are never going to get any pleasure out of sex."

"I hate sex!" I countered, crossing my arms over my chest. I was determined I was not going to look at them.

"You know that's not true, Molly", Mindy replied, "We all know how much you enjoyed it before Roger hurt you."

"That was different sex. I hate what Roger did and I hate what he looks like with no clothes on," I snapped, "and I think all men are ugly when they are bare-naked!"

"Well, we agree they are not built the same as us, Molly," said Sadie, "but I don't think their bodies are ugly. You just need some instruction on what to do to make things easier for both of you.

"No," I whimpered, pulling away, "I don't want to!"

"Okay, just watch Mindy and Susie and see what they do."

"No, I don't want to!" I shrieked, trying to scamper off of the bed, but Sadie grabbed my arm and held onto me.

"Stop it, Molly! Either listen and watch or just face the men on your own and you can be sure you will be screaming and carrying on again when that happens. Your mother will be furious if you carry on like that again. Who knows how long you will be in the basement yowling to come out? Now pay attention, or you can go to your room and wait for Roger to come. You make up your mind." Sadie's response was blunt and to the point. I looked up and, with tears rolling down my cheek, I watched.

"Just relax, sweetie. I won't hurt you. You trust me don't you?"

"Yes, but I don't want to hurt again like that." I cringed, trying to escape.

"I promise you, you will enjoy what I do. Remember how much you liked what we did before, Molly? Look at Susie and Mindy. They are completely relaxed. Nothing can hurt them here.

"You are the only one who can make certain that things go well Molly, if you continue to fight all of us the bad results will come back to you. You are smart enough to figure out what that will mean. The choice is yours." Her voice and actions were calm and reassuring. Once again I let myself trust her.

"Okay," I said reluctantly, totally malleable to her suggestions.

"But, they are too big for me, Sadie. They hurt me," I complained, feeling slightly ashamed of my willingness to back down.

"Besides, I hate their hair! It scrapes and scratches me everywhere. Why don't they shave it off?"

"You're not listening, Molly!" said Susie, "Let them touch you this way and you will be more prepared for them. It may hurt a little at first, but if you let go and just free your thoughts and think of this time right now, it will go much easier for you. Promise me you will do that?" Susie prepared to leave the room with Mindy.

"I'll try, I promise, "I whimpered, Still trying to plead my case.

This is all my fault, I thought to myself. If I hadn't been so anxious and if I hadn't liked what they did, all this wouldn't be happening. There must be something very bad in me that make men do bad things to me.

I wanted to go back to where I was before it all started. I wandered back to my room and sat on the bed trying to think how I could escape my life. I was scared and angry and I knew I was trapped with no one to help and nowhere to go. I was overwhelmed with sadness and self-pity. I lay back on my bed and drifted into a space of nothingness waiting for the inevitable.

The moment I dreaded was here I could hear Sadie coming down the hall to my room. I scrunched my eyes closed and pretended to be asleep.

"I know you're not asleep Molly, get up off the bed and come with me. You need to get ready. You have to have a bath and change into your clothes." Sadie sounded out of breath and just stood at the door to my room waiting for me to get up.

"Come on, Molly! Let's get you into the bath and into your sweet clothes. Roger and Duncan are due any minute." I stood and watched Sadie turn toward the bathroom. I was still reluctant as I acquiesced and tramped along the hall after Sadie.

I had a nice warm bath and felt fuzzy and drowsy. I was almost excited to see Duncan. I liked him the best. I was still very anxious about seeing Roger, but I was resigned to my fate. I knew I had to go through with whatever he had in mind for me to do. Maybe all the ladies were right. Maybe if I just tried and remembered to do what they said I would be okay. I was incredibly afraid, though and I knew what we were doing was wrong but I didn't know what else I could do to stop it.

Chapter 31

"Let's wait here in your nice special room, Molly," Sadie said as she finished doing my hair.

"Why do I have to put all my clothes on when they are just going to take them off again? You don't need to fuss with my hair because they will just take it all out and let it hang down my back." I slouched in my chair.

"Because it makes them feel good the same as it does for you. I love the excitement I feel when someone does it to me." she replied, smiling and smoothing my hair.

The sharp rap on the door startled both of us and I crumbled against Sadie, petrified of what was going to happen. I started to whimper into her side.

"Hush, Molly! Do as we showed you and remember to ask Roger to do what we did to help you relax. Remember now, you promised to try real hard to enjoy this."

"Wow! Duncan and Roger! We didn't expect both of you at once. This is a nice surprise, isn't it Molly?" She turned and let both of them in. She smiled at me and gave me a knowing wink.

"Yes." I gazed down at my feet and I longed to disappear.

"Come on in, both of you," she said. "I'll run downstairs and fix us all a drink. I'll be right back, Molly." She left me alone with both men.

"Hi, Molly!" both men said at once.

"Hi!" I replied. I was still looking down at my shoes, afraid to look at them.

"We thought we would both come together tonight to help you and teach you a little about what to do, so you won't be so scared about it." Duncan continued.

"Is that okay with you, Molly?"

"Sure!" I mumbled, not looking at him.

"I'm sorry I hurt you and scared you so badly, Molly. I hope you will forgive me." Roger chucked me under the chin and lifted my face up so he could see my eyes.

"That's okay, Roger." I crossed my legs and rested one shoe on the other.

Sadie returned, carrying a tray of drinks.

"Here we are, some nice warm toddies. Yours is extra sweet, Molly and not as strong as ours. I'm going to sit with you for just a little while and then I have to get ready for a friend who's coming to see me later. I'm really excited. He is lots of fun to be with and he makes me feel especially good."

"Why don't you come and sit on the bed between Roger and me?" Duncan asked, patting the bed beside him. Roger moved over.

"Here's to a fun and exciting night!" Roger said, as the three of them raised their glasses to each other.

"Raise your glass to us, Molly. This is called a toast and we do it when we want to do something nice for each other and wish each other well," Sadie explained and drank hers halfway down.

I sipped mine. I coughed and sputtered. I didn't like the taste any better this time. I made a grotesque face to make sure they all knew it.

"It burns all the way down and I don't like the taste of it, Sadie."

"I know, but it will make you feel warm soon and it will help to relax you. I need to get going now, Molly. I have to get ready for my date. I will come and see you later, but try and have some fun with Duncan and Roger."

"I'll try, Sadie, but I wish you could stay with me a little bit longer."

I took another small sip of my drink, hoping it would poison me and I would die on the spot.

"I'll see you later," Sadie tittered. She drank down her last mouthful and left, closing the door behind her.

"Okay, Molly! Let's have a little bit of fun," Duncan said as he finished his drink.
"I haven't finished my drink yet, Duncan, and I don't feel so good. Maybe we shouldn't play tonight if I'm getting sick."
"Drink up, Molly. You will be fine. You're still nervous, but we will help you with that. Stand up and face me." Duncan stood and took off his suit jacket.
"I can't drink it too fast. It makes me cough too much." I stalled as long as I could.
"Fine! Set it down on the dressing table and you can take a little sip at a time. Now come over here and stand up and face me, Molly." He took my drink and placed it on the dressing table.

I slipped off of my chair and went over and stood in front of him. Duncan spread his legs and pulled me closer to him. He started to take out the ribbon in my hair and I began to feel warm from the drink. I started to shake. I was scared. I trusted Duncan and I was certain he would not do anything to hurt me.
Duncan continued, "We're going to do this slow and easy, Molly! I want you to do exactly what Roger and I tell you to do. We don't want a repeat of the last time. You know we have paid a lot of money to be with you and it doesn't make us feel very good when you cry and carry on like you are being tortured. Remember how nice you felt when we touched you down in the lounge that time? We know how much you liked that. We are going to do the same tonight and we are going to show you how to position yourself so you won't hurt so much." He turned me around and started to unbutton my dress.
"Can I have another drink?" I asked in a shrill voice.
"Of course you can," Duncan said and he handed me the glass.
I took another little sip and felt it warm me all over. I didn't understand why the liquor made me so sleepy and made my bones feel like jelly. I hated the taste but I liked that I was slipping into

a nice warm place where maybe I wouldn't feel any hurt. I knew I had to escape this time and place so I wouldn't know what Duncan was doing to me. I didn't want to remember anything bad about him. I loved him when he walked with me and talked to me like a daddy. I had to find that place in my mind where nothing could touch me. It was a nice quiet place I felt a peace and a quietness that contradicted my real world. I loved it there and I determined to stay. I looked around in my minds eye and I saw beautiful flowers, grass and a small pond and I slipped over and sat beside it. It was very nice not to have to think about the bad stuff and to know I was safe here because no one except me had a way of entering it. I wished I could swim but then I was too small and I understood it would not be smart to break the quietness of my mind by splashing in the water. Somehow I understood the ripple effect of the water splashing onto the grass was the same ripple effect life events had on each of us. How every action affected others around and how far and wide the ripples could drift, so I stayed quiet and enjoyed the tranquility of my space. I was brought back to awareness with a jolt when Roger took a hold of me and started to nudge my chin up so he could put his lips on mine. I jerked and tried to pull away but he was having none of that.

"Relax! Stop being difficult! You're not helping one bit, behaving like this," he snarled.

"Okay!" I whispered and tried to sink my body into the bed. I squeezed my eyes shut and prayed it would soon be over.

He moved again and did what he believed he had a right to do. Strange how because he paid money for this he was able to justify rape and call it a learning experience for me. I lay there and let him do what he had to do. I was determined not to cry out as the pain increased with each thrust. When he finally collapsed on me, fully spent, I start to cry into his chest.

"Stop, Molly! You're okay. You're not hurt, but you will be a little sore. I will help you so the hurt will go away quickly. Hush, now!" He wrapped his big arms around me, calming me in that special way only he had.

"We don't want to bring your mother down on us now do we?" Roger nudged me closer to him.

"No," I said hiccoughing.

Both he and Duncan pulled the covers over us and they snuggled me to them. They both fell into a noisy sleep. I lay there thinking about how my days were mapped out for me and that there was no escape. I promised myself that no one would ever see me cry again. I would make certain that I would do whatever I had to so that I would never be punished again for not cooperating. I vowed, too, to never let the men know they gave me any pleasure, no matter what they did. I would not give them or anyone else the satisfaction of knowing they had made me feel very good or that they had hurt me. I swore I would get so good at hiding my emotions, no one could know what I was thinking or feeling. I wasn't too sure I could follow through on all that with Duncan. He made me want to be with him. I finally felt a freedom knowing I could escape into my secret place in my mind where the physical did not exist and pain could not enter.

Those were my last thoughts as I, too, fell into a deep sleep. I didn't feel either one of them clean me off or get up and leave the room.

I woke up the next morning with Sadie nudging me awake. She wanted to take me down to the bath.

"You were the best last night, Molly. We are all proud of you. Both Roger and Duncan said how much they enjoyed their time with you. This warm water will feel nice and help your soreness. You don't have to go to school today, either. It's Saturday, so you kids can have a whole day of fun." She playfully splashed some water in my face and giggled.

"Oh, you know Mom, Sadie. She'll expect us to do work in the house or the yard before we can go and play. Besides, I don't feel like running around. I am too sore. Not that she will care; she'll still expect me to help around here. She wouldn't care if I died." I felt miserable.

"Now, Molly, don't feel sorry for yourself. You can't be that sore. You slept all night. I didn't hear a whimper out of you when you sat in the warm water. There is just a little bleeding this time."

"You think you know everything, but you don't and I don't care what you think. I am sore but even you don't seem to care as long as I keep quiet about everything. You all know I won't tell so I won't get punished. I don't need you to tell me what to do anymore." I angrily splashed the water into her face.

"That's enough, Molly! Get your clothes on and come downstairs for breakfast," she replied sharply.

She wiped her face and threw the towel on the floor and left.

I felt smug because I'd made her mad. I didn't care what she thought and I didn't care what anybody else thought either. I had made up my mind to stay away from all of them.

"I'm not hungry," I snapped, getting out of the tub, "and I won't be coming down to play either. I'm staying in my room alone!" I wrapped the towel around me, stomped down to my room and slammed the door shut. I threw myself on the bed and wept into the pillow.

"God, if you are real, please help me. Nobody here will so you have to, please?" I prayed for any kind of help.

"I don't know why I have been singled out to do this stuff but maybe you can make it all go away." My prayer to Him continued."

I sat and stared at Michael. I had gotten so wrapped up in recalling those times I had no idea how long I had rambled on. I felt very tired and washed out.

"How difficult that time for you was Molly. It is very important you don't blame yourself for any of it. It was not your fault. I think we have run out of time today but I am proud of you and thank you for sharing all that with me. Call me if you need me. I'll see you in a couple of days."

"Good night Michael."

I drove home and was so wasted and worn to the nubs that I crashed on my couch and fell soundly asleep.

The next thought in my head was how bright the light was. I opened my eyes and realized the sun was glaring through the window right into my eyes. It was early morning. I felt foggy and couldn't focus my thoughts. I was still caught up in sleep mode. I showered and dressed and shuffled my way to the kitchen to put on the coffee. I sat at the kitchen table anxiously waiting for the coffee to brew; I desperately needed a jolt of caffeine to get my blood and brain moving fast enough for me to make a cohesive thought. As soon as it dripped into the pot I poured a cup, laced it with cream and sugar and walked into the front room. That first sip was so good. I savored it and sat in my favorite chair to enjoy the quiet and organize my day. I looked around the room and studied the pictures on the walls. I have always loved scenic pictures and soft colors, so my home reflects that. The walls in my front room are a soft off white with one feature wall a sea-mist green. I have no clocks on my walls because I can't stand their ticking. They are like a telephone, intrusive and hard to ignore. My favorite chair is a beige glider chair. I spend most of my down time here, loving the isolation and feeling of safety. I nestled into the glider and concentrated on how to hold onto my sanity. I remembered what Michael said about writing down my thoughts. I retrieved a pen and pad of paper.

These days, I needed a place to let go and cry, yell or simply be quiet. I worried more and more about the nightmares and the flashbacks, but I was determined to stay in the 'now' and not be pulled back to where I couldn't fight against the memory. I knew I was strong at my core and I had to believe I was going to come through this and out the other side with my faculties intact. At least, my daughter was giving me some space. I could see she was trying to understand how important my home was to me. I felt sure our relationship was strong enough to endure whatever the future had in store. I didn't feel the need to be on the defensive whenever I saw her and that in itself was progress for both of us. If I let go of that hope, I knew I would sink into the darkness of my destructive memories. At first I couldn't write anything. All I could do was think about what I could do to stay focused.

I began to dwell on my mixed feelings for Duncan and began to write:

"It was strange how my mind worked as a child and how much I loved Duncan and looked forward to his presents and his kindness outside of the special room. I can almost hear the tenderness in his voice whenever he spoke to me. We always held hands when we went for our walks in the park. He was the only one of my clients who did that. It made him exceptional to me. I often thought of him as my protector, because he was frequently there to hush my sobs and hold me to him when other men would hurt me. The day he and Roger came was like a movie that played over and over in my mind's eye. Each word and each minute of the day was vivid to me. I think of how I yearned to be rescued. I had thought, with what Sadie and the others had taught me, I was finally going to be important to my mother. I believed the men who came to see me would love me. My dreams rapidly shattered into pieces like glass when reality set in. The shards glinted and haunted me. But Duncan still remained different in my mind. I loved him from the moment I met him. That love lasted throughout the years until we moved from Moose Jaw. His kindness confused me, even after I learned what his purpose was. I know now that it had precious little to do with me. I was embarrassed by the betrayal of the response of my body to him. I was pissed that I could not control it. My love-hate relationship with him was ongoing. Even though I came to understand no one could save me from what was happening, because no one outside of those involved knew what was happening. I still relied on Duncan to provide the nurturing I longed for and in his own way he did. There were many times when he came solely to take me for long walks and liberating talks. He never wore his uniform on those occasions; he always wore a nice sweater or shirt and jacket and pants. They were mostly brown and I came to love the color of those clothes. It was very different to the browns of the uniforms some of the service men wore. Sometimes, he would pick me up give me a big hug and squeeze me to him. He would tell me how much he loved me and how sorry he was that he sometimes had to hurt me. Then he would put me down and take my hand and we would continue to walk and talk about the trees, the ducks or the birds. Sometimes we'd talk about school, but never about the house I lived in. He always smelled good to me. I loved it when he would nuzzle my neck. His clothes were scratchy but his chin tickled my neck and made me giggle. I enjoy recalling those times. The memory of our last day together is buried deep in the recesses of my mind.

I wonder how people lose their sense of humanity and replace it with a love of power and money? Children are vulnerable members of our society and yet there are predators out there who believe what they do is okay. In fact, what I learned is that some even believe they are doing well to teach children things that they have no ability to understand or control. They are pedophiles who believe it is their right to love and make love to children.

I had a sadness and anger that warred. The sadness was overwhelming at times and thoughts of death came and went like the sun on a partially cloudy day. It tore my heart apart to try to do what was expected of me in order to please my mother, with the vain hope that she would see me as her daughter and not a source of money. I'd had a taste of amazing sexual urges. At the same time, the painful reality was, that it was introduced too soon and at a time when my body was too small to enter into it without pain. I was sad when I thought how much I loved and hated Duncan. I wanted to be held by him. But I hated the sexual side of our relationship. I knew that had come with a high price, and yet for me it was worth whatever emotional price I had to pay. At least, that is how I felt at the beginning of the journey. My anger was at the world in general. The "Why?" questions invaded my thoughts, as did the self-pity that went along with them. I was angry with my siblings for having that boundless innocence of childhood. They had the fun and freedom that I was denied. I was angry with my mother for not accepting me as her child. I was angry at Sadie for teaching me things I was too young to know, and angry at her when she stood by and let it all happen. I was angry at the circumstances that put me in that place at that time. The days came and went and I became increasingly withdrawn, refusing to get involved emotionally with anyone outside my family, such as it was.

I stared down at the words on the paper and felt the dampness of tears on my face. I wiped them away and put the papers in my purse so I wouldn't forget to take them to my next session.

Chapter 32

That horrible intrusive phone rang and I grabbed the receiver and snapped, "Hello!"

"Wow! Did I get you at a bad time or what? You don't need to bite my head off!" Ross chuckled on the other end.

"Ross! I'm sorry, I was relaxing and the phone startled me. I can still feel my heart thumping. Is everything okay?"

"Yes, everything is fine. I'm just calling to remind you of our conference call this weekend. It's my turn to make it so I am making certain everyone is available. I will call on Sunday evening at six. Will that work for you?" He sounded cheerful; I always envy him his bubbly personality.

"My gosh! Has it been three months since our last call? I can never seem to get a handle on time and how it passes me by. I will be here and I'm looking forward to connecting with you all. How are Joseph and Emma?" I asked, excitement building up in me, I am always happy to hear from my brother.

"Have you heard from them recently?"

"No, like you time just whizzes by so I haven't spoken to them since our last call. It is a good thing we have these conference calls set up every three months or we would probably never find the time to speak with each other."

"You've got that right. I'm ashamed to admit I rarely think to phone any of you between those calls. I am sure we would have heard if anything exciting or serious had happened to either of them. I look forward to our chat on Sunday. Thanks for calling and reminding me, Ross."

"No problem, Molly. I'll talk to you Sunday. 'Bye for now."

"'Bye Ross."
Thank goodness he called to remind me of the call this weekend! I had totally forgotten it.

For a brief moment, I wondered if I should share with them what was happening to me. I knew each of them would be here in a heartbeat if I called and said I needed their help. Joseph has been our protector and I was certain that he knew a lot more than he let on. I decided not to involve them and vowed to keep my part of our conference call neutral and light hearted. I could fill them in on Carin, her family and the weather. I was anxious to hear about them and the news of their respective families.
I cherished the thought that they were there and as near as a phone call away.

Chapter 33

I needed to get going. It was my turn to bring the goodies for my knitting group and I hadn't even decided what I was going to bake. I browsed through the recipe book and thought about brownies. Somewhere I have a recipe that includes a little coffee They are to die for, but sadly I can never stop at just one. I then become so annoyed with myself when I eat so many and I feel sick after, although I am never sick enough to pass them up. Oh no! Instead, they just get added to the extra roll I carry around my middle and a little on each hip. I settled on the brownies and to hell with the consequences. I baked up a storm and even did a couple of dozen cookies to take over to Carin and the kids. I rushed to get ready and leave early enough to drop off the cookies.

The drive over was uneventful with my mind focused on the road and the pleasant anticipation of being with my friends.
"Hi, Carin! I can't stay. I just stopped by to drop off some cookies I baked this morning." I handed her the bag of cookies when she answered the door.
"Thank you, Mom that's sweet! Are you off to knitting and a gabfest with the girls?" she asked, taking the cookies and laughing at me.
"Yes. We are getting near the end of spring. Once the hot weather comes, we shut down until the fall. There is so much going on with each of us through the summer, that we have an end-of-season party. We each go our separate ways until September when we start again. I miss it, but I find I am just too busy to try and fit it in every week. We still have this month. I really need to get going or I'm going to

be late. I'll see you later, dear. Enjoy the cookies!" I waved cheerfully, running down the steps to my car.

"Thanks, Mom! We will! We need to get together for dinner one night soon. I'll call and we can set a date." She waved back and shut the door.

"Okay, Carin! That sounds good."

As I drove away, I was pleased to think that maybe, just maybe Carin and I could get back to being comfortable with each other again. I needed to keep the dreams and flashbacks on the back burner when I was around her and I had to keep my temper in check. I was determined to make amends with her. I knew I could keep smoothing over any rough spots that came between us. That would buy me more time. I realized if I didn't, I could be pushed into a situation that would be devastating for me and destructive to my small family. I was desperate to get things to where Carin once more could enjoy the peace of mind that would enable her to get on with her own life. She needed to stop worrying about me.

I felt good about everything as I drove over to pick up Annabelle and go to Maggie's.

Chapter 34

When we arrived, both Amy and Betsy were already here.

"Hi, everyone!"

"Hi! How are things going?" Maggie asked.

"Great!" both Annabelle and I responded in unison.

"Your front yard looks so beautiful, Maggie. You must love to work in it,|" I said as I took my favorite place on the couch.

"I do. I just wish I could keep that big buck out of my back yard. He comes and eats all of my tulips and other flowers. Deer don't like daffodils, so at least I still have some color." She was indignant at how this deer ravaged her flowers.

We sat and gabbed about generalities and about how the kids, grandkids and anyone else on our radar were.

"I need to apologize for my outburst last time we were together," I said feeling quite contrite.

"Why don't you tell us what has been going on with you lately, Molly?" Betsy asked as she took the knitting out of her bag.

"As you can see, I have not done a thing since last week."

"I told you last time I am having problems with Carin."

"Oh, come on, Molly! Open up! We're your friends," Annabelle remarked, putting her knitting down.

"We all know it is more than a falling out with Carin. If you don't trust us, there is something wrong with this picture. We do more than just get together and knit. We are a close group of friends like no other friends you know. We have laughed and cried in this group for over five years now. Let us help you, even if we can't do any more than just listen," She bit her top lip and turned to look at

159

me. We were in our usual places, and she was sitting next to me on the couch.

"I can't explain it all. You will think I have lost my mind." I fought to keep my emotions in check. I felt tears burning the back of my eyelids.
"We promise we won't think that. Right girls?" Maggie laughingly said.
"Now spit it out, Molly. What is going on?"
Annabelle reached over and took my hand and I dissolved into tears.

"You all know a lot about my past. Since I was attacked, I have been having flashbacks that go back years and years. I can't remember the details of some of the stuff, but the emotions rock me and scare the living daylights out of me. Some of my dreams are so vivid, I swear I am there in person as a very young girl but I can't pin the time or the memory down. My temper is on a short fuse and I find myself behaving in outrageous ways in public places. Carin is convinced I am slipping into dementia and wants to put me into an assisted living place. I feel desperate sometimes and helpless to defend myself because of the public episodes and outbursts." I wept, pausing briefly to take gulps of air between sentences.
Maggie was the first to offer her support.
"Jeepers, Molly! No wonder you are so uptight! Why didn't you share this with us before? Of course we can help! You know you can tell us anything. We won't judge you. Are you getting professional help with the flashbacks? It sounds to me like posttraumatic stress."
Maggie put down her knitting and leant forward in her concern.
Amy picked up the conversation, nervously pulling her stitches out.
"We are so sorry you are going through this right now, but we will all stand with you if it comes to having to prove you can look after yourself and your home. Have you explained to Carin what is going on?"

"I can't. Amy. She doesn't know about my past and the things I was involved in. She would be shattered to know about my history. I can never share that with her. I just can't," I sobbed, wrapping my face in my hands to hide my tears.

Betty moved over to sit beside Annabelle and me and remarked, "Of course you can't and neither should you, Molly. Right now, we need to decide how we can help."

Hiding my face from them, I continued, "I am seeing Michael and that helps a lot. You remember Michael, don't you?"

"Yes, I remember him," Annabelle said, "he helped my daughter when she was going through a difficult divorce and was in great emotional distress." She squeezed my shoulder to reassure me.

"You can best help me just by being here for me and understand me when I have these eruptions. Sometimes, when discussions are happening and someone says something that grates on me, I lose it. The rage I feel overwhelms me. I release it in whatever way I can and anyone on my radar gets the brunt of my nasty outburst. I am sorry, but that is how it is right now and if you can put up with me, I will be grateful. I promise I will try to keep my feelings in check."

"No problem, Molly! Unload whenever you have to and we will try and hold our tempers, providing you don't get too nasty! If you do, it will be necessary for us to smack you up the side of the head," Maggie said, chuckling.

Amy laughed. "You've got that right! Now let's get on with some real juicy gossip I heard about Angelina and Brad."

I wiped my face and blew my nose; relieved I sat back and listened. *I silently thanked my God that I have these wonderful friends with whom I can share my burden.*

"What did you hear, Amy, and are you sure it's the truth?" Annabelle asked, trying to be serious but laughing at the same time.

"I am so blessed." I said and settled into another afternoon of friendship. We spent the rest of the afternoon knitting, pulling out mistaken stitches and prattling about useless information on the pop stars of today and yesterday.

Driving home, I felt a sense of peace, knowing there were four devoted friends who would stand by me in my struggle to stay focused on the present. I was certain they would also stand with me if it came to a legal battle to fight for my home and independence. For the first time in months, I felt as if I could make it through the days ahead. I was actually whistling when I opened my front door. My two dogs greeted me like a long lost friend. You would think I had been gone for a month rather then a couple of hours.

"Okay, okay! Let me get in the house and change my shoes and we will go for a long walk today. It has been awhile since we did a serious walk but today's the day. Get down now, both of you, while I get ready." I laughingly stroked each dog and shooed them outside until I was ready to go.

I checked my machine for messages and noticed Carin's number on the call display. I promised myself to play it when I returned from my walk.

Chapter 35

It was a beautiful day of bright sunshine with a little breeze to keep it comfortable so it wouldn't get too hot. The Arbutus trees were stunning this time of year, their leaves were a gorgeous green that glistened in the sun, they still had their bark and they stretched their branches like arms reaching to heaven. Forsythia and broom were showing off their bright yellow blossoms and there were still some shooting stars and camas lilies dotting the soft green of the grass that was young and firm bearing the colors of spring. The earth shared the redolence of the new growth in soil still damp after the rains. What a picturesque journey for me to walk along the bush-lined trails! I listened to the Canada Geese, the mallards, and wood ducks chatting with each other about who knows what. Signs of their nests were visible and the mothers-to-be were sitting faithfully waiting for the birth of their progeny. The shrill song of red-winged blackbirds filled the air, while crows squawked their warnings as we walked by. Hawk and eagle soared and swooped, searching for a small morsel of food, doing their part to keep the mice and rabbit population at a reasonable level. The blue of the sky dared the blue of the creek to match its dazzling hue. The creek bubbled and meandered its way over the rocky creek bed. In the small glen, the willow tree was in full regalia, fighting with the Garry Oaks and Douglas Firs for space for their roots to spread and soak up the nourishment from the ground. The sun dappled path opened to the green landscape to the accompaniment of the soft murmurs of the creek as it passed by. The sweet buttercups, saucy bluebells and bold wild red sweet peas carpeted the glen with a riot of colors. I sat on the bench above the creek and drank in the peace and tranquility of this place and time.

My dogs were lying in the grass, stretching their legs. They laid their heads on their paws and closed their eyes to dream whatever dogs dream. I put my head back, stretched my legs out in front of me and closed my eyes, letting myself relax for a minute or two, to enjoy the simple act of doing nothing. I sensed my bones weaken and my muscles become liquid as I drifted into nothingness, oblivious of the sweet quiet world around me. Sleep captured my mind and opened it to dreams.

***

"Molly! What is your problem? You moon around and do nothing these days, but read and sulk. I am getting a little fed up with your sullenness. Go on out and spend some time with your friends or your brothers but get out of the house. I don't want to look at your sour face." My mother's words sliced through my thoughts and resentment churned in my stomach.

"I don't want to go anywhere. I don't have any friends and I definitely don't want to listen to Joe and Ross play their stupid games of war," I snarled and gave her one of my most baleful looks.

"Then go up to your room where I don't have to see you."

"Fine, I don't particularly like looking at you either."

"What did you say?"

"Nothin'" I replied and walked away.

"You better get yourself straightened up before tonight! Duncan is coming over and maybe another man who called and made a temporary appointment to be with you. But he won't confirm the time until after five o'clock. Neither one of them will put up with your moods." She rambled on as she followed me down the dark hallway.

"Oh, don't worry about me. I know exactly what I have to do and I don't need any advice on how to please them. You can be sure you will get your money and I guarantee they will go away happy. Oh, and above all, they will be more than willing to come back again for further enjoyment. Isn't that how it works?" I spat out my words, willing her to do something cruel and physical so I wouldn't be available tonight.

"Don't give me your smart talk, missy. Just get on upstairs and take your bath and lay your clothes out on the bed in the special room. Do it now before I lose my patience with you." She sputtered and shoved me in front of her.

"No problem! Don't worry about supper for me. I don't feel very hungry. I am thrilled about the big date tonight," I whispered recklessly. I couldn't stand the thought of another night of games with men.

"Oh, just go! Just go now before I smack some sense into you!" My mother turned her back and walked away.

This was my world. My life was in the toilet and I couldn't see any way out of my insoluble dilemma. I forced myself to accept what was. I still had some wonderful and special times with Duncan outside of the bedroom. It was hard for me to sort out my conflicted feelings for him but, oh! How I looked forward to being held by him!

Sometimes, when we walked, he would pretend he was my dad. It was fun when we were just being friends. He was the adult and I was his child and there was no sex involved. Those times were precious to me and I was grateful for small periods of shared words and feelings with him. I didn't feel all alone. At times it was like I was really a part of him. I needed to be wanted and cared for. He was the one person, other than Sadie and the other women, who was there for me. When he was with me in times of crisis. He picked up the pieces of my emotional chaos. He helped me to put them back together in a way that allowed me to function again. In short, he was the major adult positive influence while at the same time he was a significant part of the problem. It was far too complex for my child's mind to sort out, so I accepted whatever love and platonic companionship I could get. Regardless of the inappropriate relationship we had, he filled a crucial role in my life.

When he came just to take me for a walk in the park, it made me feel like a little girl, innocent of the knowledge of man and woman. His physical size and strength assured me of protection by his mere presence. I was smug about how I felt, because my brothers and sister did not have that father influence at that time. I would swing his arm in great glee at the thought that I was once more that child who had no knowledge or experience of the house on Ninth Avenue. I slipped into a world of make believe, where there was just sweetness and light and no sexual thoughts. I morphed into this space a lot and even sometimes when I was alone and Duncan was not near. I never forgot the times when he was just being a friend and protector.

Those were my thoughts for the night ahead. That mindset would get me through whatever I had to do to fill my roll as a sex slave.

Chapter 36

One day, out of the blue, my mother told us that we were moving to Mossbank, a small town about fifty miles from Moose Jaw in Saskatchewan. Her mother, stepfather and sister lived there, as did my father's mother and stepfather.

Joseph put down his fork and stared at my mother.

"What do you mean, we are moving?"

It was just like my mother to spoil our dinner with startling news. We were all flabbergasted and we gaped at her with our mouths hung open. Our warm kitchen suddenly felt cold. The conversation, laughter and chomping were all silenced by our stunned reactions. The hush was deafening. The only sound was that of the coal shifting in the stove and the kettle simmering on it.

"Just what I said. We are moving. We have been here for four years and it is time for us to move on. The war seems to be coming to an end and it won't be that long before your father is home and I know he won't want to live here." Mom had put down her fork and made it clear that the decision was already made.

I gawked at her with my bottom lip quivering.

"What about Sadie, Rachelle and everyone? Will they move with us?"

"No, of course not! They will stay here and run the house until it is time to close it down. We won't be going right away. It will take a little time to get my affairs in order and things sorted out here." She picked up her fork and blithely carried on eating her dinner.

"Do they know we are going to leave them here?" Emma asked.

"Yes. We have talked about it many times. They all know that when your father returns, we can no longer be a part of this." She waved her hand around the room like the house was something unpleasant and perhaps even had an unpleasant smell.

"What do you mean, Mommy? I love it here, all my friends are here," Ross wailed.

"Yeah," we all joined in.

"Oh, stop it. We aren't leaving today. It will take a few months, so don't get your knickers in a knot. I am just letting you know, so you won't be shocked when the move happens. Now all of you clear the dishes and scoot into the front room and listen to the radio. I have things to get ready for tonight."

"Will we have lots of visitors in Mossbank?" I asked tremulously.

"No, we won't. Mossbank is a very small town and both your grandmothers live there. We will visit with them and they will visit with us. You will make new friends and so will I. Now go on, all of you! I told you, I have work to do."

"Wow! We will have a whole new life when we move, Joseph! Won't that be great?" I excitedly started to clear the dishes.

"No. it won't, Molly! I don't want to leave my friends and I know all the neat places to play. I love it here." He grabbed the salt and pepper off the table and slammed them into the cupboard.

"How can you say that? We will have our daddy back and he will look after us. We won't have to be afraid of Mommy anymore, because he won't let her be mean to us. We won't have to be shut down in the basement by ourselves anymore. I just know he won't let her do that stuff anymore." I was hopping with such eagerness that I was nearly vibrating.

"We don't even know him. We don't know what he's like. He might be meaner than she is," he whined, while he put some of the dishes into the sink.

"He's been in the war for years and all he has been doing is killing soldiers and living in the bush and desert and stuff. I am more afraid of him because I don't remember him." He yelled at Ross and Emma to get a tea towel and dry the dishes.

He was stomping around the kitchen, shoving things into the cupboard and the sink. He dropped a heavy cup on my hands that were submerged in the dishwater.

"Be careful, Joseph. You are going to break something," I told him, wrenching my hand out of the water.

"I remember him a little bit. I don't really though. Do you think he will be mean like she is?" I mumbled. I tried not to think about anything else.

"I don't know," he snapped, "Just leave me alone. I want to be by myself right now!" He turned away with his head down and his shoulders slumped. He looked very sad, walking away from me.

"I don't care. I'm glad to be going away from here," I muttered to myself, Emma and Ross.

"Yikes!" I screamed, as Pippa jumped on my lap and jolted me awake. I leapt off the bench.

"Whoosh!" I inhaled, as Christine jumped up on me with all her weight on my tummy.

"Take it easy! I'm awake, okay? Both of you settle down. I'm sorry I fell asleep. Let's go home. By the way, both of you were asleep long before I drifted off, so don't look so pompous."

I was still a little disoriented, trying to figure out if I just imagined it all, or if it was a dream. Either way, it was disconcerting to me. I seemed to be on a fast track, taking me back to my childhood years whenever I let down my guard.

I remembered, though, how excited I was to know we would soon leave Moose Jaw and all it held for me. It would take another year before we left. In those years, I became adept in pleasing men in a variety of ways and I was one of the biggest money earners in the house. I had learned how to hide my emotions and I was always on guard against my mother's wrath. I had resigned myself to the fact we would never be close. I spent many tearful and terrified days and nights in the darkness of the basement. To this day, I have a terror of being alone in a closed darkened room. I have never owned a house with a basement, nor will I ever.

Dusk was settling in as we made our way back home. I didn't want to be on this part of the trail in the forest when it was dark, so I quickened my steps.

I mulled over Joe's words when we first learned about leaving Moose Jaw. I thought about how sad he must have felt. He, too, had learned to deal with our mother, who was nearly as harsh with him as she was with me. I believe that she loved him, though, because I saw her hug him several times. She always made sure he looked neat and clean when he left for school. She was rather ambiguous with him and expected him to behave much older than he was. I wondered how devastating that move was for him? His best friend, Ward, was left behind as were many of his happy memories. I felt very sad in my heart for him as I continued my way home.

Chapter 37

"Hi Beth! It finally looks like spring is happening." I was smiling as I walked into the reception area the next morning.

"Yes, it's nice to see a clear blue sky, sunshine and flowers poking up everywhere. I guess we shouldn't complain about our weather when I hear of the conditions some cities have to endure. Michael will be right out, Molly. He's just finishing a telephone conversation."

"Thanks, Beth." I took a seat and picked up a magazine, but I didn't get a chance to read anything because Michael came out.

"Hi, Molly, come right on in."

"Thanks, Michael. I'll see you shortly, Beth."

I took a seat and, as usual, I questioned why I was there and what good it was doing.

"Well, how has your week gone, Molly? Any more frightening incidents happen?"

"I don't know. It seems that I always have to be on the move or alert because if I am not, I find myself drifting back to the past. Some of the things I see and remember are truly confusing. I really do wonder if I am on the verge of insanity."

"We both know that is not true." He looked at me, a little amused.

"I don't know, Michael. Sometimes I feel as if I am on the outside looking into my mind and I can't pull away from it. It is like the world slips into silence. I see people's lips moving, but I don't hear them because I am in my own place of nothingness. If I sit down to relax, I immediately go into another flashback. How the hell am I supposed to function this way? No wonder Carin thinks I can't look after myself. I am beginning to think the same. Do you have any answers that make any sense?'

"Yes, as a matter of fact I do. You are under a lot of stress right now, Molly! You have endured a major physical assault at the hands of a stranger whom you cannot confront. In addition, your family is threatening to take away all that represents your independence and is pushing you into a corner. You have to accept your need to come to terms with both of these things. Once the flashbacks have been met head on and put away forever, you will become more stable. It is going to take time and it will be painful, confusing and mysterious. We may never resolve them all, but I know for certain there is a reason why you are seeing what you are seeing. You will come through it much stronger than when you began. You have to be willing to fight along with me, Molly. If you give up, then you could well lose all that is important to you right now. The flashbacks won't stop until you come to an understanding of every one of them."

"How am I supposed to unravel them when I don't remember them? I don't want to remember them because I don't see the significance of them right now. I don't want to live in the past. I just want to forget it all and get on with my life as it was before." I kept my eyes down and started to fidget with the buttons on my sweater.

"That's all well and good, but obviously your mind is not ready to put it all behind. The fact that you can't confront your aggressor is playing a part in your flashbacks. This same problem shows up in your dreams. You can't confront the reality because you have buried those memories where your mind won't let you go yet. It will take time, Molly, and you have to be willing to accept what is happening until we see how this plays out." He sat back in his chair and ran his fingers through his hair. He seemed harried. I wondered if it was my fault?

"That's just great. Do you think Carin will be willing to wait to see what happens? If I have another incident, as she puts it, what do you think her reaction will be?"

I stood up and walked away from him. I picked up and studied a small angel he had on a little table in the corner of the room. I turned it over in my hand and wondered if there is an angel out there for me? I felt exasperated, numb and utterly powerless.

"Let me talk to her, Molly. Maybe I can explain what is really going on here, so she can be brought onside. Maybe she can help you through it." His smile was warm and I believed he would do whatever he could to help me.

"Not a chance, Michael. She has never had any idea of my past. I don't intend to reveal it to her. I will never give you permission to talk with her or anyone else.

Why don't you tell me about the last flashback and anything other memory that is troubling you.

"I guess I'm still a little stuck in my thoughts that overtook me when I was walking my dogs. We had been told by our mother that we would be moving and leaving our friends behind. It was such a shock for us and the women who lived and worked in the house were like family to us. The thought of leaving them was very disturbing. My brothers were very upset. I was of mixed emotions, for me it was an escape from a lifestyle that I abhorred. The days following her announcement we dazedly continued our daily chores and our routine was pretty much as it had been. The changes were gradual, with things being put in boxes to take or to give or throw away.

Chapter 38

We were all getting our things ready to pack in a gradual way. Joseph was still moaning about how he didn't want to go. Ross, too, was deploring the fact that he would be leaving behind his best friends. "I don't know what you two are so sad about. I think it is a great adventure to move to a different town. Don't forget, we will get to know both of our grandmothers really well, because Granny Louise and Aunt Lucy live there. Nana Kate and Uncle Greg visit there every spring and summer. It will be lots of fun, and we won't have to see all these people anymore. Mommy said none of the ladies would be moving, so none of the men will be visiting anymore and that's really good." That was my way to try to bolster their moods.

"How do you know that's good? I love our friends and some of the men give us good gifts and chocolate. They sometimes come in the day and play with us. You don't know if our grandmothers will want to have us around all the time. I like it here and I want to stay here. So there!" Ross exclaimed.

"Well, I don't care about you or Joseph. You can wish all you want, but we are moving and it will happen soon because Mommy says she wants to be settled into our new place when Daddy comes back. I heard her telling Rachelle the war is coming to an end. We are winning, so Daddy will be coming home soon." I smirked and left them to sulk. I skipped out of the room, more happy and full of hope than I had ever felt.

"Molly! Come here!" my mother shouted from the kitchen.
"What, Mommy?"

"You need to get ready for tonight. You have a couple of men coming in to see you. Wear your little pink nightgown, the one with the rabbits on and the ribbon that ties at the neck. Get Rachelle to help you with your bath and hair." She continued to pack some of our dishes in a box and marked "special dishes" on it with a dark pencil. She was bustling around the stove at the same time, getting supper ready.

"I don't want to. Can't I stop now that we are going to move? And where is Sadie? She's never here anymore? I miss her lots."
"Just do as you are told, Molly! I am too tired to listen to your whining. Go on upstairs and find Rachelle."

My mother never looked at me when we talked. That day she looked sad and alone.
"When are we moving? Will it be soon?" I kept my head down. I struggled against the urge to cry. I shut down my feelings. I didn't want her to see how upset I was.
"Yes, we will be leaving at the end of next month, so we have to get all of the packing done by then. We need to earn a lot of money, because it will cost a great deal to move everything and find a new place to live." She started to set the table.
"Joseph, come on out here and help with the table. I need your help so I can get supper on to cook." She turned away from me and called him from the doorway.
He yelled back at her.
"Why can't Molly help you? She is right there and I am in the middle of painting my new model airplane. It is a Messerschmitt and it's going to be a beauty."
"I'll help you, Mommy. I like to set the table. Joseph can help put the supper on to cook. I'm not sad we are moving. I am really glad. I can hardly wait! Will we live in a house all our own, or will we have people living with us again?" I fired questions at her, trying to get her to forget about sending me upstairs.

175

"We will have our own place. Now get out of here and get ready. Joseph can help me and you can help by doing as you are told. Joseph! Get in here now! I am fast losing my patience with you!"

"I'm coming. I don't know why I have to do this girl stuff. How come Molly gets to do all the fun stuff?" He grumbled his way into the kitchen. He glared at me and stuck out his tongue.

"How can you say I have fun? You don't even know what I have to do!"

"Molly, do not say another word. Get yourself upstairs right now! Joseph, you keep quiet and do as you are asked."

I was quite certain my mother didn't think of me as her child. Maybe she considered me one of her employees? I wonder if she was unable to love me because I had become like the other ladies? I was someone who simply worked for her and brought in money. I left the kitchen. I carried a deep sense of rejection in my soul. I found Rachelle and passed on the instructions from my mother. My legs were like pieces of wood as I dragged myself to the bathroom.

"Rachelle, can you tell me where Sadie is?" I inquired while she got the water ready for my bath.

"No, honey, I don't know where she went. She has been gone a long time. I think she might have gone back home, wherever that is."

"I know and I miss her lots. This is her home now I hope she comes back soon, don't you?" I sniffled.

"Mommy doesn't like me to talk about her and she gets mad at me when I ask about her. Do you think you could find out for me and then you would know too and you could write to her and ask her to come home?" I anxiously ran my sentences together.

"I don't know about that, Molly. I think we should just wait and see what happens. Come on, hop into the bath and let's get you smelling nice and clean and into your soft nighty. Do you want me to weave ribbons through your braids tonight?"

"Okay," I shrugged my thoughts deadened.

As I climbed into the tub of bubbles, I asked.

"Do you know who is coming? Is it someone I know or you know?"

"I don't know, Molly. I know it isn't Duncan or Roger. They are both on duty at the base. Things have been very busy there lately. People say the war is coming to an end. Let's hope that is true. I think one of the men is from the base too, and he heard about you from Roger. I overheard your mom and Sissy talking about tonight. Sissy answered the phone when one of the men called to set up a time to be with you." She dried me off and took me to my special room to get me ready.

All this fuss confused me. I get coddled as if I was a toddler unable to dress or bathe myself. Then I get thrown to the wolves, but am not allowed to cry out or get help. I sometimes felt loved and other times I felt abandoned. While I was getting prepped for my date, the lump of fear that sat in the pit of my stomach reared its ugly head. It wasn't the pain as much as the futility of knowing that for a sum of money, I had to perform and do whatever the buyer wanted. I was nothing and knew I meant nothing to anyone except for a brief moment when my body was needed to fulfill a fantasy. I was tortured with the futility of my life.

I succumbed to the familiar cold, flat, wooden feeling and sat numbed, waiting. I tried to hide myself and my emotions in that dark place in my mind until this night was over.

"Molly, come downstairs now and we'll wait in the lounge for your company," Sissy declared, coming into my room. She relieved Rachelle so she could get ready for her guest. She snapped me out of my reverie. I looked at Sissy with sightless eyes.

"I thought we were going to be in this room tonight, Sissy?" I was curious by this change.

"You are, Molly, but this is the first time Henry has come, so your mom wants him to have a couple of drinks and maybe a dance or two with you before coming upstairs."

"I hope I don't have to have any of that booze to drink. I don't like the taste of it, Sissy." I scrunched my face and shuddered, remembering the taste.

"Maybe we can put some sugar in it for you and heat it up a little, Molly. We'll give it a try and see if you like it better." She led me down to the lounge. I saw my brothers and sister getting ready to go out with Mindy.

"Where are you going?" I asked.

"We're going to see "The Three Caballeros" with Mindy and we won't be home until late. Too bad you can't come with us, Molly. Why are you in your nightgown? Did you do something bad again and now you have to go to bed early?" Emma questioned. She had a look on her face that said I'm special and you're not.

"That's none of your business. You'd better get a move on or you'll miss the bus." My mother shooed them all out the door.

I wistfully watched them trek out the door to do something I would love to be doing, but I was trapped here. I watched my mother as she laughingly hurried them away and wondered again what was wrong about me.

"Sit down, Molly, and I'll go and fix us a drink so we'll be ready for Henry when he comes." Sissy walked over to the sideboard and mixed the drinks.

"When is he coming?" I looked at her longingly, wishing I could be going to the movie. A small tear slipped out.

"Now stop that, Molly! I already told you we need money for the move. We all have to do our part. We'd all like to cry over our lot in life, but a fat lot of good it would do if I cried every time I had to do something I didn't want to do. Where do you think you kids would be without me looking after you and this house while your father is away?" My Mother scowled and pulled me away from Sissy's side. She shoved me on to the couch.

"Henry will be here in a few minutes. Now pull yourself together and sit up straight. Sissy, finish fixing those drinks while I answer the door. That is probably Henry now. I don't want any trouble from you tonight, Molly. Just get on and do what you've been taught to do!" Mother left to answer the door.

"Molly, this is Henry." Sissy introduced him to me after Mother had ushered him into the room. She gave out the drinks and I scrunched my nose, sniffed and tasted it.

"Mm.! This is good Sissy! Thank you for making it warm and sweet." I smiled at her.

Henry was tall and quite nice looking. His blond hair was curly and hugged his face. He had the greenest eyes I had ever seen. He had on his Air Force uniform, but he had a different kind of hat than Roger and Duncan. He carried it in his hands. He had a deep resonate voice and seemed really nice. He sat down and shyly lifted my hand from the couch and gently curled his around mine.

"Yes, thank you for the drink. It hits the spot after a busy day at the base. It feels good to relax," he warmly added and settled himself next to me.

"What kind of hat is that, Henry?" I asked.

"It's a pilot commander's hat, Molly. I'm a pilot in the Air Force."

"Do you fly planes in the war?"

"Yes. I am leaving in two days to go overseas and help end this war."

"Will the war be over soon?" I took another sip of my drink.

"We believe it will be over before the end of the year and that is just a few months away, Molly."

"That's really good." I started to feel warm from the drink.

"Come and snuggle up a little closer, Molly. You smell real sweet." He reached over and put his arms around my waist.

"Your uniform is too scratchy, Henry, and it makes me itch." I scratched at my face.

"Why don't you take Henry up to your room, Molly," Sissy chuckled, "and you can help him get out of his scratchy uniform."

"Okay. C'mon Henry. I'll show you where my special room is.

I was tipsy from the drink Sissy had made me.

I took Henry's hand and staggered up the stairs to my special room.

Henry shut the door and stood me up on the bed and knelt in front of me. Even tho' I was nearly eight years old I was very small for my age and I had a slight build.

"Do you want me to take my uniform off, Molly, or do you want to help me with it?"

"I'll help, but I'm not too good at undoing buttons. I am getting better though. I have to do it good because I will be going to grade three next year and I will have to do them quick and by myself" I studied his shiny buttons and wondered how long it took to get them to look so sparkly. He smelled different from the other men. It was a spicy, sweet smell and I didn't like it, but I knew I didn't dare tell him. Sometimes the men got very mad really fast when I said things about them that they didn't like. When his clothes were off, I started to feel edgy.

"Can I take your ribbons out of your hair, Molly?"

"Sure."

"You have lovely long hair and it feels like silk and smells nice." He kissed the top of my head.

"Please, Henry. I don't feel so good. I just want to go to sleep. The drink is making me feel sick and sleepy." I tried to push him away.

He was having none of that and so once again my body felt like sludge from the drink and my mind closed against what was happening to my body and slipped into that place of quiet nothingness.

When I awoke, he was gone and Sissy stood at the side of the bed. She told me it was time to go downstairs for my next date.

"I don't want to come down. I want to sleep, Sissy," I wailed, still half asleep and groggy from the drink. I rolled over and turned my back to her.

"You don't have to come down then, Molly. I will bring him up to you, but let me do your hair up again and put your nighty on. Here's a cloth to wash with and make yourself fresh again." She gave me a damp cloth soaked in lavender water to wash my face and I did a quick sponge bath.

My next encounter was not nearly as gentle as the one with Henry. I was incredibly sore and felt wretched. I was full of shame for what

I had done tonight. I wanted to curl up and die. I never wanted to look in a mirror again. I loathed and blamed myself for being such a willing partner. I let men do what they wanted just so I could get money for my mother. A part of me had hoped that she would come to love me because I did these things for her. That dream was quickly dying. I knew I got what I deserved for being such a wanton tramp just like she said.

I was sorely distressed and I missed Duncan. I knew he understood how I felt. A little piece of me was excited about the move, but a deeper part was afraid of what was ahead. There would be no one to help me, like the women in the house had done over the few years we had lived here. I did understand that Duncan was outrageously busy at the base these days. I rarely saw him. I hoped he would come to see me soon, so I could talk to him about how scared I was.

I had more clients coming and going, as did my mother and the other ladies. Days and nights seemed to run together. I didn't know these men as well as I knew Duncan and Roger. I found myself fighting the inner demons that assailed me on the days I knew I had dates. These men were strangers to me.

One day when I was in the middle of helping my mother pack the doorbell rang and I ran to answer it.

"Duncan!" I threw myself into his arms and he picked me up, twirled me around and hugged me to him.

"Is it okay with you, Rose, if I steal Molly for a couple of hours? I won't get much time to come by before you leave."

"Go ahead! But have her back by three o'clock. We still have lots to do and I want to get it done before tonight."

"Thanks, Mommy!" I squealed and wrapped myself tight in Duncan's arms.

He put me down, took my hand and we walked out the door together.

"How have you been, Molly? I am sorry I haven't been around to see you, but things are crazy busy right now.

"I know, Sissy explained why you haven't been able to come. I have been really lonely and I am scared, Duncan."

"What or who is scaring you?"

"I am afraid of moving away from our friends and I love my house. I don't much like the men that have been coming to see me, but we could stay here and not do that stuff. My mommy says we can't do it when my daddy comes home. I don't understand why we can't stay here and do other stuff that is okay with him. I want to tell my daddy what my mommy makes me do. I know he will be really mad at her and he will make her be nice to me. I think he will want to know what we have been doing while he has been over there fighting the war. Don't you think that too, Duncan?"

"I understand why you are scared, Molly. It is scary when we have to do things that are different. Moving away from your friends and all the places you are familiar with is frightening. That's not unusual. I was pretty scared when I had to leave everyone I knew when I joined the Air Force, but it didn't take too long for me to make new friends. I would never have met you. I would be very sad about that. You are the most special little girl to me. I love you more than anyone else, Molly."

"But you are an adult, Duncan. It is easier for you to move. Kids like to keep the friends they know and like. What about you? I won't ever be able to see you again and I will be sad for that. Do you think my dad will be mad at you for playing with me like I am an adult?"

"You don't know that I won't come and visit with you, Molly. You never know, I might be stationed near you after the war. There is an Air Force base in Mossbank."

"Really? I didn't know that. Will you promise you will come and see me if you get moved there? You won't be able to play with me like we do in this house, Duncan, but we could go for walks and talk and you could help me feel better if I am sad."

"Molly, we need to talk about the things that happen in the house here. Do you think your daddy needs to know about it? I think he will be very sad to know bad things happened to you and he couldn't be here to protect you. Your mommy has done the best she could.

Think how hard it is for her to be alone with four little children to look after by herself. She had to do something to bring in more money, so she could look after you all. It is too bad you are so cute and that some of us like to be with little girls, but I never meant to hurt you, Molly. I hope you will always remember how I love you more than life itself. If you think hard, you must know I never was mean to you. I always treated you with gentleness. Some of the other men might have been too hard on you and that is too bad, but I don't think it would be fair to tell your dad and make him feel bad about leaving you all. He did what he thought was right in going off to the war and you don't want him to regret that, do you?"

"No, I guess not, but I want him to love me and look after me. How can he like me if my mommy tells him how bad I am? If he sees that she doesn't like me, maybe he won't like me either. I wish I was dead sometimes, Duncan, and then I wouldn't have to worry about anything. I really want my daddy to love me and keep me safe!" I leaned into him and cried.

"Molly, he won't be able to help but to love you! Just be you, and he will see what a wonderful little girl he has, I promise! I have always kept my promises to you. You know I would never lie to you about this. It is very important that you never tell anyone about what happened in the house. Once you move away no one will ever need to know. It will be a secret kept by all of us. Your dad would be too hurt and ashamed that he wasn't here to protect you, so you must never tell him. You want him to be glad he went to help win the war, don't you?"

"I guess so," I said sadly. I will do as you say, Duncan." I was very disappointed and downhearted.

"No matter what happens, it is most important that you keep that promise to me, Molly, even if something bad happens to me. Will you make that promise now and remember, I have never broken a promise I made to you?"

"I promise, Duncan, but I hope nothing bad ever happens to you. Will I see you before we move?

"Yes. I have one more time with you before you leave. I can't remember the date, but I will come to you. We should go back now, Molly. Are you okay now?"

"I guess I am. I wish you could come with us, but I know you can't. If you get moved to the base in Mossbank, promise me you will come and take me for walks there, okay?

"For sure I will do that!" He hugged me and we walked back to the house, hand in hand.

Chapter 39

The next couple of months were filled with packing and arranging little parties to say our goodbyes. Each of us kids had a separate farewell party that was special for our friends. Mine was a dress-up party, where each of us wore an old-fashioned dress that touched the floor and we had funny hair-dos. It was great fun. We each borrowed dresses from our mothers and even wore the weird hats with feathers poking up. We had cake and ice cream. That was a special treat. Sissy made my cake and it had quaint dresses painted on the icing.

Joseph had a pirate party and they all had funny eye patches and painted mustaches. Rachelle made the mustaches with her eye pencil. They all made swords out of box tops and they tied scarves around their waists. All our women in the house loaned their pretty colored scarves. Their special treat was hot dogs. Their party was really noisy.

Ross's party was an Army convoy party. They had funny mustaches painted on too. They all had weird signs and paper badges pinned to their hats. They wore brown and blue blouses, borrowed from our women. They used cardboard boxes for jeeps. Joseph drew and colored different symbols on the sides. Their special treat was caramel popcorn balls.

Emma was too young to have a good-bye party because she didn't have any friends, so mother had all the women dress in pretty clothes and they had colorful cup-cakes. We all ate one.

Mother and her friends had a night party, but we couldn't go and we weren't allowed to sneak any peeks. We obeyed her because we didn't want to spoil her special party because she had done such nice things for us.

I knew it was getting close to the time of the move because most of our stuff had been packed and not many people came anymore. Duncan and I had our last time together. I would never forget that traumatic night. It was the worst. He was the best friend I had from the adults I knew in Moose Jaw.

A week later I lay on my bed in my room and I let the sadness that smothered my soul wash over me. I remembered our walking times. He had been such a good friend to me. I wished he hadn't gone away. I wanted to have him back just once more to tell him how much I missed him. I needed to tell him that I wanted to stay here and wait for him. I knew that was not possible. I was numb, knowing some things were forever and nothing could change what was already finished.

I missed Sadie too, but I knew that I would never know the real truth of where she went or even if she left. I shuddered to think of what might have happened to her. I squeezed my eyes shut and struggled to keep the grief to myself. I never let anyone see how I felt. Nothing could break the code I had kept with myself to hide my deepest feelings, no matter how much it hurt my heart. I had three more nights with clients and then, one morning, when I came down for breakfast, my mother proclaimed those magical words that spelled freedom for me.

"Today's the day!" Mother told us at the breakfast table.

"The moving truck will be here at nine o'clock this morning and we will be on the five o'clock train this afternoon to Mossbank." She was dressed in a very pretty dress and she floated around the kitchen like some prima donna. She fluffed her shiny black hair and smiled like a Cheshire cat. She looked as if she had spent a long time getting her make up just right. She was very happy. I wondered if she was as happy as I was to be free of this house and the memories it held?

Sissy had braided my hair in French braids with red ribbons weaved in. My skirt was dark blue and my blouse was very white. My shoes and socks were clean. I had my last bubble bath and I smelled like roses. I was still small, but I had grown some. The past five years had changed me dramatically.

Ross and Joseph were in long pressed pants and a clean dress shirt. Their hair was plastered down, and their faces and hands were scrubbed clean. Their shoes were polished and shone like a mirror. Emma was dressed in a pretty pink frilly dress. Her light brown curly hair was pulled back in a ponytail. The little curls that sprang out framed her darling face. She had hazel eyes and a sweet smile. Her hair ribbon was pink and her shoes were white. We all looked freshly scrubbed and our excitement shone in our eyes.

"Do we have a house to move to, Mommy?" Ross asked.

"Of course we do, sweetie, but our furniture won't arrive until the end of the week, so we will stay with Granny Louise and Aunt Lucy until then." She finally sat at the table.

"Where will we all sleep? Does she have enough beds for all of us?" I wondered aloud. "We will make do. You older kids will sleep on the floor for four days. We should be thankful we will have a clean, warm place to stay."

"What about eating?" Joseph put in.

"We'll eat there too; you know how good a cook Granny is. Don't you remember her home baked bread and buns with her own jams and jellies? We'll be well fed. Now let's all go up to our rooms and get everything into boxes that we will take with us on the train. You know what needs to be done, so I will expect you all down here with your own boxes that have your names on and all the things I put out for you to put in your box. Rachelle will tie your box tight, Molly. Mindy will tie yours, Joseph. Sissy will do yours, Ross and Susie will help you pack your things Emma and tie your box up for you. She will help you get ready to go. Now, everyone! Go and do what needs to be done, so when the taxi comes to take us to the train station, we'll be ready to go." She turned away from us to clean up the breakfast table. I noticed tears tumbling down her cheeks.

"Why are you crying, Mommy?" I was afraid she was sick or something bad had happened.

"It's nothing. Just go on up and do what I told you to do and never mind what doesn't concern you, Molly." She sighed and wiped the tears away with the back of her hand. I turned to leave and glanced back to see her leaning against the counter. She stared pensively out the window. I had a sense of her sadness. I was sorry I couldn't say something that would make her feel better. I knew anything I said would only make her feel worse, so I quietly left the room.

By the time the taxi came, we all were very tired. I just wanted to go to my bed, but of course, our beds were on the moving truck. They were on their way to Mossbank. For the first time, I was having second thoughts about moving from this house that I had known and loved in many ways for most of my life. I was sad to be leaving my friends and the women who had lived with us. They were like family. I loved them more than most people I knew. I started to cry when they each hugged and kissed me good-bye. I clung to Rachelle and asked her to tell me when she found Sadie. I promised to write and tell her my address. My mother pulled me from her and told me to get into the taxi.

"Like always, you have to cause trouble, don't you Molly? I told you to forget about Sadie. You've known all along that none of our friends can come with us, so why you have to make a big scene and delay us is beyond me. I am sure you just do these things to draw attention to yourself. You are not the only one who is feeling sad, young lady, but you have to blubber and wail louder than the rest of us. Now stop it and get into the car! If we miss the train, you will be good and sorry, believe me!" She rattled on and on and the hatred I felt for her boiled and churned in my stomach.

"I am glad we are leaving this horrible place," I sobbed in my frustration and hurt, "and I don't care what happens to any of our friends. It will be more fun in a new place and I can meet new friends and maybe they won't have to hurt me all the time. I wish I could be invisible so no one would look at me." In my mind I slung barbs at her.

"You can be such a little bitch, Molly! I don't know how I failed to teach you better manners. You never give any thought to other people's feelings and just spew garbage and hurtful words out of that big mouth of yours. One day, someone is going to shut you up in a way you won't like, believe me!" She railed at me from the front seat of the cab.

"You don't know anything about me! You hate me and I hate you!" I screamed. I was practically hysterical. I felt the hot rage seethe inside me and take on a life of its own.

"Mommy, why are you and Molly crying and yelling at each other?" Emma whimpered, reaching up to try and get on her lap.
"It's okay, little one. Mommy just feels a little sad to be saying good-bye to our friends. Molly is being Molly and we know how little she cares about anybody! Her only concern is for herself. Pay no attention to her. She is just trying to get everyone's attention like she always does. The more nasty things she can say, the better she feels." Mother lifted Emma and cradled her in her arms.

There were no words I could think of to say that could possibly express the rage that burned inside me. I felt the hurt and betrayal in the deepest part of my being. I was beside myself with grief and isolation. I turned my face away and wept great, wracking sobs into the back seat of the taxi. By now, Joseph and Ross were crying and she tried to console them. I twisted away from them all and nestled down into the corner of the cab. I yearned with all my heart to disappear forever. I squeezed one last look at my house as we drove away and for an instant, I was certain I saw Duncan at the window of my special room. My heartbeat quickened. I ached to say good-bye to him one last time. I knew that could not be him in the window. I curled upon myself and wept deeply into my arms. My only hope was that my life would be very much better in Mossbank and that it wouldn't be too long before my dad returned home from the war.

I was frantic about what I was losing. My brain was bursting with confusing thoughts about Duncan and how much I loved him and yet, at times, loathed the ground he walked on. I felt the hurt at losing his friendship and the loss of Sadie. I wondered why she never said goodbye or if she had any control over what happened to her? I made a wish in my heart that my dad would be strong. I wanted him to hold my hand and take me for walks in the park the way Duncan did when we were just being friends. I hoped my dad would never find out about the things I did in Moose Jaw. I hoped he only found out about the nice side of Duncan. I wanted him to know about the times that Duncan swung me up into his arms and held me and we watched the swans swim by on the little pond. Duncan was special when we were away from the house and there were just quiet words and no funny touching.

I tried to think of my Granny Louise and how wonderful her house smelled with breads, buns and cookies that always seemed to be in the oven. I remembered her as being kind and loving with me. My mother always treated me nicer too when Granny was around. I guess she didn't want her mom mad at her for being mean to me. Maybe when we were living there, I would tell her what bad things my mommy did to me. Maybe then things would really change and my mom would have to love me and take better care of me. I had to remember, though, to keep the secrets of the house in Moose Jaw forever, so no one could take us away and put us in a place where we might never see each other again. I didn't want my mommy and my friends in the house to go to jail, either. I will always have to be really careful what I tell my Granny. All those thoughts jumped around in my head while we made the journey to the train station.

I closed my eyes and shut out all the chaos and noise of my siblings' chatter and crying. I shut out the hurtful words of my mother and slipped into my quiet place where memories were no more and I was just a little girl. I pretended in my mind's eye that I had a little doll that I dressed in frilly pink clothes and put ribbons in her hair, so everyone would see how pretty she looked. I would love her because she was just a little girl. I had become very good at shutting out the world around me. I had a place I slipped into, a pretend place that was always warm and the people in my make-believe place loved and cared for me.

We arrived at the train station. It was a bustle of activity, with people getting off trains and people rushing to get on. They wept, called out their good byes and laughed in their greetings. It was a collage of humanity with a huge range of emotions. I stood frozen and watched and wondered how anyone would know what to do with us. I clung to my brother Joseph's hand and he to Ross's and he to Emma's who was clinging to my mother. We were finally moving and someone took our small suitcases from us and led us to our train. People helped my mother get us on the train. The porter showed us where to sit and he told her our bunks were already made up. We all crawled into them and I fell to sleep immediately.

It seemed like no time before Mother was waking us up and telling us we were in Mossbank and to get dressed. We all rushed to get into our clothes. I peeked out the train window and saw my Granny and Aunt Lucy waving excitedly at us. I squealed with delight and went charging off to greet them. The porter hooked an arm around my middle.

"Whoa, where are you going in such a hurry?" He was holding me tight and I couldn't move even though I was squirming trying to escape his grasp.

"My Granny and Aunty are waiting for me," I gasped, afraid of what he might do to me.

"Wait, and I will help you down those steps. They are too big for your small legs. Come, now, and I will take you and your brothers off."

He led us to the door, climbed down, and then lifted each of us off onto the platform. I was certain my legs were whirling in mid-air as I tried to run to my Granny and Aunt Lucy.

"Granny! Granny!" I exclaimed, running into her arms.

"Oh, Molly! It is good to see you again!" She hugged me to her. She was warm and soft.

"Hi, Molly!" my Aunt Lucy said, enfolding me in her arms.

It was wonderful to be there. I felt safe in the knowledge that these two women loved me and would take care of me. I knew they would not let my mother hurt me anymore."

It was such a good feeling Michael to be with family that loved me as much as they did. That day was wonderful and the times after filled my world with joy.

I'm very tired and I'd like to stop here Michael." I pulled my jacket off the back of the chair and headed for the door.

"Okay, Molly! We covered a lot of stuff today and I understand your weariness. Let's leave it for now and I will see you next week. Remember, you don't have to do this alone. If you have any more frightening dreams or outbursts, please call me. We can talk it through." He stood up and walked me into the reception area. He looked troubled.

"Right, Michael. I will see you next week. Good night, Beth." I was aware of the tears burning my eyes as I left. The memory of that wonderful day when we arrived in Mossbank tugged at my very soul. I knew in the days ahead I would have to reveal to Michael what the end of the war really meant for me. I felt as if I was walking a tightrope and there was no net beneath me. If I fell, I would crash and burn.

PART TWO

THE TRADE
TIMES, DREAMS,
NIGHTMARES AND
MEMORIES LONG LOST TO
THE YEARS OF CHANCE.
DAYS, WEEKS AND
MONTHS OF THOUGHTS
WRAPPED IN A TIME
WARP.

Chapter 40

Melody, Frances and I had finished watching an old movie from the 1940's "Meet Me in St. Louis" starring Judy Garland. These were my travelling friends, we often went on a road trip and a weekend away we were like sisters. Sometimes we didn't see one another for two or three months but we could talk and share anything. I had put the kettle on for tea and was staring off into space waiting for it to boil. Melody and Francis came into the kitchen and sat down at the table.

"You seem miles away Molly, are you okay?" Melody asked.

I turned and poured the water into the teapot and told them how the movie took me back to the time of the move to Mossbank.

It must have been pretty exciting, I never have been on a train, even though I have lived in Victoria all my life. Francis declared.

"Share the experience with us Molly what was it like to move away from your friends." They both said together and laughed.

"The first three weeks of our move to Mossbank were a bustle of activity. Summer holidays from school gave us plenty of time to explore our new surroundings. We unpacked slowly and put stuff away while we stayed at Granny Louise's home. It was a peaceful and carefree time! At the end of the third week, we all moved into our new home.

This house was much smaller than the one in Moose Jaw. There were only three bedrooms and they were tiny in comparison to what we had enjoyed before. It was great for me, however, because I knew there would be no 'special' room here. I delighted in making the bedroom I would be sharing with my little sister Emma into a room where I could come and shut the world out. Our room was a creamy blue color with lighter blue lace curtains that I loved. They had a deep flounce on the sides and bottom.

My mother began to organize the household, while she put the boxes of things we had been using at Granny's into our new bedrooms.

"Molly, I want you to help Emma put her things in the bottom two drawers in the dresser and you put yours in the top two. When you are done that, I want you to take Emma outside and play with her, while I help the boys get their things put away. I have some laundry I need to do as well, I will be busy for the next couple of hours, so keep a close eye on her."

"Okay Mommy, I will take good care of her." I placed the box of clothes onto the bed. I began to put our things into the designated drawers.

"When Joseph and Ross have finished, can we all go and explore?" I asked.

"Yes. Just make sure you all stay together," she answered wearily.

I helped Emma put away her clothes and I unpacked mine and put them away. I took Emma by the hand and we went into the boys' bedroom. It was small, like ours. The walls were cream with a different blue from ours. My mother gathered up the dirty clothes and told the boys to finish up. I helped them put the last of their clothes in the drawers and we all explored the house together.

The kitchen had long wooden cupboards and everything was painted white. The bottom cupboards looked like clapboard. All was white and boring. I stared at the strange drain board that had no sink or taps. I wondered if they were hidden in one of the underneath cupboards? The stove burned wood and coal and had odd looking feet that looked like claws. The front of it was black and had white around the oven door. It had four small round lids on the top. The lid lifters were black and there were only two. One stayed in the top right lid all the time. There was a tall piece attached to the back and top of the stove and it was black, but trimmed in white as well.

Where there was coal there must be a coal bin, so we ran outside looking for it. We found it at the side of the house and I suddenly stopped and asked Joseph.

"Where was the bathroom? Did you see a bathroom?"

"No!"

I spied a pump in the back yard when we were walking back in the house. We all went back inside and we went through the house looking for a bathroom. We found a large pantry and a cooler off to the side of that. There was a big piece of ice on the bottom shelf to keep the food cool. We found mom and asked.

"Where is the bathroom, Mom?"

"There is no bathroom. We have an outhouse where you will go to the bathroom," she replied nonchalantly.

We all stared at her stunned.

"How will I take a bath?" I was totally dumbfounded by this bit of news.

"We have a big metal tub that we will fill up with hot water and we will heat it on the stove," she answered.

"Where will we get the water to put in the tub?" Joseph asked.

"From the pump outside and we will catch and store rain water in the spring and summer and melt snow in the winter. That water is much softer, so we will wash our hair in it. The well water is much harder."

"Oh, that will be fun!" Emma squealed, bouncing up and down on her stubby legs.

"Huh! I didn't know water was hard except when it froze. What does the water feel like when it comes out of the pump? How does it come out of the pump if it is hard? How do you get any water out of the pump and where does it come from?" Ross was wondering aloud.

"Wow! This is so weird, Mommy. Is the tub going to be the kitchen sink and will we do our dishes in it too? I asked.

"Don't be worrying about stuff like that. Just go out and play." Mom was busy trying to get organized. She shooed us all out of the house.

We traipsed out and went in search of this outhouse. When we found it, we were mortified at what we saw. The smell was beyond anything and the thought of having to come out here every time we had to go to the bathroom was daunting. I tried to imagine it in the cold winter when there was so much snow on the ground. It would be dark as pitch and I shuddered at the vision I pictured. We shuffled away from it and I kept my bleak thoughts to myself.

Chapter 41

Our house was bordered by farms and there were wheat fields that seemed to go on forever. The corn crops were still small, but with the heat of the summer sun they would soon flourish and bear the delicious corn on the cob we all loved.

Mossbank was quite different from a city like Moose Jaw. It had only one main street, one post office, one service station and one dry goods store. The one main street was a wooden sidewalk that ran down the center of the town. The boards were narrow and close together, so it was easy to walk along them. Looking back, I think it must have been made that way to keep the mud from oozing between them when the snow melted. My Aunt Lucy ran the post office and she and Granny Louise lived upstairs with my old Grandfather who had no legs. I think they got shot off in the First World War. The service station was owned by my Nana Kate and Uncle Greg.

The first time I went into the dry goods store I was in awe. It was a very large, barnlike building. The floors were worn down wood. Surprisingly, they were not rough but smooth and shiny from all the traffic coming and going over the years. There were shelves that held fabric, some that held small tools and others, hardware, small appliances, dishes, pots, pans and food, anything you could think of was for sale in that store. It was a place to get lost in and spend time just staring at all the stuff. The candy counter was my favorite. There were a million varieties of penny candies kept in big jars on the counter near the cash register. The big freezer bin held the popsicles and ice cream. The soda pop was kept in the part with ice. I remembered reaching into the water when the ice melted and pulling out a bottle of pop. My favorite was ginger beer. The ginger beer was in an earthenware bottle with a cork and it was sweet and spicy. Each bottle cost a nickel if you drank it in the store, but seven cents if you took it away. When you brought the bottle back you got two cents back. I loved the licorice pipes and the jawbreakers. In the winter I could always smell a hint of smoke from the pot-bellied stove that was always lit during the cold months. The owner of the store kept a running tab for us. It was from him that I learned about debt and paying it off quickly. We gathered pop bottles and returned them for two cents. He recorded the money in his record book that he kept under the counter. When we wanted a bottle of pop that cost five or seven cents or a Popsicle that cost a nickel, he took that off the credit. When we wanted a penny candy (or in the case of jawbreakers, you got three for a penny,) he marked that as a debt. We couldn't buy anything else until we paid that debt off. That is how everyone shopped in Mossbank. During the good times, the farmers had a large credit, but in the hard times debts would be the norm and the cycle carried on.

Mossbank was a place where I learned many basic lessons and I was able to become a child again, even if it was to be for just a brief time. It is a town that rests in my heart. It was full of some of the most cherished memories of my young years and some of the worst. We had one whole year to wait before my father returned from the war."

I sighed and drank my tea.

"Wow, look at the time, I need to get going" Melody exclaimed.

"Me too, I enjoyed our "night out" even though we stayed in." Frances yawned.

I retrieved their jackets and we said our good nights.

I sat down in my glider and reflected on that time and how happy I was to be gone from Moose Jaw.

"Molly, come and see the field," Joseph called out to me after school one day.

"What's wrong?" I yelled, running into the back yard to see what had happened.

"Oooh!" I gasped, looking at the field.

"Isn't it beautiful?" Joseph stared in awe.

It was breathtaking. I stopped and stared for a couple of minutes, taking in the golden color of the wheat. It swayed to and fro in the gentle breeze that drifted through the plump golden heads that waited to be harvested.

There are no skies as blue and endless as a prairie sky on a sunny day.

The heads of wheat bulged with the burgeoning crop, gleaming with a gorgeous soft golden yellow. They were not like canola when it is in full bloom, but it was equally wondrous to see. Little did I know this field would be my sanctuary and a place to hide. For now, I drank in the wonder of nature and the stark beauty of a simple thing like a wheat field on a hot fall day. Within a few days, the wheat would be harvested and flattened, leaving only the memory of its beauty.

"Oh, Joseph! Aren't you glad we moved here?" I breathlessly whispered to him, clinging to his hand.

"Your drawing is getting much better with all the mallards, pintails, snowy owls, meadowlarks and orioles you see every day. I love your paintings and I know one day you will be famous."

"You exaggerate so much, Molly. I'm not that good, but I love to draw and paint all the birds. Their vibrant colors are amazing and I love the challenge of trying to get them just right." He spoke dreamily, lost in his own thoughts.

"When are you going to paint another horse?" I said as we continued our wandering.

"The last one was beautiful. I hope I can paint one day, but I would like to paint children, I think, but maybe birds like you."

The wheat came up to our shoulders. We lay hidden in the middle of the field and watched the pintail ducks fly down to their nests. We sometimes tried to search out the nests, but they were usually too well-hidden and camouflaged.

That was what the days were like all that first summer and fall. There was no place to swim. The earth and soil dried out and dust was everywhere. I loved the memory of my feet and legs laden with the dust of those summers. We ran, picked choke cherries, Saskatoon berries, and even wild strawberries. I was a child again. I was carefree and happy. The memories of Moose Jaw slowly faded into a place I only recalled in nightmares. My mother had found a new boy friend. He had many friends in the service who often came to our house to party, but I was not included. I was liberated from that lifestyle and I cherished the joy of it, each and every day.

Chapter 42

There was an Air Force base located just outside Mossbank, and many of the airmen came to see my mother. There was always something going on, but it did not stop my brothers, sister and I from running and playing throughout the summer. When fall came, we all went to school and that was another real eye-opener for me.

"It looks small for a school, doesn't it Joseph?" I asked. We hesitantly approached the schoolyard.

"Yeah. I wonder where I will go? I don't think all of us can go to the same school. It isn't big enough."

"It looks like a big house and it doesn't have any swings or anything to play on. There is a big box with stuff in it and a baseball diamond in the middle of the yard, but nothing else." I looked around warily.

"It is such a bright red," Emma said, gripping my hand.

"Aw, it's probably just the place where all the kids get together and get put into their classes and meet the teachers and then go to the right school." Ross put in his two cents worth in his usual carefree manner.

"Like where else do you figure?" Joseph turned to Ross and asked.

"I don't remember seeing anything in town that looks like a school, do you?"

"Naw, but we didn't look at all the places. There goes the bell!" Ross said.

"We best get inside and find out where we are supposed to go."

We all ran into the building.

"Wow! There aren't many kids here, are there?" I looked around and no one seemed in a big hurry to go anywhere.

"No. I wonder where they all are," Joseph remarked hesitantly.

Everyone just stood around in the hallway. I saw a man approaching us and I felt uneasy. I am sure it was the strangeness of the situation and the lack of knowing what was expected of us that contributed to my fear.

"Gather round children, and we will assign you to your classrooms and teachers. I am Mr. Hague and I am the principal." He seemed to relate to how uneasy we felt when he identified himself.

Suddenly I was okay. I was relieved that he was going to tell us what to do and where to go.

Miraculously, we all ended up in the same classroom with the same teacher, a nice lady named Miss Jones.

We giggled and giggled all the way home at the strange school we were going attend.

"Holy cow! Did you think we would be in a school like that or even that there were such schools for kids to learn?" Ross chortled and ran ahead. He was jumping like he was playing basketball.

"Golly no! I am in the first row," Emma said, skipping along beside Joseph.

"That's because you're in grade one. Each row has a different grade, unless there are too many in that grade to fit into one row, then they take as many rows as they need. In our classroom we have two rows of grade three and one of grade one and kindergarten, one grade two and one grade four. That's how come we're all in the same classroom with the same teacher. I wonder how we will be able to learn anything that way?" Joseph said, head down and deep in thought.

"I'm glad we are all together. This way we can help one another learn. It will be fun and maybe some of us can learn faster and move into the next grade before the end of the year. This is so great." I was pulsing with excitement. I loved to learn and I learned fast so I was certain I would move ahead faster than the other kids.

We were in school for only a short time on the first day. When we were let out, we walked through the schoolyard. We each seemed to be lost in our own thoughts. I didn't like the starkness of the schoolyard. The ground was dry, dusty and hard as cement. I couldn't imagine what games we could play here. A wire fence surrounded it, but there was no gate, just an opening where it started and ended.

"Stupid! Why bother to have a fence and no gate?" I wondered out loud.

"What did you say, Molly?" Emma asked.

"Nothing. It's not important."

Chapter 43

After the first week, we settled into this very different school. City schools were more fun but we were adjusting to the change.

"Let's you and I go into the wheat field today after school, Molly. I want to see if I can spot a pintail duck so I can paint it before the colder weather sets in and they move on. I want to paint a female." Joseph reminded me it was now mid-September and the snows would soon start.

"Okay," I said, "but we have to drop Ross and Emma at home first though, because Mom will be mad at us if we let them walk home alone."

The wheat field looked barren and colorless now that it had been harvested. Joseph spotted his duck and quickly sketched it. I saw an old shack and went to investigate. It was shabby and grey. The paint, if ever there was any, was long worn away with the years and elements. Some of the boards were missing, but the roof seemed in good shape. I wondered at it being at the edge of the field. It was close to the Williams' farm. I thought maybe it was a place where they might have stored equipment and stuff when they first moved to the farm. I gave that thought thirty seconds of my time, then moved inside the shack. It had a wood floor that was dusted with dirt and just old boards on the walls. There was nothing in it, but I thought it would be a neat place for us to play. I heard Joseph call to me, so I ran back and quickly told him about it.

That shack would become my protection for brief times of my life in the years ahead. This would become my place of safety from my father when I had to escape and find solace alone. For now it had no significance, but it wouldn't be too many days before it took on a whole new meaning for me. Joseph and I stood back to study the exterior and I was surprised at the beauty of it standing against the darkening sky.

"We better get home before it gets dark, Molly."

"I know. Let's go now, Joseph. It's been a nice day, though. You got your sketch done and we found a secret shack where we can come and play. It could even be a fort." I giggled at the thought.

Chapter 44

"The war has ended and your dad will be home in a couple of months," My mother told us at breakfast one day late in September, 1945.

"Oh, Mommy, that is good! Aren't you happy?" I bounced excitedly in my chair.

"Of course I am happy! What a stupid question to ask, Molly," she snapped.

"We don't even remember him. What will he be like after all this time in a war?" Joseph asked. He had a deep frown and his lips were pursed. He seemed lost in his thoughts.

"Who cares? I'm glad he's coming home and that he is okay," Ross sputtered and reached for another piece of toast.

"Jimmy's dad was killed in the war and Mary's dad has no arm and lots of other men and women are dead or hurt real bad."

"That's right, Ross! We are very thankful that your daddy is in one piece and will be home to be your daddy again, real soon," Mother responded. She reached over to squeeze his shoulder.

Chapter 45

Time whizzed by. Finally, the day arrived when our father was to arrive at the train station. We were all pacing and chattering like magpies, waiting for the train. I don't know how many times we asked our mother how much longer it would be before it came. Other children and families were waiting for their loved ones to arrive as well.

The train blew its whistle as it trundled slowly up to the platform and soldiers came off. I looked and looked for my dad but I couldn't find him. It had been four years since I had seen him, so I didn't recognize him at first. He spotted my mother and then turned toward us. They both started to walk toward each other. They embraced and he hugged all four of us against his legs. He was very handsome. He had really blond, curly hair and blue eyes. To me, he seemed quite tall. I would never forget the feeling that gripped my heart when I felt his arms go around us. He knelt down and embraced each of us, except Emma. He picked her up and held her to him. She was just a baby the last time he had seen her. He reached over to my mother and they held each other again for an incredibly long time. They were both crying and laughing at the same time. We were baffled by their behavior.

We had a special supper that night with lots of fresh vegetables and a big roast of beef. It was marvelous! My dad ate it slowly and savored it. He told us how wonderful it was to eat a home cooked meal!

The days that followed were awkward at times. Sometimes he was sad and he just sat at the table and wept for his friends who were killed or maimed in the war. I overheard him tell my mother one day that he was lonely. I went outside and cried for him. I yawned and got up from my chair. I went to bed feeling a little sad. I saw it was after midnight and I had a busy day tomorrow. An early appointment with Michael and then other mundane chores.

Chapter 46

"Hi Beth! I'm a little early for my appointment. I was just a couple of blocks away, so I thought I'd come now and read while I wait." I took a seat and put my jacket and purse on the chair next to me.
"No problem, Molly. He is finishing up some notes he needs to send off. How are things going? Keeping busy as always? Oh, excuse me." Her ringing phone interrupted her.

"Hi, Molly! Come on in." Michael smiled as he came out of his office and directed me in.
"What's been happening over the past week, Molly? I haven't heard from you, so I assume things are settling down?" He took his usual place and I took mine.
"I'm good. I still linger over memories a lot and tend to spend too much time reliving them."
"We've been over this before. You know how important it is to address the memories as they break through. Why don't you tell me about what has been going on?" He put his notepad on his lap, looked up and smiled at me.
"I can't seem to get Mossbank out of my head these days and that's going way back. I remember many of the good times my siblings and I had there. Then the memory of my father crashes in on me and I feel as I am suffocating with the shame." I started to rub my hands together and fidget in my chair.
"Why don't you tell me how that started."

Chapter 47

One day, my mother took my brothers and sister to Moose Jaw with my Grandmother. My dad and I were alone in the house. I never wanted to go back to Moose Jaw, so I stayed home with him. He came and sat down next to me and asked how things were going at school.

"I do really good in school, Daddy. I am already up one grade higher than I should be. My teacher won't let me go any higher because she says I am too young to be with the kids in that grade." I was happy to be alone with him and telling him how smart I was.

"Good for you, Molly. Do you know what you want to be when you grow up?" He put his arm around my shoulders.

"I think I want to be a nurse or a doctor," I replied snuggling into his side. "You smell really nice," I told him. I loved his smell and the feel of his soft white sweater. He was strong and firm. His stomach was hard and his arms seemed especially strong to me. He put his hand on my tummy. I felt fantastically safe and warm nestled into him.

"Wow! Those are big plans, Molly. What makes you want to be a nurse or doctor?" He looked at me with those wonderful blue eyes and I melted into his side even more.

"I love to see the insides of animals and bugs and things. I once fixed a bird's wing when it fell to the ground. Joseph and I picked it up and I bandaged its wing to it side. We kept him in the outhouse until it got better and then we let him go and he flew away. Another time, we found a snowy owl. He was sick and nearly frozen to death and we made a warm box for him and fed him stuff and he got better. I love seeing that, don't you? You must have seen lots of bad stuff in the war. Did you help people when they got hurt?" I shifted away a little so I could look up at his face. He looked sad, then quickly turned away. I thought he must have been thinking of the bad things that happened overseas. It seemed like a long time before he answered.

"Not so much. We never had a lot of time to stop and help our buddies when they got shot or hurt. We had men we called medics and we called for them and they took care of our injured friends." He moved away and I was sure I saw tears in his eyes.

"I'm sorry, Daddy. I didn't mean to make you sad again." I leaned my face into his tummy and put my arms around him.

"That's okay, Molly! Let's go into town and get a treat. Would you like that?"

"That will be fun! I love banana popsicles. Can I have one please? Maybe we can call in to see Granny Louise and Aunt Lucy." I jumped off the sofa and pulled him toward the door.

"Hold on a minute! I need to wash up first. I don't want to call on anyone today. We can go for a walk after we get our treats, if you like."

"That's okay, Daddy. We can walk around and maybe find some berries, but I think they are all done now. Maybe we can go out to the Williams' farm and get some corn and you and me can have corn on the cob for supper tonight. Is Mommy coming home tonight?" I was jumping up and down and twirling round and round, I was that excited.

"No, they are stopping at her friends' house for the night and they are coming home on the train in the morning."

"I don't like going back to that house, Daddy. I hope you will always keep me with you when Mommy goes to visit in Moose Jaw." I looked at him and choked down my fear, thinking about those times in that house. I was no longer bouncing. I stood there and looked at him, hoping he wouldn't guess how bad a person I was. I knew that Duncan was right. It would be a mistake to tell him about the house in Moose Jaw.

213

"Why don't you like visiting there, Molly? You lived there for quite a while. You must have had friends you would like to see again?"

"Its okay, Daddy, I don't want to see them anymore. At first I was sad to leave there, but now I love it here and I am safe and I play a lot with my friends and Joseph, Ross and Emma." I didn't look at him.

"Did something bad happen to you there?" He tucked his fingers under my chin so I had to look at him. I pulled away from him, afraid I would start to cry.

"No. Are you nearly ready to go?" I was horrified that he might guess what I did there. I ran out the door to wait for him outside.

"Okay, okay! Keep your shirt on I am coming! Where do you want to go first into town or to the farm?" he asked as we went outside. He held my hand and we swung our arms together as we walked along the road. My dream was coming true! We were walking, talking and holding hands like Duncan and I used to do. I didn't have to pretend he was my daddy, because now this was my real daddy. My heart felt sad when I thought of Duncan but today I was too happy to be sad.

"I would like my treat first, if that's okay with you." I looked up and he smiled at me. I was safe at last. I was overjoyed that he was home and I was going to spend the whole day and night with him.

"Let's go get that Popsicle for you right now." He twirled me around like a ballerina.

"Can you paint and draw like Joseph, Daddy?"

"No, sweetie, but my brother is a wonderful artist."

"Do you think Joseph will be famous one day?"

"I don't know. We will have to wait and see. Do you paint and draw, Molly?"

"Not as good as Joseph, but one day I hope to be good."

"Keep practicing and you will do well at it. When you love to do something you should do it, even if you aren't good at it."

Chapter 48

It was a great day! We talked about the birds that came here, about how good Joseph painted and just about stuff. We bought our corn and ate it. I was starting to get very sleepy.

"It's time for you to go to bed, Molly. You can hardly keep your eyes open, and we have had a busy day." He tugged on my braids affectionately.

"Okay. Can we do something tomorrow, too?"

"We'll see. Maybe we can all do something together." We walked together to my room, swinging our arms in unison.

"C'mon, Let's get you ready for bed."

"I can get myself ready. Thank you for all the good things we did today. Good night, Daddy."

I stood by my bed and reached for my nightgown that I had tucked under my pillow that morning when I got dressed.

"I want to help you, Molly. For too many years I missed tucking my kids into bed at night."

He came over and pushed my shirt over my head and slipped my nighty on.

"Take off the rest of your things, Molly and climb into bed and I will sit with you for awhile."

"I love you, Daddy and I am really glad you weren't killed in the war," I whispered and crawled under the covers.

He lay down next to me and he caressed the side of my face. He planted a soft kiss on my cheek.

"Let's undo these braids. They must be hard to sleep on." He blew in my ear and I giggled because his breath tickled me.

"Okay." I sat up while he undid the braids.

"Do you like your hair free of those braids? I like to see your shiny hair, loose and wild." He loosened the last of the braids and buried his nose in my hair.

I snuggled up to him and he wrapped his arms around me.

"Can I climb under the covers with you for awhile, Molly?"

"Sure."

He cuddled me closer and touched my face. He trailed his fingers down my neck. He moved slowly, so I still didn't feel threatened by him. I was thrilled that he loved me and thought I was nice to look at.

Then I started to feel uncomfortable with the way he was touching me.

I knew this was wrong and I was confused that he was doing the things Duncan did. I knew it was my fault. There had to be something really wrong with the way I behaved. I made men do bad things to me.

"You have a lovely body, Molly," he said.

I couldn't believe this was happening to me. What was wrong with me? Why couldn't men see I was just a little girl and I wanted to be like other little girls?

"You do like that!" he laughed and tucked me back under the covers.

"Good night, my little wild one." He chuckled and left.

"Good night," I whispered back.

I buried my face in my pillow and yelped like a wounded dog. I was crushed and shamed by my wanton behavior. My poor dad! He must have thought me a tramp. My mother did too. I didn't understand how I made men do bad things to me. There had to be something really bad inside of me that forced them to do this stuff. I was certain my own daddy would never want to be alone with me ever again. I stifled my wracking sobs and prayed that God would change me. I was burdened with these thoughts when I fell asleep.

The next morning, my dad treated me as though nothing had happened. He didn't comment on my swollen, tear-ravaged eyes, nor did he mention my lewd behavior. I was grateful for that. We met my mom and everyone at the station later in the morning and, true to his word, we all went on a picnic together. We took a bus over to Johnson Lake and the rest of my family had a super day.

I hid my shame inside of me. I wanted to erase the night before. I felt hopeless and wondered if he would ever forgive me. I had to conceal my emotions and I did my best to cover them. We had never learned to swim, so we were not allowed to go near the lake on our own. It was a big deal for us to be allowed near the water, although none of us wanted to go in. It was late in the year and not that hot. The day was fresh and the food was good. It turned out to be a wonderful family day.

Chapter 49

The next time my dad came into my room was when my mom and siblings were out. I can't recall why we were alone in the house at night. He came in and crawled into my bed and the nightmare started all over again. This time, I felt deeply betrayed. I had believed my dad would come home to protect me but instead, he turned out to be one of the worst perverted pedophiles.

The nights held terror for me once again. I would beg my mother to take me with her when she took my siblings anywhere, but she wouldn't. I remember one incident that happened not long before she left for good.

"I'm taking the kids to a movie in Moose Jaw today. The movie "National Velvet" is playing and the kids love horses. Molly can stay with you and I will be back on the seven o'clock train," she told my dad at the breakfast table that particular Saturday morning.
"I want to come too, Mommy, please," I pleaded.
"No, you know you don't like coming to Moose Jaw. I don't want to listen to your whining about all the things you hate about Moose Jaw for the whole day." She hadn't noticed the anxiety in my voice. She carried on with what she was doing. She simply ignored me. I always felt I was invisible to her.
"Please let me come! I promise I won't say one bad thing about Moose Jaw I swear, cross my heart and hope to die!" I hoped she would see my desperation.
"No, Molly, you can stay with your dad and keep him company."

"Why can't Joseph or Ross or Emma keep him company? Why does it have to be me?" I moaned.

"What's the matter with you? You like staying home. Now stop your whining," she snarled in that sharp voice she reserved just for me, "You're not coming and that's that." "Molly, why don't you want to stay with me?" my dad asked, looking hurt.

"Just because I want to ride on the train and see the movie," I sighed.

"I'll take you on a train one day just the two of us will go to Regina for a week during the holidays. How does that sound, Molly?" He clasped my cold hand in his warm hand.

"Will you take us too, Daddy?" Joseph, Ross and Emma spoke at once.

"That's enough all of you! Joseph, you take Ross and Emma and get yourselves ready to go. The train leaves in an hour. Molly, you can help me clear up the dishes and don't start bawling. Your dramatics are not going to change my mind. I will never understand you and your sour moods."

While they were getting ready to leave for the train, I ran over to her.

"Please can I come, please?"

"No! Now stop that nonsense!"

I grabbed her legs and clung to them.

"Please take me with you Mommy, please!"

She dragged me across the floor in an effort to pry me loose.

"Maybe we should take her with us," Joseph said, looking sad.

"Don't be ridiculous! This is absurd behavior even for you, Molly. Now let me go. Go to your room until you can settle down. Come on kids, your dad is waiting in the front yard to walk us to the station." She held Emma's hand and turned away from me. Joseph turned back and gave me a sad little smile and shrugged his shoulders. He was as resigned as I was. Utter despair overwhelmed me. I felt horrid pain rip at my heart. I knew there was nothing or no one to help me.

Chapter 50

I watched them go and I knew I would pay dearly for my conduct when my dad returned. I was right. He came through the door and bellowed, "Molly get over here right now!" He was in such a rage; I was amazed he was not foaming at the mouth.

"What the hell was that about?"

"I wanted to go on the train and see the movie Daddy. That's all." I was quaking.

He grabbed my arm and shook me until my teeth rattled. Then he grabbed my chin in a vice grip. I was afraid he was going to crush me.

"That's just the kind of behavior that will get us both in a heap of trouble. I have made it very clear to you that no one can know how much I love you and the ways I show you that. You want to get me sent to prison? That is exactly what will happen. You will be sent to a place for children who behave like you until you are grown up and that will be the end of your being anything other than a tramp for the rest of your life. Is that what you want? What about your brothers and sister? Do you want them to end up in an orphanage?" He yelled in my face, his spittle spattered on mine.

"No, I wasn't going to tell; I promise I will never tell." I was so terrified of him I tripped on my words.

"Just remember that! Now come here. You and I have some lovin' to do. You know how much you like it." He pulled me into his arms.

I shuddered and I did what he wanted. He pushed me into the bedroom he and my mother shared.

Dreams shattered dreams.

"You know, the shame is not yours to bear."

"You don't know the real truth, Michael, so don't try and pretend it was not my fault." I avoided looking into his eyes as I remembered my humiliation.

"It all seemed to be good at the time, Michael. I believed he just wanted to love me as his daughter, but it was never like that."

I went on to explain how the situation with my father began. I was hunkered down in my chair, too embarrassed to look at him. Tears were streaming down my face.

"You were introduced to sex long before you should have been. You responded in a normal manner, although it was much too soon for you to be exposed to those kind of emotions. You have nothing to be ashamed of, Molly." His voice was soothing and kind and I felt his sadness as he tried to reassure me.

"How can you say that? I knew what was happening. It's not like I hadn't done anything like that before. I liked it and I thought it was okay until he started to touch me where I knew he shouldn't. I didn't want it to ever happen again but he wouldn't let me stop. He was cruel beyond words and had a terrible temper. If it wasn't my fault, why did he pick me? Why did it have to be me? I am his daughter, for heaven's sake! Why didn't he go to a hooker or someone else? It all seems such a blur and I had never been more afraid of anyone in my life." I sat wringing my hands trying to make sense of the thoughts tumbling through my head.

"You can't take the blame anymore, Molly. He knew exactly what he was doing and he took advantage of the fact that you could not fight back. He knew the animosity between you and your mother would be the perfect barrier that would protect him. He knew she wouldn't listen to you, nor would she believe you. The worst part of all this, is that he knew she wouldn't protect you. He knew, too, that she was the last person you would go to for help. Can you see the connection between the relationship with your father and the one where you were beaten up? You are not Superwoman! You can only do so much to protect yourself. When you are confronted with someone bigger and stronger and high on drugs, there is little you can do to help yourself. The important thing now, is not to put yourself in that position again. You shouldn't be going to those places alone and definitely not at night. What happened between your father and you, set you up to accept the blame for it all."

"If that's so why didn't I do something once my mother took Emma and left? Why didn't I stop it then? Why didn't I tell my grandparents, if I was so innocent? I could have done something when I got older, but I didn't. I just kept going along with it until I moved out. Can you believe that?" I was angry at Michael's naivety and my voice became louder and louder.

"Yes, of course you did. You had it drilled into your head that if you told anyone, he would go to jail, taking away the support for you and your brothers. Look at you now, Molly, you still carry that shame. Do you really believe you could have confessed to the women who loved you that you were involved in a sexual relationship with your father? What about his mother? Do you believe you could have gone to her with such an accusation about her son? You were under his control and he had been using you and controlling you all those years. You accepted any form of love you could find and did whatever you had to do to get it. It wasn't and isn't your fault."

"Oh, and I guess it wasn't my fault that I chose to become involved in the sex trade and make lots of money doing it?" I spat out the words.

"That's not what I am saying. You made a choice but you made it with the wrong information. Do you honestly believe if Carin's father had targeted her at the age you were and the size you were, that she could have done anything to help herself? Think about the facts and not about how you felt. Look at other children and try and see your own life through the eyes of a child. I believe you will start to see you could not do anything to stop what happened. You were already well programmed by the time he came home. Your dreams of being protected and loved by your father were shattered and you simply followed the pattern that abused children fall into.

"I guess you're right, Michael. It really doesn't matter now anyway does it? I am an old woman now and I should be able to let that stuff go. I was weary of this conversation and the logic he was trying to sell. I slipped into my jacket and left the room.

"Right, Molly. I will see you next week, he called after me. "Please think about this session, and if you need to, remember you can call me anytime. You still have my cell number, don't you?"

"Yes, I have it. Bye, Michael. See you next week, Beth." I shut the door. I breathed in the fresh, cool air, grateful to be out of the hot seat.

Chapter 51

I wondered if Michael could possibly understand how deeply ashamed I felt and have always felt, not just about my father but about my life? I suddenly found myself in front of Carin's home.

"Hi, Mom. What brings you here? I thought you had taken a short trip or something. I haven't heard from you for awhile." She was standing in the doorway, looking quite attractive. She was dressed up, so I thought she might have just come in. She was wearing a lovely beige pantsuit. Her curly hair was pulled back and looked charming. She is only five feet two inches but, like me, wears heels. She is slim and looks younger than her forty-two years. She has her father's eyes and disposition, but she and I are alike in many ways, particularly in our need for privacy.

"I thought because I am out and about, I should stop by and see how you and the kids are doing? I have been keeping busy myself, although I can't tell you with what. It just seems the days rush by and before I know it weeks have passed. I'm sorry I haven't called or anything, but then there is nothing to stop you from calling or coming around, is there Carin? Can I come in or have I caught you at a bad time?"
"Yes, actually I was just getting ready to go out. I am meeting Bill and we're going for dinner and a movie when he gets off work today. I'm sorry, Mom. If I had known you were coming over, I would have arranged our movie for tomorrow night, but it's too late to cancel Bill now. He will have left for the restaurant."

"No problem, Carin. I will call you next week and maybe we can get together and do something then. I am sorry I caught you off guard by dropping by like this. I'll call you." I turned and walked to my car.

"Please don't be upset, Mom. Next time, just call ahead. If I don't hear from you I'll call you next week." Her voice carried a sad note. I was disappointed by this turn of events. I had paid little attention to her feelings.

"That would be a nice surprise," I said sarcastically as I left.

That went well, I thought to myself! I wondered if Carin and I would ever have a reasonable conversation again? The scary part of all of this was the thought that she could gain control of me and my assets if she convinced the powers that be that I was not capable of handling my affairs any longer. I knew I would have to keep that in mind whenever I lost patience with her. I was getting drawn into an extreme case of self-pity. The fault today was mine. She was absolutely correct. I should have called ahead. Things were getting better between us and I needed to keep that in mind. Carin had been gracious and it was very unfair of me to use that tone. I promised myself that I would call her the next day and apologize.

Chapter 52

A hot cup of tea and a bowl of soup helped to make me feel better as I relaxed in my comfortable chair and switched on the television. I knew I would to have to start that shawl I wanted to give to Helen for her birthday. I would do that right after the news. I really wasn't into what was being reported in the news. I started to think about my parents and wondered how different my life could have been. I was plagued with the parallel path my life was once again travelling along. It seemed I had as much control over my life as I had as a child. I knew that if I continued to lose control I would be a candidate for assisted living. My home would no longer be a place of refuge for me. I felt my stomach churning at the dilemma with which I was faced and I thought back to the tumultuous last year in Mossbank.

My nights were continually filled with horror. I would lie in my bed and wonder if he was coming for me. I wondered, too, why my mother let him get away with this stuff or maybe she didn't know?

"I want you kids to come into the kitchen and sit down. I have something important to tell you," my mother announced one afternoon.

"What is happening?" I asked Joseph.

"How should I know?" He seemed wary.

"Let's sit down and find out," I whispered

"I am going to be moving back to Moose Jaw," my mother declared.

"What? When?" we all asked in unison.

"The end of the month."

"No way! We don't want to go back there." Joseph, Ross and I yelled incredulously.

"You don't have to come with me. I am taking Emma and you three will stay with your father."

"How can you just go away? You're our mother. You are supposed to take care of us." Ross started to cry.

"I don't want you to go away, Mommy."

"You'll be fine with your dad and brother and sister. I can't take you all. I am going to live with Ralph. He and I love each other, but I can only take Emma because she's too young to be without me right now. You have to be strong and I know your dad will take good care of you." She was incredibly blithe about it all.

"What do you mean you can't take us all? You're our mother. Mothers don't just walk away from their children." Joseph was gawking with his mouth open.

I sat and stared at her and I, too, wondered how she could walk away from her children.

"How can you do this, Mommy? He can't look after us as good as you. Please don't leave us alone with him, please," I begged.

"We're wasting our breath, you guys", Joseph sneered, "She's made up her mind, haven't you Mom?"

"Yes, and remember who you're talking to young man! Take that sneer off your face. I'm still your mother."

"You sure don't act like it. You don't care about us. Why don't you just come out and say it like it is, instead of lying to us. You've never taken care of us the way other moms do, except for your precious Emma. I for one wouldn't go with you if you begged me. I'm glad you're going. I don't care if I never see you again." He left the house, slamming the door after him.

"Wait for me Joseph! I want to come with you." I ran after him, tears streaming down my face. I was flabbergasted by this news.

And so my mother and sister left. I never saw either one of them again. They were like smoke they simply disappeared into a new life. I longed for the comfort of having a woman in my life and

I missed my sister. I tucked them both away in a small corner of my heart and struggled forward with my life. My father now had full reign over me. This was a different kind of hell. There was no reprieve. No hope glimmered on the horizon. There were just days and nights where I had to do what was demanded of me. There was no escape except for the run down shack next to the wheat fields. He had hinted that he would want to leave Mossbank and move to Vancouver where jobs were more plentiful and we would be nearer his mom and step-dad.

I yawned and finished my soup.

I can't be moping around here all day. I thought to myself. I wondered how I had endured so much for such a little child. I was not even twelve years old and yet I felt years older. I was very unhappy to leave my grandparents and aunt behind but like everything else I had no say after all I was just a kid living under the strict rules of my father. He of course always reminded me how grateful I should be for everything he provided. Try and get into my head and find the meaning of that statement. Gratitude was the last feeling I had for him, he stole even more from me than the horrific years in Moose Jaw.

I slammed my way around the kitchen, grabbed my coat and went for a long walk to clear my head before going to bed.

The days tumbled one after another. I was unsettled most of the week. I was almost glad when the day came on which I had an appointment with Michael.

Our session started slowly and I began to talk about the move and what it had meant. I stopped abruptly when embarrassing memories invaded my thoughts.

"Don't stop Molly, nothing you tell me will go any further than this room. I am writing short pertinent notes only." He smiled and sipped his tea, leaning back in his chair completely relaxed.

I sighed and started to talk again.

"We left Mossbank soon after Mother left and moved to British Columbia. Vancouver is different from Mossbank in many ways and it proved to be a learning ground for me. Life was much the same here. I still shook each night when he called me and made me to do his bidding. I acquiesced and lived in dread of his volatile temper and incessant sexual demands.

The years slipped by. I was happy at school and continued to get good marks. I was in Junior high now with just three years left before I graduated and would be able to go to University.

One day, he took me to a place on Hastings Street, in Vancouver. We walked up about twenty stairs passed the first floor and on up to the second level into a two-level apartment. I had no idea what we were going to do. I worried about it when he told me we could earn some pretty big bucks here.

"What are we going to do here, Dad?" I was apprehensive and sensed it meant trouble for me. It was usually that way when I went anywhere new with him.

"Wait and see. I don't even know if he will accept my offer. I have to talk to him some more and he needs to get a look at you, to see if you are suitable for the job."

"What job?" I asked, surprised. "I don't have time for a job, Dad, with school. You expect me to look after you and my brothers and keep house. Give me a break, please!

"Quit your whining and stop asking so many questions. I just explained to you, I don't know for sure there will be any job for you. Quiet! Here he comes now." He leered at me and I shut up!

"Hello, Jim! Is this your daughter?" The guy offered to shake my hand after he shook my dad's.

"Yes, this is Molly." My dad put his hand on the back of my head and nudged me forward.

"Hi, Molly. Turn around and let's see you walk over to the far wall and back again."

"Why do you want me to do that?"

"Molly, just do as you are ask and don't ask stupid questions," my dad snapped.

I walked across the room and back again. I studied the man and instantly disliked him. He had a sleazy look and I hated the way he leered at me. I was quite well developed and in that way, I looked older than my fifteen years. He was tall and very broad in the shoulders. He looked as though he hadn't shaved for a couple of days and his clothes were unkempt. His shirt looked as though it had never seen an iron and his pants hung on his hips over his potbelly. They looked like his shirt, wrinkled and dirty. He lit a cigarette and tossed the match on the table, nowhere near where the ashtray sat. His fingernails were long and dirty. His after-shave smelled sickly sweet and I wondered if he used that in place of a bath and deodorant? I knew I would never be able to work for him, no matter how much money he paid me.

"Take off your blouse, Molly and let me see what you've got."
"No way am I taking off my blouse!" I retorted and I looked to my dad to support my decision.
"Damn it, Molly! Do as he says before I cuff you up the side of your head." My dad grabbed me and shook me.
"Why do I have to disrobe for the likes of him?" I was disgusted with both of them.
"Because I say so, that's why! Now just do it or do you want me to do it for you?" My dad had that razor-edge tone to his voice that I knew so well. His eyes were flat blue and he looked like a snake.
"No," I said and wearily took off my blouse. I stood there for him to leer at me.
"Come over here, Molly and stand in front of me." The creep sneered, his cigarette hung out his mouth.
I walked over to where he stood and he turned me around and undid my brassiere and then turned me to face him. I was mortified! I stood there like a zombie. I knew my dad was going to let this pervert do whatever he wanted with me. I covered my exposed breasts but he pushed my hands away.
"Yes, she will do nicely," he grinned. "We're set up in the other room. You'll have to wait out here, Jim. I think she'll do better with you out of the room. You're sure she knows what to do? You did say she had experience, right?" Creepo leered at me and, taking my arm, moved me toward a door.

"Oh, yes! She's had lots of experience. I trained her myself. She will cooperate fully, won't you, Molly?"

"Yes." I felt miserable and I am sure my response reflected my feelings. I still didn't know what I had to do but I sensed it was not going be too pleasant. I thought for sure that I would throw up if this creep touched me anywhere else. I knew I couldn't fight them. I carried the scars from my dad's anger whenever I had defied him and so I went along peacefully.

"Come with me, Molly. I'll introduce you to your costar and the cameramen." He clasped a hold of my hand and led me into the adjoining room.

I stopped dead in my tracks when I saw the huge bed, the cameras and the three men who stood around talking. One of them had on a dressing gown. The other two were in street clothes. I could hear muffled sobs coming from an adjoining room. A man and woman were speaking harshly to whoever was crying.

"Who's crying?" I asked, looking around the sordid-looking room. I was stunned at the stark, bare concrete walls. There was only one wall that had a normal look to it and it was behind the bed. There was a beautiful picture of a naked woman in a demure pose. That wall was painted pale green. There was a comforter on the bed and the sheets were stark white that complemented and brought out the pleasant primary color of the comforter. There were pale yellow roses on vivid green plants and smaller pink ones against its cream background. There was a small table covered with a pastel yellow cloth. A white lamp with a pink lampshade gave a rose hue to that corner. It was all most appealing. The rest of the room had a variety of furnishings stacked in one corner. I assumed they were brought into play when a change of backdrop was needed to film the movies. My heart went cold, because I knew what this room was. I seethed with humiliation, sadness and anger thinking about what my father had done.

"God in Heaven, I pray I am in the middle of a nightmare from which I will very soon awaken," I gasped silently.

231

"Stay here, while I go and see what the hell is going on." The creep's sharp words pulled me back to reality. I knew for certain this was no dream and I prepared myself for what was going to happen here. The man stomped across the room and opened another door. I could see a bed and two small children lying next to each other, with a grown man and woman lying next to them. They were all naked and I knew immediately that the creep produced and distributed child pornography. I was horrified. The children in that room were not more than six years old and they were both crying.

"Stop that racket right now and get on with it! You both know what to do, so do it before I knock your heads together," Mr. depravity yelled, then shut the door and came back into the room where I stood dazed. I detested this man, but knew I was powerless to do anything.

"Okay, Molly. Take off your clothes and slip into these things." He handed me a g-string, a tiny brassier that barely covered my areolas and a flimsy see through, short nighty.
"Where can I change?" I asked quietly.
"Right here!" He laughed at me. "You don't have anything we haven't seen before." He stood with one ankle crossed over the other and leaned against the concrete wall. He looked almost bored but not bored enough to look away.
"Right," I whispered and took off the rest of my things and started to put on the thong.
"Wait, just a minute, Molly. You can't be filmed with all that pubic hair. Come over here and climb up on the table. Lie down while I shave off some of this hair. Make sure the next time you come, you shave it the same as I do it. No one wants to see a lot of hair covering up the gateway to paradise, now do they?" the creep said as he slowly shaved my hair into a triangle shape. I learned later it was called a bikini cut. I was petrified I was going to upchuck; I had to swallow several times to get my stomach under control. I loathed his touch that much.

"Hey, Tom! If you want me to do the movie with her, don't you think you should leave that part of it to me? She's got a nice build and she's still young and fit. She'll photograph real well." The guy in the dressing gown shouted and crossed over to the bed. He lay down.

"Yeah, you're right," the creep said. "Molly, get down and finish putting on the things I gave you and lie down next to Larry. Are you guys ready with the cameras?"

"Yep, we're all set." Mat, the one who was holding the camera put out his cigarette in an ashtray and the other one turned on some very bright lights that were focused on the bed and Larry.

"Come to papa, Molly! Let's see if you're as good as your old man says you are." Larry started to undress me as soon as I lay down. He covered my body in kisses and caressed me everywhere. His hands were all over me like a slow dance and then he was on top of me. The men behind the cameras were making gauche remarks and he worked himself into a frenzy of passion with me as the object of it. Finally it was over and Tom, the creep, told me to put my clothes on. He met me in the other room where my dad was waiting. They treated me like some mannequin who had no feelings and needed no comforting. I was simply a prop. I dressed as quickly as I could and I swore to myself that I would never do this again. I could still hear the children protesting in the other room. I promised them under my breath that somehow I was going to find a way to stop this animal.

"You did swell!" Tom, the creep told me when I came into the room where he and my dad were leaning against a wall, smoking and laughing about something.

"Good girl, Molly! That wasn't so bad now, was it?" My dad chuckled as he counted out the money the creep had given him. He handed me ten dollars. I slapped his hand, turned and walked away.

The creep turned to my dad. "Now you know that's the end of this deal. Any money I make off the film is mine. Yours is a one shot deal. Every time I use Molly, I will pay you the sum agreed upon.

You and she are not entitled to nothing more, no residuals from the pictures. You got that straight?" Tom leered at my breasts.

I snarled at them, "You're disgusting. You and your sordid partners!"

The creep, wearing his sickly smile, replied.

"Yeah, but it's you on the bed, sister. Not me. I guess the money's worth doing business with someone disgusting like me."

I jerked my thumb toward my dad.

"It's him that will do anything for money, not me!" I could no longer deal with my chaotic emotions.

"Aw, look at those tears! Funny, I didn't see you crying in there when Larry had his hands and mouth all over you," the creep scoffed.

My dad interrupted our sniping at each other.

"That's enough! I don't need to hear anymore. I don't want to know what goes on in front of the camera."

"I guess not, you just want her for yourself. You're a dirty old man," the creep said, ridiculing my dad.

"You're way off base, Tom. Just shut your mouth. Come on, Molly. Let's go home." He took my arm and pulled me out the door.

"Right you are, Jim. You stay on your high and mighty horse judging me. It's guys like you that hire out your kids to do your dirty work for you. You like the smut, but you think because you don't watch it, your hands are clean. Think again, buddy boy. You're worse than any of us. Don't call me, Jim, I'll call you if I decide to use your kid again." The creep slammed the door behind us.

"I'm never coming back here again!" I said fuming.

"You'll do as I say!" My dad lit another cigarette, and shoved his hands in his pockets and walked away. I had to run to catch up with him.

Chapter 53

Two weeks later we were back at the same place. I was in agony. I struggled to contain my pent-up emotions. Disgrace, helplessness and fury were the sensations I had to tamp down if I were going to make it through another film. I couldn't make eye contact with my dad or the creep who made the flicks.

"Come on in, Molly! You know the drill. Go into the staging area where they are just finishing up. I hope you prepared yourself like I told you last time or do you want me to do the honors each time you come?" His lip curled up on one side. I assumed it was a smile. It looked more like a leer to me.

"No, I did as you asked, Creepo." I mimicked his sardonic look.

"What did you call me? I couldn't quite hear. I bet it was a nice compliment."

"Yeah, right," I responded, moving into the other room. I gave him a scathing 'hate you' look. I heard him mock my words when I shut the door.

Mat, looked up as I entered the room.

"Hi, Molly. We're just about done with Jill's part. Your clothes are laid out on the table over there. Go ahead and get ready."

"Hi, I'm Jill. I've heard a lot about you, Molly. Why don't you and I go for coffee after you've done your shoot?" She held her hand out for me to shake.

"I dunno. My dad usually wants me to go home right after I'm done." My heart felt like lead in my chest. They all behaved as though this stuff was normal.

"I'll ask him. I've got my car and I can take you home after. We won't be late, if that is okay with you?"

"Sure." I answered woodenly.

Jill was petite with straight blond hair. Her face had quite a few blemishes, but she wore lots of make-up and did a good job of applying it. It looked quite natural. Her smile lit up the room. Her eyes were a smoky gray and added to her impish look. She had a boyish figure and wore costly designer clothes that complemented it. She was outgoing and had an exuberance about her that drew me to her. She was in her early twenties.

"That was a good shoot. You're damn good for a kid your age," Jill told me over her cup of coffee. The coffee shop was one of the dreariest places I had seen. The tables were black Formica with colorful flecks throughout. The chairs were covered with red naugahyde. I think the walls were supposed to be white, but they were marked with stains and crude remarks scattered over them. The tabletop had some names carved into the hard surface. The wood underneath was probably dirty. The floors had cheap looking linoleum that was marred with black scuff marks, as well as with various other bits of who-knows-what crushed on it. Cigarettes gave off a stink that coated the back of my throat. I noticed the burns on the tabletop where careless smokers had dropped live ash. I assumed they let it lay in its inert form to permanently mark the table. The whole place was dimly lit and dingy. It made me feel even more depressed than when I had come through the doors with Jill.

"Yeah, well I've had lots of practice," I told her between sips of my milkshake.

"Tell me about it, Molly. What kind of practice can a kid like you have had? I bet your old man keeps you for himself." She peered at me across the table.

"Not really," I said fidgeting, afraid she would guess and get us all arrested.

"Okay, let's leave that alone. You don't have to tell me anything, but you know I get it. Have you ever thought of charging for what you do? You could earn a lot of money and I know just the person to help you." She lit a cigarette and blew the smoke at me. She had a strange look on her face as she visually examined my body from my breasts down. I fiddled uncomfortably and I wondered what she was thinking.

"My dad will kill me."

I slurped my milkshake. I avoided any eye contact with her.

"He wouldn't need to know. I could teach you how to fool everyone, even your dad and mom." She shifted in her seat across from me and reached over to touch my hand. My hands were cold and wet from the condensation dripping down the outside of my milkshake glass. I pulled my hand away and wiped it on my pants.

"I don't have a mom."

"What do you mean you don't have a mom? Everyone has a mother somewhere."

"Not me. My mother left long ago. She has this need inside of her that that drives her to attach herself to any man. She wants to be the perfect woman to whom all men are drawn. That does not include motherhood."

"No problem. I want you to think about it, Molly. I'll be around at the studio. I assume you're still in school? What are your plans when you graduate?" She deftly changed the subject.

"I want to go into medicine: maybe be a nurse or a doctor." I smiled at her as I thought of my dream.

"Good for you! You know, it requires large amounts of money to pay for a University education. I can show you how to save what you earn and you could probably pay as you go. I must dash. C'mon, I'll take you home but I'll watch for you at the studio. Think about what I'm offering you and I promise I can show you how to work this so no one knows what we are doing." Jill grabbed her jacket and purse and threw down some coins for a tip.

"Don't forget what I said, Molly. Give it some serious thought." She dropped me off at my house.

"I'll think about it. And thanks for the milkshake."

That meeting would change the course of my life, Michael. Jill turned out to be my dearest friend for many years. I don't regret our friendship but I regret where it led."

"I can see why that would be Molly. How did it play out?"
"I went along with everything. I wish I had been strong enough
to resist. I would have normal like days with my grandparents and
siblings but for the most part I lived a nightmare."

Chapter 54

"What's up with you these days, Molly? You've been moping around here the last couple of times you've come to visit." Nana Kate put her arm around my shoulders. She lived on the north side of Vancouver and I loved to visit with her and Uncle Greg, my step grandfather. She was my dad's mom and I wasn't sure if she really knew what her son was like. I wondered if she was completely fooled by him? Everyone else seemed to be.

She was small of stature. She had had one of her breasts removed in a radical mastectomy. She'd had breast cancer and had gone to a very well-known clinic in New York. In those days, they removed the whole breast and the lymph nodes to ensure they eradicated all the cancer cells. She never had it recur. Her hair was gray and always done up in an attractive style. She went to the hairdresser every week. She was feisty and had a wonderful sense of humor. She was in her sixties when we moved to B.C. I loved her dearly. We had Sunday dinners with them every week. She was very English and we were taught to always leave a little food on our plates. I can't recall if it was to compliment the cook or to show that we were not greedy. I didn't understand it then and still don't.

We called her husband "Uncle Greg." He was born in Tacoma, Washington but he moved to Canada to be with my grandmother. He was six foot three, lean and fit. He loved us and was very generous, often buying us treats and encouraging us to pick and eat as many cherries and apples from their trees as we wanted. Many times he would slip us each a dime or a quarter and send us off to buy some candy or ice cream. I genuinely cared for him.

I adored her and enjoyed being in her home. Her kitchen was bright with moss green walls and white trim everywhere. Her appliances were all white and she kept her house spotless. She had a huge window above the sink that overlooked the side garden that was full of gooseberry bushes, raspberries and boysenberries. The cherry tree branches reached and hovered over the berry patch like a guardian. She had two cherry trees. One was a Bing and that was the one that stretched its arms into the frame of the window. The Queen Ann cherry tree was huge and its green leaves and rambling branches provided shade for the vibrant begonias nestled beneath the canopy of green. The kitchen had a little mudroom off it that led to a beautiful back yard. The back was like a painting. The flowers were all different shapes, sizes and colors that flourished under her green thumb. Her favorites were the dahlias of which she had a diverse mixture. Some were small, with single daisy like petals; some grew like a tree with huge flowers; others looked a little like porcupine. The vast array of colors blew my mind. I was happiest when I was in the midst of nature and it was truly at its best in her garden. I loved to be alone to wander among the range of colors and mixture of the different plants, trees and shrubs.

"Nothing Nana. I've been thinking about University and how I'm going to be able to pay for it, that's all. I really want to go into medicine and I know it's going to cost a lot of money that I don't have. I know dad won't be able to pay." There was sadness in my heart that was weighing me down.

"Well, you'll do like every other young person. You'll get a job and pay for it as you go along." She was bustling around the kitchen.

"Yeah, sure what job will pay me that kind of money?"

"You'll work it out. In the meantime, come and sit with Greg and me and have some lunch." My grandmother had the same lunch every day, beer, crackers, cheese and tomatoes. I enjoyed sharing the crackers, cheese and tomatoes, but my drink was always juice.

We talked about school and other mundane things. I cherished both of them very much and I really wanted to confide in them, but

I knew that could only lead to trouble. I chatted with them a little longer, finished my lunch, thanked them both and left for home.

The following week I came home from school and my dad informed me that I had an assignment with Tom the creep later that afternoon.

"Please Dad don't make me go there again." I pleaded

"It's already a done deal, you'll just have to live with it."

"I have too much homework." I wailed.

"Go on up and get started on it and you can finish it after you get home or in the morning."

"I really want to keep my grades up, if I get good marks on my assignments and class tests than I don't have to write finals at the end of the year and I might even qualify for a scholarship"

"Since when don't you have to write exams at the end of the year?" he sneered.

"That's how it is in grade 10 and all through high school." I was hopeful he would change his mind.

"Well, whatever, just go and get as much of your work done now. I'll call you when it is time to go." He walked away.

I trudged up the stairs defeated as usual.

It seemed like seconds later. I had barely started a major assignment that had to be in the end of the week.

"Come on, Molly! We're going to miss the bus and we'll be late for your appointment," my dad roared from the bottom of the stairs.

"I'm coming! Ready to do your will, O master," I grumbled.

"Pack up that attitude and leave it here! You'd think you were going to a funeral, with that long face and surly look."

"I don't want to make any more of those disgusting movies."

"You enjoy the new clothes I bought for you, don't you?"

"I'll go without new clothes and anything else to stop going to that creep's place."

I took a seat across the aisle from him, so I didn't have to talk with him. I didn't speak all the time we were on the bus. I was beginning to hate him as much as the creep.

My stomach churned with fear and revulsion. We arrived at our stop and I refused to talk with my dad as we walked to the creepy porno place.

"We're here, so just pack it in right now, young lady! I'm still calling the shots as long as you are under my roof, so you'll do your share to bring in the money. Got it?"

He lit his cigarette and blew the smoke into the air. It hung there suspended in space and then dissipated as the fresh air consumed it.

"Yeah, I get it."

"Hi, Molly! Off you go! They're just wrapping up," the creep chirped when we walked through the door.

"Hi, Molly," Jill said as she dressed in her street clothes.

"Hi, Jill."

"How about we go somewhere after your shoot, Molly? I'll clear it with your dad if you're game." She had a cheerful perky manner about her.

"Sure, that would be cool." I was relieved to have somewhere else to go, other than home and someone else to talk with, other than my father. I knew I wouldn't be able to concentrate enough to do my schoolwork when I was finished here.

I hurried through the shoot, anxious to get out of there. I co-operated completely. They were all pleased by my change of attitude.

"How pathetic they were!" I thought, changing into my street clothes. I watched them watching me and I deliberately and provocatively removed the sheer under garments. I seductively slid the stockings down my leg and just as slowly put on my brassiere and panties. I laughed out loud at the slavish looks they had on their stupid faces.

"Men! How mundane and pitiable you are," I sneered.

I slinked in my most sexy walk past them and out the door chuckling and winking at them as I passed them by.

"Bitch!" I heard Tom growl on my way down the stairs.

"Have you given any more thought to what we talked about Molly?" Jill asked over her drink.

"Yes, I think I'd like to get involved with you."

"Great! I know you know all the poses and moves needed for the porn flicks but I need to see what you can do when you are in a room alone with a john." She studied my reaction to her statement.

"I know what to do."

"We can go to my place and you can show me what you know. I might be able to show you some new moves that will make your job easier and keep you safe and clean." She was munching on a fry.

"My dad will expect me home in time for supper."

"I told him I might take you out for supper tonight and that we would probably be late getting home. He told me to have you home by ten o'clock."

There was confidence in the way she answered. She appeared comfortable with whom she was. I wondered what it was like to be in control of your own life?

"Do you think he knows what we will be doing?" I asked hesitantly.

"No chance of that! I don't think he even cares what we talk about or even do! Let's go and we can get started." She tossed the tip on the table, grabbed me and pulled me behind her. She was like a little girl in many ways.

"You'll do nicely, Molly! You have a great body and an innocent look about you. You're going to do well and make lots of money. I'm going to take you to my friend's place and introduce you. At the same time, I'm going to show you how to work the pole for dancing. That is one of the most popular things men like to watch and it's not easy to do, once you've got the hang of it. No pun intended!" She was very excited at the prospect of my working with her and seemed genuinely pleased with the way I behaved with her.

"Roy, this is Molly, the young woman I was telling you about." She introduced me to her friend who answered the door to her knock.

"Hi, Molly! How old are you?" He looked at me with reservation and he made me feel nervous.

"Old enough!" I quickly answered.

"You might think so, but answer my question. How old are you?" His lips were pressed together and his hands were on his hips.

"Fifteen," I mumbled, afraid I wouldn't get the job or the training.

"We have to make you look older, but not much. Jill, teach her how to use make-up and get her hair cut. Buy her some appropriate clothes and high heels. Lose the bobby sox and saddle shoes. No crinolines, no flared skirts and tailored blouses. Tight sweaters and short tight skirts; you know the drill. Has Jill explained in detail what we expect from you? I have a strip club called the "Jailhouse" and I can use another young woman like you. Are you comfortable getting naked in front of a bunch of leering men?" He sauntered across the room, poured himself a drink and turned and watched my reaction to his question.

"I've been doing porn flicks for the past four months that require me to do all kinds of disgusting poses and things in front of men and cameras. I think I can handle standing naked. Jill showed me some of the dance moves and I can learn how to use the pole," I replied arrogantly.

"That sounds good. I'll leave the details of how you are going to get away from your parents to do this. What I don't know won't hurt me." He turned and dismissed us.

"Okay, Molly, you're in! We have to get you home right now, but I will make up some story to tell your dad about a job I think you can do after school. I'll tell him there might be some shifts at night and on the weekends. Leave everything to me. I'll see you tomorrow after school and we'll start your lessons." She ran her words together and seemed quite enthusiastic about the whole scene. That confounded and confused me. I was determined to do anything that would eventually get me away from my father. I wasn't able to do much right now, even if I had lots of money. I had to look after my brothers and the house as well as finish high school.

"Jill, do you know anyone who owns a gun?" I choked on the words. Fear crept in my belly and sweat smeared my clothes. My hands and part of my face were slick with perspiration.

"Yes. I have a friend who owns a Beretta. Why do you ask? Are you okay Molly? You look as if you are going to pass out. What gives?"

"It's nothing. I get a little freaked out when I think about guns. You know how it is. Some things make you feel weird and scared. Something like when a snake crawls across your feet."

"Just thinking of that gives me the creeps! You're not going to need a gun, Molly. To start with, you'll be working in the club. When I think you're ready to branch out, I will set you up with a pimp so you will be well protected. These guys take their job very seriously. After all, you're their meal ticket. I'm going to see if Ralph, that's my guy, will take you as part of his stable. That's a ways down the road. You've got more to learn before we go there. There will not be any reason for you to have a gun." She appeared to be worried.

"I don't want to keep it. I just want to borrow it for one night."

"What are you thinking, Molly?" She glanced over at me.

"I can't tell you. Just please introduce me to your friend," I replied in a flat monotone.

"I can't do that until I know what you're up to." She stared out of the windshield.

"Can't you just trust me? I can't tell you Jill, but I desperately need to meet your friend." I was starting to get mad at having to explain myself to her. I was soaked in my own sweat and shaking. I hoped she couldn't smell the putrid fear that oozed out of every pore.

"Don't tell me you are going to try to be my mother and question everything I do," I said in a huff and crossed my arms under my breast.

"Forget I asked! I should have known you would be just like everyone in my life. Do your best to take control of everything I try to do. Just drop it for now!" I resented her attitude.

"Yeah, that's a good idea. We're here now, Molly and it looks like your dad is home. I'm coming in with you to talk with him about your prospective job. Remember, don't interrupt and don't look surprised by anything I say."

"I won't, but what if he finds out?"

"He won't, I promise." She squeezed my hand to reassure me.

I never thought he would be this gullible and I was amazed at how easily she convinced my dad that this was an ordinary job. It worked! I was launched into a career I never thought I would do.

Chapter 55

School became a respite for me. My outrageously busy life outside of it left my head spinning most of the time. I continued to do well in school. I believed that one day I would be the surgeon I dreamed of becoming.

Jill and I became very close friends. It wasn't all about practice, we went to a couple of movies, and "Strangers on a Train" was my favorite. "At War With the Enemy" with Dean Martin and Jerry Lewis was hilarious. We always had a milkshake and fries after at a soda shop on Georgia.

One day, after we had finished a practice, Jill surprised me.

"Okay, Molly! I think you're ready for your debut on stage tonight. How do you feel?" Jill was breathless after our rigorous training session on the pole.

"Good. I think I can do this. Who would have thought pole dancing required one to be an athlete?" I eased down off the pole.

"Let's go over your exit off the pole. I want to see you do that a little smoother. You're still taking a hop off it, like a gymnast does. You want to come off like a cat, willowy, sexy, and slinky and in perfect control. Try it once again for me, Molly. That's it! Well done! You're going to knock 'em dead tonight. I am more excited than you I think." She chuckled to herself. She brought a big gaily-wrapped box and handed it to me.

"What's this?" I took it from her astonished.

"Open it and see," she whispered and slipped her hand down the side of my face.

"Oh Jill! Do you really think I should wear these? They're so skimpy and what are all these beads and things?" Surprise and joy lit my face.

"That's a g-string and it goes under your short cover up. You'll see the beads and things fit perfectly and they enhance where men's eyes are drawn. Go ahead! Put it on and perform for me from your entrance to your exit."

"I don't know, Jill. It all seems so sleazy." Hesitatingly, I slipped my hands through the soft silky fabric and marveled at the feel of it.

"Don't get cold feet on me now! Come on, I'll work with you and I'll show you it's not sleazy. It's pure art. Watch me as I go through my routine. After I'm finished, tell me if you still think it's sleazy."

I watched as she went through her act and I was mesmerized. I didn't feel embarrassed or ashamed and I realized that I could do this without feeling any guilt. I was convinced she was right and that it was truly a form of art.

"That's very sexy! Okay Jill, I will try to do as well, but I know I can't compare to your act. I hope I don't follow you tonight." I giggled to hide my concerns.

"You won't. You're on first and I have to follow you, so don't upstage me, okay?" she laughed and poked me in the chest. We both changed into street clothes and went over to the club for a rehearsal.

"Wow, Molly! That's terrific!" Roy smiled and patted my behind.
"Do as well tonight and you'll be a big hit. I guarantee there'll be lots of moola tucked in your g-string when you come off the pole. Remember to take off your brassier, one strap at a time, nice and easy. You want to bring the guys along bit by bit until you are down to your string. That's when you hit the pole and drag that out until their eyes are bulging. Come off slow and catlike."

That night came and went, as did many more after that. I was amazed at how much I enjoyed it. I was earning good money that made it even more worthwhile. The attention and accolades I received from the patrons of the club cheered me.

I closed my eyes and in an instant I was sucked into a vortex where the darkness was complete and I could feel it clawing and tearing at the deepest part of my soul where all my nightmares and monsters hid. I knew in that place I was sinking into the very space I had struggled against most of my young life and yet it seemed so much better than my present home life. I released my monsters and fears and chose to become a part of the darkness. To me it was better than any of the other things I had to do for my dad or Tom. I always felt dirty and utterly ashamed with them. When I was home and in my bed at night, my dad started to come for me more and more. I suspected he knew what I did at the club and he was taking advantage of me. He knew too that I would never confess anything to him.

"I'd like a break Michael. Would it be okay if we continued next time?"

"I hate to stop here but why don't we do that and you can come back tomorrow and we will continue on. It's crucial we work through all this history Molly. Can you come back tomorrow?

"I guess I can, I would rather wait a week though. It ekes out so much energy and I find it hard to keep going back."

"Let me know in the morning if you decide not to come. The sooner we get through this the better you are going to be."

I went home and crashed for a couple of hours. I took out my dogs and cooked supper, ate it and went to bed.

How crazy is this. I wish it was one of them having to drag through all this garbage.

I went back the next day and after the usual preliminary remarks I started to tell him one of the worst things that I had ever done. I tried to keep my voice calm as I talked but inside my heart was pounding and I was scared.

"It was just another day in paradise, my dad had informed me we had another session with Tom."

"Molly, hurry! We have to catch that bus. You have the movie to do today and you know how Tom hates it when we are late. Don't shuffle your feet like that and straighten your shoulders. Stand tall and act like a young woman and not an old lady shuffling off to her doom."

My dad was a stickler for ramrod straight posture. I knew it stemmed from his army training.

"Right, like I'm supposed to be thrilled to be doing movies showing every part of me in disgusting, revealing poses and doing outrageous things with men I despise. But, hey, don't sweat it! I'll get that jaunty spring in my step just for you, *Daddy*. I know how much you love me and want me to be a success. Ooh, and maybe I'll be sought after by all the porn producers in Canada!" Sarcasm spewed out of my mouth.

"Just get a move on and keep your smart mouth shut. You're damn lucky you've got a roof over your head, clothes on your back and food in your belly." He shoved me out the door.

"Yeah, you and my mother make great book ends. You could make a picture book illustrating how to be perfect parents."

The bus-ride was riddled with silent tension.

"Hi, Molly and Jim! Molly, Jill's segment is done and they're waiting for you, so go ahead and get ready. I've got a full slate today. The kids are doing their thing and I've got another segment right after you are done, so I don't want any unnecessary takes. Try to do it right the first time and make sure you at least look like you're having fun, will ya?" Tom mocked me in that derisive tone of his.

"Right!" I sneered. I hated everyone in the room, including my dad.

"Come on over here and snuggle up to me, Molly," my partner in crime called as I finished getting into my skimpy porn clothes.

"What's that noise?" I asked.

"The kids in the next room are giving everyone a hard time. The mother's got a hot temper and they're at the receiving end of it. It will settle down in a minute. Meanwhile, let's you and I do a little rehearsal while the set is being lit up and the noise quiets down. You look damn hot in that outfit. Come over here and let's play doctor." Larry slurred his words and I saw what a slime he was. I longed to punch that smirk off of his face. At the end of the shoot, I was full of pent-up anger and distraught by everything that went on in this place. I knew I had to do something to stop it all. I felt sorry for the little children, and knew exactly what they were going through. I worried that they would feel abandoned by their mother and everyone else. It was all excessively depraved and sick. I could remember how I felt in Moose Jaw when the men did horrific things to me and how alone and desperate I felt.

"I'm going to go for a walk. I'll catch a later bus," I told my father and wrenched away from him.

"Don't be late, you've got school tomorrow."

I walked away. The storm inside me was building. I thought my fury would explode and I would shatter into a million pieces. I walked around like that for an hour or more and made a decision to do something about it. I couldn't stand the thought of another encounter with Tom, Larry or any of them. I couldn't get the picture of those little kids trapped in that horrific room with those animals pawing them, all for a couple of bucks. I seethed with hatred and rage.

Some of the children I had glimpsed over the time I had been involved seemed to have no one to love them, they were always alone with one of the crew when I watched them come into the suite. I wondered if they had been stolen. I shook with the despair and wrath I felt.

"Jill, have you thought some more about getting that Beretta for me?" I bellowed over the phone. It was slathered with the moisture that poured off of my hands that made it very difficult to hold on to the receiver. "I need you to help me, Jill. Don't ask me any more questions. Please help me to get it." I was frantic.

"I haven't given it anymore thought. Why, what's going on with you, Molly?

"You're riled over something. What is it? Let me help you. Getting a gun is not the answer!" She sounded panicked.

"Just don't ask questions and get me that gun!"

"I can't do that but, I have a friend I think you should talk with. He's into some pretty bad stuff but he's a good guy and we've been friends for a few years. Let me get him to call you and you can tell him why you want a gun. Don't get yourself into something you can't get out of. Where are you and at what number can he reach you?"

"I'm going to do some quick shopping Jill, it's stuff I will need to pull this off." I choked on the words trying to process everything I would need to do in a few short hours. I knew if I didn't do this now I would possibly never have the courage to do it ever.

"Okay, I just wish you would tell me what you're up to, I know I could help if you would let me. I will get my friend to call you in an hour. Please Molly don't do anything you are going to regret." She whispered the words into the phone.

"I won't Jill I promise." I murmured.

I gave her the number of the pay phone and left to pick up some more appropriate clothes. I changed into everything in the ladies washroom. I was a basket case by the time I returned. I slipped into the booth and I waited for her friend to call. I slid down the wall of the phone booth. I wrapped my hands and arms around my head. I moaned and sobbed into my hands. I stayed crouched in that position until the ringing phone jarred me into awareness again. Jill's friend listened to my request for a gun. I shakily tried to explain what was happening with me and the children.

"I'm coming to meet with you. I'm only ten minutes away. Stay put. I'm driving a black convertible. Watch for me."

True to his word, he arrived ten minutes later. He took one look at me.

"You are not getting a weapon from me, little girl. You are in no condition to handle a gun and I doubt you have the guts or the ability to fire one."

Chapter 56

Three hours later, I stood across the street from the creep's apartment. Jill's friend was with me. He had coached me on what to say and told me what we were going to do. I had made it clear I would do whatever I had to do. He promised to help me and explained he would show me how to get out quickly and cleanly, leaving no trace of myself behind. He would wait for my signal downstairs. He gave me his word he would not come up before the signal. He was going to walk me through the process. This was costing me almost all of the money I had saved, but I didn't care. I knew I couldn't keep doing those despicable movies and I was determined to help the little children who were being forced to do the kiddie porn. Those movies were wicked and ugly. I was driven by revenge and dread and I wanted the nightmare to end now. The panic I felt and the fury of the past few months had choked out of me all sense of right and wrong.

"Have you got everything clear in your mind, Molly? You can't have any slip-ups; otherwise it's curtains for you. Are you sure you want to do this thing? You're going to have to live with it the rest of your life."

"I'm sure. I know I can't live with myself and let that creep keep using kids like he does. He's destroying the lives of sweet little children who are not even six years old. I swear the last two were no more than five." I babbled at him louder than was wise, but I was hyped-up and anxious to get it done.

"Why don't you just turn him over to the cops, Molly? They'll do a number on him before he even gets to court, I guarantee."

"I can't. I don't want to be dragged through the mud and I sure don't want my grandparents, or anyone else in my family dragged into it. Besides, he'll get out of prison and do it all again. Creatures like him never stop. They're money-hungry, lecherous, sick bastards! So nothing changes and the only way to end his career is to kill him." As I poured out my venomous words I became too agitated to stand still.

"Jesus, Molly! Don't go in there all het up or you'll botch it. You have to calm down. Let's go over the drill again. Tell me what you're going to say and what you plan to do." He was calm as he took my shoulders and turned me to face him.

"Breathe deep breaths." He spoke quietly in my ear.

I settled down and went over everything I had to do again and again. He finally gave me the go ahead.

"Hi Tom! It's Molly! Are you alone tonight?" I asked over the telephone. I knew he was. The pay phone was across the street from the studio. His was the only car parked outside on the parking lot.

"Molly? What are you calling me for? Yes, I'm alone. Why?" He sounded anxious.

"Can I come up? I want to talk with you? I won't stay long, but I need to see you, Tom. Please say yes," I pleaded in my little girl voice.

"Okay, sure come on up."

"What's this about, Molly? Does your old man know you're here?" He looked worried when he opened the door.

"Damn! Its ten o'clock shouldn't you be home and in bed?" He ran his hands through his already disheveled hair. I was scared at the way he looked. I was certain he knew that this was a trick.

"No, I have a part time job and there's no school on the weekends. My dad knows I'm working late tonight. My ride won't be there until midnight, so I have lots of time." I removed my jacket revealing my skimpy sheer blouse. I was not wearing anything under it. I hiked my short skirt a little higher and sat on the sofa next to him.

"What game are you playing at, Molly? You could get burned here, ya know." He sounded suspicious. I was worried that he didn't believe my act. He shifted away.

"I know. Maybe I want to be burned by someone who knows what they are doing," I purred.

"Okay kitten! Once we start, there's no stopping the action. Right?" He lit his cigarette and blew a smoke ring. He glanced at me to make sure I was watching.

"Right! Do you have anything to drink? I'd like to fix us a nice little relaxing cocktail. In my new job I have learned a few different recipes for really smooth drinks," I purred, hiking my skirt a little higher.

"Yeah. I've got some good scotch and soda." His mouth sounded dry and his pupils dilated when he leered at my breasts.

"That sounds good. Show me where, and I'll do the honors." I slid off the couch in a way for him to see a little more skin.

"The sideboard is over there and there are ice cubes in the fridge in the kitchen. The light switch is on your left. Glasses tongs and everything else are in the sideboard. I'll go slip into something a little less cumbersome while you do that." It was obvious by the bulge in his pants that he was getting turned on.

"Okay." I slinked over to the sideboard and he headed for another room to get changed. He was almost trotting.

I chuckled nervously as I watched his reaction to my performance. While he was changing, I slipped the powder Jill's friend had given me into his drink. I poured a double shot of booze into the glass to hide any taste, even though Jill's friend informed me that there was no aftertaste to it. My hands were shaking. I was a wreck.

"Okay, my little pussy cat! Are you ready for daddy?" he purred. He had on a satin dressing gown, loosely tied so I could see he was naked under it. His manhood peeked out of the front opening.

"Ooh! I see your little friend is at full attention." I leaned provocatively against the sideboard.

"Did you say little, I don't think so darlin." He drawled.

"You can find out real quick. Come on, sit here and let's do this slow and easy. He patted the couch beside him.

"I need a drink to cool me down first. It seems you do too." I handed him his drink and snuggled next to him. My own mouth was dry and I started to perspire. I was petrified.

"Gawd! You sure know how to get my blood boiling, little girl! Let's start by taking off this blouse so I can get a close look at the girls and maybe cop a little feel." He leisurely undid the buttons on my blouse and slipped it off my shoulders. I lifted my arms and he took it off. I was embarrassed to feel my own response to his touch. I hurriedly took a small sip of my drink and hoped he would do the same. He picked up his glass and drained it. He smacked his lips together and handed the emptied glass to me.

"How about you fix me another one of those? And while you slink your way across the room, why don't you do a little strip act for me. I have a feeling you know exactly how to do that," he chortled and opened his dressing gown a little more.

"Mmmm! I know exactly what you mean!" I took his glass and sauntered to the sideboard, seductively exaggerating my walk. I poured the drink and slipped the rest of the powder into his drink. I undid my skirt and wriggled my bottom to keep his eyes focused there and not on what I was doing with his drink. I turned, let it fall to the floor and stepped out of it. I let it dangle on my foot and tossed it off. I stood and let him look at me naked to the waist except for my little glittery g-string. A very thin black garter belt fastened my nylons. I rocked back and forth and slipped my fingers under the corner of the garter belt. I smiled and waited for his response.

"Jeez, you look so damn hot! Come on back to me, darlin'. I'm going to burn you slow and easy and you'll be begging me to do you."

I tiptoed over and gave him his drink. I slipped back half way to the sideboard and remained there undulating back and forth. I fiddled with one of my garter clips. I unclipped it and I rolled the stocking down. I turned and bent down, exaggerating the move and slipped it off my foot. I could hear his breathing get heavier and faster. I knew he was going to finish his doctored drink before I finished my strip tease. He was pounding it back. I was getting into it now and I began to feel more confident. I turned back to do the same with my other stocking. This time I moved a little closer to him and tucked my thumbs in the top of my g-string. I nudged it down revealing the triangle of hair.

He fondled my breasts and drooled over them. I hated him, but there was no doubt he knew what he was doing. His hands roamed over me. He was panting by this time. He tried to kiss me and I shrank back.

"What's wrong? Remember our deal, kitten? There's no turning back." His words were garbled and I watched his eyes lose their focus.

"Damn! That booze is going to my head. I don't feel so good." He was almost incoherent as he massaged his forehead. His head lolled back a little.

I quickly moved over him and pushed him down on to the couch.

"Hey, you're not backing out are you? Because I'm just getting started," I murmured in his ear. My breasts were fully in his face and his arm flopped down when he attempted to touch them. He tried to get his mouth around me, but he could not quite manage it. My hands roamed down his body. I opened his dressing gown and his hard-on was now soft. He was gradually losing consciousness. He slumped back. His mouth went slack and foamy drool slithered down his chin.

I was shocked and pumped at the same time. My hands were trembling so hard I had to stop and gulp in some air. I shook Tom to see if he responded, but he just fell over. I fought against the nausea that threatened to overtake me. I pushed it aside and refused to think of backing out. Tom is an animal and I had convinced myself he didn't deserve to live. I was so terrified but I knew I couldn't turn back. There was no telling what he would do if I didn't follow through.

I got up and went over to the window. I signaled Jill's friend to come up. I picked up the glasses and washed them. I put everything away and thoroughly wiped anything I had touched with the lint free cloth Jill's friend had put in my purse.

I answered the soft wrap on the door and let Jill's friend in. It was such a relief to see him. I needed him here. He quickly took Tom's pulse and indicated that it was very faint. He handed me a syringe. I took it and injected Tom between the toes with the full contents of it. I was in full control of my nerves by now and I was almost euphoric with the power I felt within myself. There was no turning back now. I was damn glad Tom would not be filming any more children nor would his smut be seen anymore. I kept that as my focus otherwise I think the horror of what I was doing would have undone me. I moved away from him. Jill's friend moved over to take Tom's pulse again. This time there was none. He looked up and shook his head, signaling Tom was dead.

"Come over here and help me move him to his bed."
"He's so heavy I don't think I can lift him," I said as I tried to lift his legs. His body was completely slack and for the first time I understood the meaning of the words 'dead weight'. I started to hyperventilate with the reality of that dead body.
I was beginning to freak out. I wanted to get out of there. I couldn't look at Tom's lifeless body. Every part of me was trembling with stark terror.
"Just do it, Molly. We have to get him into his bed and get out of here," he snapped.
I lifted his feet and we dragged him into his bedroom and put him into the bed.
"Good girl! Now we have to make sure there's no trace of you anywhere in this apartment. Is this where you do your films?"
"No, upstairs there are three bedrooms with all the lights and cameras." I started to cry and shake uncontrollably.
"Hey, hey! Get a hold of yourself! This guy was an animal. You did society and a hell of a lot of kids a big favor. By the way, you look hot with no clothes on. I'm only human. Maybe you should cover up, eh?" He laughed and winked at me.

"Gawd! I forgot I was nearly naked. I'm so sorry." I fumbled, trying to cover my exposed skin but unable to do it with any kind of competence.

"Don't apologize. The view is stunning and if I had more time, I might even see if you'd let me taste a little of it," he chuckled, taunting me.

"Get dressed and let's get out of here. I have to get you over to Jill's in half an hour."

I quickly slipped into my clothes and we carefully went over the apartment with a fine toothcomb. We made sure we had left nothing behind. We crept out and drove over to Jill's.

"You look awfully flushed and agitated, Molly, but don't tell me what you've been doing. I don't want to know. I've got to get you home. Promise me we will never speak of this night again. If I formerly introduce you to my friend in the future, you will act like you have never met him before." She looked as stern as she sounded.

"I promise, Jill." I was still in shock from the after effects of what happened tonight. I was equally exhilarated with the adrenalin rushing through me and staggered at what I had done. I could hardly think straight. I was awash in the power of it.

Over the next few weeks, I rationalized that what I had done was a good thing. I huddled within myself for days and even weeks scared silly the police would know what had happened and come to take me to jail. But none of that happened and eventually it became another buried memory.

There was great consternation in the newspapers when Tom's body was discovered and his dirty little secrets were made public. The outcome of their investigation indicated he had died of natural causes, according to the article. The films discovered in the apartment were loosely described as "kiddy porn." The police allegedly destroyed all the ones they confiscated. Both Jill and I were greatly relieved to know our porn flicks would never be viewed publicly.

Jill thumbed through the newspaper. She never asked and I never said I knew anything about what happened. She put the paper down and said.

"We received the money for the movies we had completed but now we don't have to worry about anyone ever seeing what we had done. I am certainly happy about that! It wasn't as bad for you, Molly. You're still a kid. No one would have come down hard on you, but they sure would be disgusted with me. I think it's time to introduce you to my guy. Are you interested in broadening your field, Molly, and moving into the sex trade?" She looked up with a funny little grin on her face. I always remember this stuff like I was there, it is as if I am seeing a movie"

I sat ramrod still in my chair and stared at Michael, waiting for him to respond. My heart was still galloping in my chest and I was sure he could not only hear it he could see it banging against my ribs. I had never related that story to anyone ever and now I was mortified and scared spit less that he would have to turn me over to the police.

What the hell was I thinking telling him about Tom. Who in their right mind admits to murder when they have escaped discovery for so many years. What is going to happen to me now?

Those were my thoughts as I sat and waited for Michael to say something.

"Say something Michael, anything, what are you going to do?" I whispered.

"Molly that's quite a bombshell you dropped on me. Do you believe you killed him or do you think over the years your intense hatred and need for revenge has you believing it actually happened?"

"I think I would rather not respond Michael, can we leave it alone?"

"Maybe you're right Molly some things are best left to time. I don't need to know anymore about it. Fill me in on how things developed for you after that. It must have been an extremely traumatic time for you."

"Jill was determined to get me into the sex trade. I honestly didn't have too many uncertainties about it because most of my life I had been forced to share my body at the demand of my parents. I really knew very little about anything else. I certainly had no illusions about my morals or lack there of." I continued to relate the events, once again becoming entangled in the memory. I was back in that space and time, our conversations were vivid as where my emotions.

"I don't know, Jill. What would I have to do?" I was taken aback by her casual attitude. You'd think she had just asked me about the weather.
"Pretty much what you did in the films, but with more class. You'd be doing the things men fantasize about, and are willing to pay someone to realize the fantasy. It can be good sometimes. You will meet some interesting men. You can do the same for women if you want. I prefer men, but I like a change every now and again." She smiled wickedly.
Memories of Sadie and Rachelle flooded me when I remembered how good they could make me feel.

"I know what you mean, but that is not my thing." I said in a sleepy voice.
"I know I said I would set you up with Ralph, but another friend of mine has expressed an interest in you. He has watched your show at the 'Jailhouse' and is very interested in meeting with you. His name is Bud and he's a good guy. I think you'll like him. He's not bad to look at. I call him eye candy. Are you up for it?"
"Sure, why not?" I replied.
"Come over after your last show tonight and we can talk business. You should think about moving in with me, Molly. Once you graduate, we can set up a nice place for the two of us to relax in. I've been looking for a room mate for awhile and a bigger place. You will graduate in a couple of years. In the meantime, I can get a bigger place and you can spend weekends with me. You can still do your thing at the 'Jailhouse' a couple of nights a week and work with me on the weekends. I'll tell your dad it's easier for me to drive you back and forth from here on the weekends. I'm sure he'll go for it."

My dad agreed with Jill and I had his permission to spend the weekends with her.

I met Bud that night. He invited me to take the job temporarily and I became a member of his stable. In a heartbeat, my life had taken a new turn in the road. Bud was to be my pimp if I worked out okay.

"You've got a client tonight, Molly. Did Bud tell you?" Jill informed me during my first weekend with her.

"Yes, he called me earlier but it's not until seven o'clock. I think we are going to meet for drinks first and then go over to one of the hotels. Bud has booked a room. I'm really nervous, Jill. What if I don't know how to do the things he wants?" I asked, pacing back and forth in front of her large sofa.

"You'll do fine. How long has it been since you engaged anyone sexually?"

"It has been about eight years if we don't count a certain person who just uses me for his own pleasure. I certainly wouldn't call what I did with Larry engaging, would you?"

"Whoa, maybe we should practice a bit. Do you know any moves that get a guy going?" She lounged back on the couch and threw her arm across the back of it. I noticed how attractive she looked against the pale green backdrop of the couch.

"Sure, I can do all that. It's just I don't know too many different ways to do sex." I took a look at her to see if she was having second thoughts about inviting me into her lifestyle.

"Come to mama and I will show you some fancy footwork and back work." Laughing, she pulled me down next to her on the sofa.

"It's been a long time since I fooled around for my own pleasure." She slipped off her shirt and bra.

"Move over closer to me, Molly. I called Bud and he's on his way over. In the meantime, let's you and I get down to some sweet action here. I'm going to take off your top and bra and I don't want you to be offended. Look at this as a training mission. We will be the ones this time to reap the benefits." She pulled my sweater over my head and neatly undid my bra, releasing my breasts into her hands.

Lord, I hate who I am! I can't stop my body from reacting to her words and her touch. It was like being with Sadie and Rachelle again and all my friends in Moose Jaw. I remembered how much I loved the way they made me feel. I was hungry for that warmth and love again. I was no good and it didn't matter to anyone how I behaved. I would never mean anything to anyone. I closed my eyes, shut my thoughts out and let my emotions take me to that wonderful place. I was vibrating with anticipation. I had surrendered to this side of life, knowing it was the only place where I would be accepted. I would gladly walk this road I had chosen from now on. I submitted to Jill. She nuzzled me and we both engrossed and trying to tear off the rest of our clothes when we were jolted to a resounding halt when the doorbell rang.

"Cripes! Who can that be?" She leaped up and shoved her arms into her blouse.

The bell chimed again.

"Open up Jill! It's Bud," a voice called from the other side of the door.

"I forgot I called him." She ran to answer the door.

I grabbed for my clothes as they walked back into the room.

"No, wait Molly. Let's go through this together with Bud. It'll be like a dress rehearsal for tonight without the dress part."

"Yeah, Molly. Stand up and let's see what you've got." Bud swaggered into the room.

I stood up and felt very shy all of a sudden. My head was down and eyes cast downward. I shuffled from foot to foot. I experienced that familiar shame and felt dirty all over.

I wondered where my brain was? To think I was getting back into this smutty life!

Never mind, I reminded myself, this was what I had surrendered to. I had to get over my phony act of trying to believe I was better than this. I was not. If I didn't go with what was happening here, I would be left with my father and whatever life he could give me. I understood what that meant. There was no question in my mind which direction I should take. I swallowed what pride was left and made my choice. I stepped further into the room. I reached my hand to Bud, and when he

263

took it I moved closer. It mattered not to me that I was as naked as the day I was born.

He was five feet eleven inches, well built with no fat anywhere. His hair was dark, straight and shoulder length, which added to his mystery. He had a little crooked smile that made him seem dangerous. He had wonderful blue-gray eyes that smoldered under long, dark eyelashes. He had that soon-need-to-be shaved look about him. Dark whiskers peaked through wind-roughened skin. He smelled like new fallen rain, sun and wind. Whatever soap he had used to shower, left him smelling clean and fresh. I could sense that warm fuzzy feeling creeping up my toes to my legs right to my core. My breasts ached to be touched. I was confused by my emerging passion. This was completely foreign to me. I was always aware of my emotions and I had been in complete control of them for the past few years. What was this about? I wanted him to touch me. I really wanted to feel his hands all over me. I moved hesitantly in his arms and his hands touched the side of my face. I looked into his eyes and leaned into him. He pulled me to him and laid a soft kiss on my lips. I pulled his face to mine and deepened the kiss. I had never kissed like this before. I wanted him now. "Tennessee Waltz" was playing softly on the record player and I slipped into a bone melting stupor. I could barely stand on my feet my knees wanted to buckle and I yearned to be held in his arms. I ached to feel the power of them around me.

"Wow," he said in a husky voice, "do you want to take this into the bedroom?"

Jill interrupted. "Oh, please! Not on your life! You're staying right here and I'm going to watch or maybe we should all truck into the bedroom and I could be involved too."

"We can all go into the bedroom and you can watch if you want, Jill, but I want her to myself this first time. She's hot and I want to see what she can really do when she's wound up. This is strictly to do with my business. Now back off!"

"Alright, don't get your shorts in a knot. And yeah, I believe that crap that it is business. You're not fooling me or anyone else."

"You don't have a lot of experience do you, Molly? Oh you may know the moves, but how about the emotions and fire that goes with it when you relax and join in the fun?" He nuzzled my neck and led me into Jill's bedroom.

I couldn't respond, my vocal chords seemed to be paralyzed.

The lessons began. I completely forgot that this was an audition for a job with his stable of girls.

I never took my eyes from his. I watched the gray take over the blue. His pupils dilated and his nostrils flared. I was still aware enough to know his passion and desire were driving him right now. I was as aroused as he. We continued to explore and touch and taste, until a spectrum of colors exploded in my head. I climbed and reached a crescendo that crashed through me. I took as much of him as he took of me. We lay spent and gasping for breath. We stared at one another in awe and I was astounded at what had happened. I had never experienced such a depth of feeling. It was a hunger like no other. This was a new feeling for me. I had no shame or remorse. I expected nothing in return. Tears sprung from my eyes. I was discovering what it was like to be cherished by another, not for who I was and what I had to sell or offer. It was simply my inner self, the 'me' I had hidden from the world since I was a very small child. I knew this was over the top, but I couldn't help how I felt. I had never known such fire. I had never before felt any connection when I had been intimate. I realized, too, it might only be me who felt these sensations and thought those thoughts. My body was still thrumming.

"My gawd! What just happened with you two?" Jill gasped.

"Whadya talkin' about?" Bud shuffled away from me. "Nuthin' different happened. She will do nicely, Jill. Her inexperience is refreshing and should earn some extra bucks until she progresses beyond it." Bud started to get dressed.

He spun around to me and pulled me into his arms

"Oh, you'll do nicely, my little firecracker! You'll do very nicely." He moaned against my chest. You're going to be mine whenever I want, and I'm going to want often."

"Anytime!" I sighed, "That was amazing! Thank you, Bud. Jill, how are you doing?"

"Jeepers! I need some lovin' real bad. I hope you guys have some left for me

"Have you ever done a party à trois, Molly?" He looked at me with those intense, smoky eyes.

"No. I saw my mom and a couple of men go into her room once, but never watched."

"Let's give her a lesson here, Jill. Molly, a party à trois earns three times the rate, so it would be good for you to feel comfortable doing it.

They proceeded to show me the positions and moves to make. At the end of the afternoon, I knew I was knee deep into a dark lifestyle. I knew what I had experienced before was nothing to what was ahead of me. I was extremely apprehensive, but at the same time, I was anxious to start making money. I convinced myself that it wouldn't be too bad. At least now I would be paid for what I could do. I wouldn't have to share the money with anyone, including my dad. Suddenly, I felt a sour taste in my mouth and a gut wrenching pain. I felt as if I were going to throw up right then. The room started to spin, sweat broke out on my forehead, my palms were soaking wet and I could hardly breathe. I threw my head back and gasped, desperate to get air into my lungs.

"Whoa! What's wrong Molly? You're as white as a sheet. Here, sit down, put your head between your knees. Bud, get some water quick!" Jill pushed me over to a chair and plopped me into it. She shoved my head between my legs.

"What's happening? Is she sick? I don't want no dame that's gonna be nuthin' but trouble, Jill. You gotta' be honest here. What's goin' on?"

"I have no idea, Bud. I've never seen her like this. C'mon, Molly. Talk to us. What's happening?" Jill shook me and placed a glass of water to my lips.

I took a couple of swallows and tried to focus my eyes on something. I took another sip. I grasped the glass and gulped the rest of the water.

"Are you okay, Molly? Jeez! What happened?" Jill leaned against Bud, looking extremely worried.

"What if my dad finds out what I am doing? He'll kill me and probably you too, Jill. I can't do this. I am too afraid. He has a way of finding out everything I do. He'll be furious and he will probably take any money I make before he kills me. You can be sure he will want to be involved. If I'm going to do this, I don't want him anywhere near me!" I did not take any breaths as I blurted out my fears and my fear of him.

"Is that all, Molly? You don't need to worry about your dad. I can control him. I promise he will never find out. We have been able to hide what we do from him up to now. What makes you think he can find out about this?" Jill took the glass from me, poured more water into it and drank it down. She smiled at me and shook her head.

"Who is her old man and where does he hang out?" Bud glared at Jill and me waiting for one of us to answer.

"He's nobody believe me! He's been doing her since she was a little kid. If he tries anything, we can take care of it. We can pull his chain anytime we want. We have enough on him to make him snivel and crawl on his knees and do anything we tell him. Do not worry, either one of you. I've got his number and I will know exactly what to do if the problem ever comes up." Jill ruffled my hair and patted the side of Bud's face.

"You really had me going there for a minute, Molly." She laughed her way into the kitchen.

"Are you okay with this, Molly?" Bud held my hand in his.

"Yeah, I think so. I trust Jill. She's met him and has been able to fool him up to now. I don't think there is any reason to doubt her. Anyway, I want to start earning some money so I can start saving for my education. I plan to graduate with honors so I will be able to go to university as soon as I have enough money saved. I am really excited at the prospect of making something of myself. The sooner the better bring it on!" Those were brave words but it was all bravado."

"You know Michael I can't believe how easily I slipped into the role of a prostitute. It was such a natural transition for me. I was actually excited by it all. Not only was I now in control but also I was going to be paid. It must seem bazaar to you and in a way it seems crazy to me from my position now but back then that was the way it was. I wonder if Jill had ever threatened to expose my father."

"I can understand that Molly but looking back do you honestly believe you were in control?"

"From my perspective at that time compared to what had happened prior to that time absolutely. I had more control over my actions than ever. Oh I understand where you're coming from Michael. You think because the clients were paying they got to dictate what I did. That is certainly true but at the same time I got to set out the boundaries, which was a great improvement. Granted there were times when the boundaries were compromised but that did not happen often."

"Molly it's a beautiful day out there why don't we go for a walk around the bog and you can tell me how things progressed. I have the rest of the afternoon free. I'll leave my cell number with Beth if any emergency calls come in and she'll put it over to my doctor's answering group when she leaves for the day. It will do us both good to get up and move."

"Sounds good to me. I enjoy nature above all else. We are so blessed by what God has provided in the way of natural beauty in this city" I stood and put my jacket on and waited for Michael to make the arrangements to have any urgent calls forwarded to his cell phone.

"This is a great idea Michael." I said as we walked along the edge of the pond that was still full of water. Soon with the heat of the summer the water level would recede and the ducks and geese would have to find a new home until the fall.

"What was it like for you to be caught up in the sex trade at such a young age. You must have been in your early teens."

"I was and by the time I was almost seventeen I was completely immersed in it." It was easy for me to slip back to those years as we walked along the trail.

" I was anxious to go on my first date and with the help of Jill and Bud I was well prepared. Bud took me to the bar where we were meeting my first client. Bud ordered drinks all around and introduced me to Joel, my client. He was older than I expected, but he was well dressed and clean. His fingernails were buffed and polished. His demeanor and appearance reflected money. He was arrogant to boot. He kissed my hand. I was blown away by his genteel manners.

"I've got to run, so I'll leave you two to it. The room number and everything is in this envelope. You have all night tonight and the price is one thousand dollars. That's the agreed upon contract. Take it easy with her. You're her first client. Treat her gentle and I promise, you'll be well pleased with the results. If there is any problem, you have my number. I will expect to hear from you in the morning. Molly, a taxi will be waiting for you at ten o'clock tomorrow morning to take you home. You have my number as well. Call me if there are any problems. I expect you will both be satisfied with tonight. I'll see you tomorrow, Molly." He stood, shook Joel's hand, touched my hair and left.

"Well, Molly, do you want another drink or do you want to go over to the hotel and we can get down to business? After, we can have some dinner or dinner first and then down to business. We have all night, so we can do whatever suits you, sweetheart."

"Let's go over to the hotel and maybe we can have a couple of drinks and see how we feel after that. Is that okay with you?" I was edgy.

"Let's go!" He clasped my hand and we went to his car and drove to the hotel.

"We'll sit here a minute before we go up to our room," he said and put his arms around me. Have you ever 'done it' in a car Molly?"

"No, it doesn't look like it would be very comfortable." I felt sleazy thinking about it.

"Oh, but it can be, and it's nice and dark here. It will be quiet for at least another hour or so." He leaned over, touched my face and ran his finger down my neck. He reached under my top and fondled me.

"Let me show you. Is that okay with you?"

"Sure, I guess so," I responded meekly.

"Lift up, while I move over to your side of the car."

I did as he asked. I was very uncomfortable with this, but I had to do whatever this guy wanted. If I didn't do a good job on my first date, it would be over for me. I would be back with my dad full time and going nowhere. I let my date do whatever he wanted. I went along with him and followed his lead. When he started to get into the rhythm of his passion, I worked him until he finally finished. He heaved a deep sigh and tried to kiss me on the lips.

"Wait, just a minute. Lip kissing is not my thing. Please respect that I have boundaries and kissing is one of them. When I want to kiss someone, it will be for real not for money! You have to understand that right up front. I have other boundaries as well. I will spell them out right now, so you're not caught unaware." I listed the things I was willing and those that I was not willing to do.

"Are you okay with all of this, or have I blown it?" I was incredibly stressed and afraid I had made a big mistake, but I recognized my own limits. I knew I had to make them clear right up front.

"Hey, baby, it's alright. I'm not new to this game. I understand. I should have known. Lots of you girls have the same hang-ups. I'm good with it. I promise to respect all of them. Hey, some of them are too kinky for me anyway. I'm only out for a good time. Good clean sex is all I need to keep me happy. As long as you're into that, we've got no worries baby. The night will be long and sweet. You in the zone, darling?" He sucked on my neck. I giggled because it tickled.

"Yeah, I'm good to go. I think we are going to have a blast. You sure you can keep up?" I snickered as I snuggled into him.

"Try me babe. I think you'll be well pleased and quite amazed. I like you, sweetie. I hope this is a start to a long and happy arrangement. Are you up for that?" He kissed the tip of my nose.

"I'm not sure. Let's see how the night ends. I'll let you know then, but I think you might be right."

Let's get decent and go and have those drinks. Our room is on the fourth floor. The night is young and we are just getting started, my sweet."

When we were settled in the room Bud had rented, he poured me a strong drink.

And so my first date went well. Joel and I spent a whole night of experimenting with positions and other things, and it was reassuring to begin in this way. He was sweet and fun. He was fascinating to talk with. This would not be the last time we were together. Joel became a regular and a very good friend over the time I was in the trade. Those may sound like empty words to anyone who has never sold their bodies for money, but my experiences before and after that taught me that some johns are easy to be with and others were best forgotten.

Other dates were not so great but most were reasonable. Some were exciting and lots of fun.

One time, I was in one of those shops that had many romantic gadgets, creams and oils. I had heard that oils were good to use, so I bought a couple of bottles to try that night. My date was middle aged and he agreed it would fun to try the oil. Neither one of us had ever used oil, so I slathered it all over him and he smeared it on me. Needless to say, we spent our one and a half hours trying to stay on top or even beside one another! If I was on top, I would slip and bang my head on the wall in front of the bed and he banged his head if he were on top. Side by side gave the same results. We were simply too slippery for any kind of successful intimate connection. We laughed until we hurt. It was so funny! When my ride came to get me, we still had not had any sexual contact. My date was such a good sport about the fact I had not fulfilled my side of the contract, he paid me the full amount he and Bud had negotiated. He told me he had so much fun it was worth every penny. He became one of my regulars, but we never used oil again.

Another time, I had a contract to go a fair distance out of town for a four-hour date. Bud drove me out and he arranged to come back and pick me up at the end of the time set. The little inn we used was quite secluded. This was one of the client's requests. I never enquired as to why anyone wanted to go to out of the way places. I left all of that up to Bud. The date went well, but when I arrived, he asked if he could drive me back to town. He had always wanted to have someone perform oral sex on him while he was driving. I telephoned Bud and explained the situation. I told him I was comfortable with the arrangement and that my date would drop me off at one of our regular hotel drop off points at the prearranged time.

"Are you comfortable with no conversation, because I will be a little busy and won't be able to answer any questions." I chuckled on our way down to his car.

"I've driven many miles with nothing but the sound of my tires singing along the road, so I don't think I will have a problem with the silence. I expect I will be a little busy too. He peered sideways at me and beamed with anticipation.

"Okay, hop in and start driving. We need to get a move on. I have to meet up with Bud in couple of hours." I pulled my hair back in a small ponytail to keep it from interfering with my task.

Everything was going well as we drove down the road. It proved to be a little more difficult for him to concentrate on his driving than he had anticipated and that was almost the end of both of us. When he climaxed, he lost control of the car and we veered off the road into a farmer's field. We came to an abrupt stop not two feet away from a huge bull. My date sat with glazed eyes trying to refocus. I was not convinced he had come down from lala land because he looked at me and asked.

"What the hell happened?"

"I think we're in some deep kaka here," I whispered, eyeing the bull that seemed hypnotized by our headlights. He stood and stared back.

"Oh my gawd! Is that what I think it is?"

"Uh huh, and I for one am not getting out to push us out of this, nor am I going to be the one to go in search of the farm house to see if we can use the phone to get help." This was definitely not part of my contract.

He retorted, "You don't expect me to get out! What if that animal decides to come after me?"

"There's always that possibility, but if he decides to charge your car, it's going to do quite a bit of damage. The bottom line is, you will still be the one to go for help. I am not getting out of this car."

The bull started to stamp his feet and paw at the ground.

I continued, "Listen, dork head, if you hadn't lost control while you were getting it off, we wouldn't be in this mess. Now get out of the car and get us some help before he decides we are interloping on his turf. If you get out and go for the house, he will probably think you are the farmer. Either way, you have to make some sort of move here. Be a man!" I smacked at him and reached for the door on his side so I could shove him out.

"Okay, okay, I'm going, but you just better hope that thing doesn't charge me." His face was so close to mine I could see the terror in his eyes. I didn't give a damn how scared he was!

"No, YOU had better hope he doesn't charge you. That is more your problem than mine." My only thought was to get out of this mess in one piece.

The upshot was that he made it to the farmhouse and called Bud who in turn called a tow truck. It arrived an hour later and pulled us out. The farmer came and moved the bull into a paddock. I don't know what it cost my date or Bud and I never asked. Bud laughed about that for months after. Me, I really didn't see the humor at all. I never again performed oral sex on anyone who was behind the wheel of a moving car.

Another funny incident that could have been disastrous happened on a date a friend of mine went on. She was new to Canada.

"Hey, Molly," she called out one night, when a group of us was sitting at a bar getting a bite to eat.

This establishment was one of my favorite hangouts. The bar was a beautiful cherry wood that gleamed and exuded a kind of warmth when I leaned my arms on its surface. The drinking glasses shimmered. They had none of those little hairline cracks I had sometimes seen in the more seedy places. The subdued lighting added to its charm and Frank, the bar tender, was always friendly and courteous. Even though he knew whom we were and what we did to earn money, he never made any derogatory remarks neither did he talk down to us. The carpets were a rich red and the walls were painted black. The atmosphere was perfect for me.

"Hi Samantha! Where are you off to all decked out?" I asked, "You look lovely."

"I'm going to a party to do a table dance."

"Where?" I sipped my drink. I enjoyed the sound of the ice as it slid down and tinkled the side of my glass.

"I don't know. Bud's on his way to let me know the details."

"Here comes Bud now," I said and waved him over.

"Hi, Molly, Samantha." He sat down next to me. "Your ride is on the way, Samantha. This is a perfectly straight forward date. You are not required to perform any tricks. These guys are having a stag party and they want some hot chick to do a strip tease without the pole. Just get one of them to clear a sturdy table for you to work on, and you should do very well." He munched on a fry he had swiped off my plate.

"Here they come now, Samantha. Are you okay with this? If you're nervous about going with them on your own, I can change the arrangement" Bud had such a sweet way about him. I watched the quiet interplay between the two of them.

"I'm okay. Don't worry Bud, I'm good to go," she beamed.

I found out later how this date played out. Samantha told me all about it.

She was driven to a swanky house where she was captivated at the opulence. There were half a dozen big guys with tattoos all over their arms, faces and backs. They put her in a big town car and drove to an out-of-the-way clubhouse. Samantha didn't have a clue where she was or who these guys were. She was protected by her ignorance.

"Wow! You guys have a nice place here. Do you always gather for parties so far out of town? How many are here and where is this place?" She rattled off the questions.

"You don't need to know any of that." A big guy who was shirtless came up and took her arm.

"Well, anyway it is very impressive." she continued. Then a guy grabbed her arm.

"Can you dance?" he asked.

"Sure, but where do you want me to perform?"

"Here, in this room, in the middle where all the guys can get a good view. You understand what we want from you? We want everything off and we want to see some very revealing dancing on your part. The guys might reach out and touch you, but that's all."

Samantha rolled her eyes and continued to tell me the rest.

"I can handle that. I'll need a sturdy table to work on. Can you get someone to set one up? I'm sure I can make you guys happy." She still didn't know who they were.

The evening went well and they drove her back to the hotel where she and I were staying that night. We had a double score for a guy around midnight. I asked her how it went when she got back to our room. She explained the engagement and filled in the rest of it.

"It was good, but there were sure a lot of them and they were all big and had tattoos over their bodies. Motor cycles were everywhere."

"What! Where were you and who were the clients?" I gasped.

"I don't know. Some group of guys who have a club house where they all gather. Dope and booze was everywhere." She was so blasé about it all as she continued her story.

"Jeez, Samantha, I hope you didn't ask them any questions or try to get information from them?" I asked, knowing full well who the biker gang was.

"I did, but they didn't answer any of my questions. They just told me to dance and they seemed happy with my performance."

That date was with the most notorious biker gang in Canada. It was pure luck and Samantha's innocence and lack of knowledge that got her through the night unscathed. Bud told me later he had no idea who the major players were. He had made the arrangements with a clean-cut man in a suit.

There were some freaky calls as well where we only just escaped with our lives and limbs intact. There were always guys that wanted to do perverse acts, but we all had our boundaries. There were certain tricks I would not perform. Bud knew each of our preferences. He did his best to make sure the clients understood what to expect from us. There were times when things went very wrong.

One date I was on was particularly scary.

"This is the place, Molly. You have one hour here and another date in two hours, so make sure you're ready to go right on schedule." Mark, my driver for the night, explained.

"Right Mark, I'll be ready when you come back," I answered in my usual off hand way, not thinking that anything would go wrong. I always went in with a positive attitude. I never expected things to go south.

"I'm staying in the driveway, Molly. Bud doesn't want me to leave, just in case things go sideways. This is a private house with no back up, so I'll be here if you need me."

"That's good. Mark, but didn't Bud screen this guy?"

"Yeah, but he said he didn't feel too good about it, being in this house rather than in a more public spot, like our regular hotels or bars." His frown and worried expression left me a little cold and slightly uneasy.

"Okay, I'll be vigilant and if I need you, I'll holler. Make sure you don't turn the radio on, so you can hear me." I got out of the car, went up the steps and knocked on the front door.

"Hi, you the dish from the bar?" the john asked as he opened the door for me.

"Yes, you spoke to my agent and I'm yours for the next hour." I was hesitant because I could smell booze on him and he looked a little scary to me. He had on a dirty singlet undershirt. His hair was oily and messed up. He was unshaven, stunk of cigarettes and stale sweat. He was about five foot ten and flabby. His pants hung loose on his hips, with no belt and they looked as though they had not been washed for some time. I doubted they had ever seen the bottom side of an iron. I was extremely uncomfortable and considered calling Mark to end the contract before it began. He yanked me by my arm and jerked me into the bedroom. He shut and locked the door with a key he put in his pocket.

"Wait just a minute! You'd better unlock that door or I'm out of here. My driver is right outside and will hear me yell if you refuse," I told him shakily.

"Uh, okay. I didn't mean to scare you. I thought you'd feel more comfortable knowing we wouldn't be disturbed." He unlocked the door.

"Thanks." I was somewhat relieved. "We'd better get on with this. You only have about fifty minutes left, so what's your pleasure?"

He told me and it was way beyond anything I was willing to do.

"Hold on! Didn't my agent tell you what my boundaries are and that I refuse to go outside those limits?" I shoved him away and glared at him.

"Oh yeah, he told me something like that but, hey, you're a hooker and I paid good money to have you do what I tell you." He shoved me onto the bed.

I struggled against him and opened my mouth to scream, but he put his dirty hand over my face. He heaved me under him, covering my face with his chest. I tried to squirm out from under him but he was too heavy. His hands were everywhere. He pawed my whole body and then he flipped me over onto my stomach. He jerked my hands behind my back. He shoved my face into the bed so I couldn't scream. I was frantic and I was sure I was going to suffocate. He tied my hands behind my back with a piece of rope he had on a small table beside the bed. I was completely at his mercy. He turned me over and sat beside me on the bed. He held my head down with his hand pressed against my forehead.

"Now, are we going to do this right, or are you going to keep giving me a hard time? I can rape you like this, or you can do as I ask and no one will be hurt. What's it going to be? You've wasted another ten minutes of my time, and I'm getting pissed off. I'm going to let your head go, but if you so much as make a sound, I'll punch your teeth down your throat. Got it?"

I nodded. Tears erupted down my cheeks.

"Aw, aint that sweet! A whore who cries because she can't have her own way! I'm gonna untie you and then we're going to get down to business, right?"

"Yes, I'll do whatever you want," I whimpered.

He untied one of my arms and tugged me further onto the bed. He reached and pulled another piece of rope that was attached to the brass headboard. I squirmed and tried to get away. He slapped my face and threw himself over top of me. His face was not two inches from mine.

"Lie still or no one will recognize you when I get finished with your face." His breath was foul and I fought against the nausea that enveloped me.

Once again I nodded and let him tie my hands to the posts above me. He did the same to my feet, splaying my legs. He removed my skirt, ripped off my nylons and garter belt. He stripped the rest of my clothes off, tearing my bra and panties. He drooled and slobbered all over me and did all that he wanted. He was crazy looking. I just lay there and let him brutalize my body. I was terrified he would kill me if I made him any angrier. He slumped over me when he was done and leaked his saliva on the top of my chest. He told me that I had given him a good time. He said he knew I enjoyed it too. His voice was gravelly and his words sounded guttural. He blathered on about how good he was and that no one will ever satisfy me like that again and that he hoped he hadn't raised the bar too high for others.

"Answer me!" He gushed spittle in my face and snatched a fistful of my hair yanking my head back.

"Yes, you are a great lover, I enjoyed it all," I sniveled.

He undid my bonds and let me get dressed. I wobbled out to car and Mark. I was scarcely able to walk on my shaking legs.

"Let's get out of here, Mark Don't ask any questions. Just move and don't stop until we're back at the hotel."

"What happened? Are you okay Molly? Jeez! Tell me what happened? Do you want me to go in and teach that jerk a lesson he won't soon forget?" Mark twisted around from the front seat of the car and the furious expression on his face spoke volumes.

"I want you to shut up and get us out of here!" I screamed. I was scared he was going to do something stupid and get us all hauled into the cop shop.

"All right, but Bud's going to pissed off when he sees the welt on your face."

"He won't get a chance. I'll plaster make up over it. Just make damn certain we never do business with that pervert again, Mark, and you remember the address and his name and put it out there so no one else gets caught up with him, ever." I seethed with rage.

"Count on it," Mark replied.

"Wow, we have come full circle Michael we have walked the three miles around the bog."

"Yes, we covered a lot of ground not just with our feet but you have revealed a lot more of your past to me today Molly. I think we should call it a day. I'm glad we had no interruptions."

We walked back to his office and we shook hands and said our goodbyes. I yelled a thank you to him as I got into my car and drove off.

The first thing I noticed when I opened my front door was my answering machine flashing. It's strange how I always think of emergencies when I see the red light flashing. I hung up my jacket, put the kettle on for tea and played the messages back. One was from Tiea, one of the women who work the streets, she sounded very distressed and asked that I call her back as soon as I got her message.

I called and she answered on the second ring.

"What's up?" I asked after identifying myself.

"I need your help, Jaden messed with me last night because I wouldn't go on a date. I'm hurting real bad Molly."

I'm coming over, stay put. Where is Jackson?"

"He's here with me, I'm real scared, can you find a safe place for me and him?"

"We can talk about that when I get there. I'll be no more than 15 minutes."

I hung up the phone, turned off the kettle, locked the dogs in the kitchen, grabbed my car keys and left.

"She was a mess when I got there, her face was black and blue, she could barely open one eye and she showed me the deep bruising on her ribs and upper arms."

"Good grief! Did you call the police?" I asked, removing my coat.

Little Jackson ran over to me with his upraised arms. He was a very sweet little toddler, barely two years old. I pulled him into my arms, nestled a kiss on his head and let him curl into me. He had that sweet smell of a baby.

Tiea kept her place spotless and Jackson was always scrubbed clean. Her apartment was small and sparse; she had a mattress on the floor, a very small coffee table and a dresser. Jackson slept in one of the dresser drawers. He was a happy little guy and deeply loved.

"Tell me what happened?"

"Jaden assaulted me when I wouldn't go on a date he arranged. I have been on one with the guy before and he was brutal. I told Jaden but he wouldn't listen, all he was worried about was the money. I stood my ground and refused and he beat me to hell and back. He's threatened to beat Jackson up if I don't do as he says." She started to cry.

"Where is your family? Is there anyone I can contact for you who can provide you with a safe place to stay?" I rocked Jackson as I questioned his mom.

"Not here, my family including Jackson's dad live in Alberta and I don't have the money to get us there. What am I going to do?" She sounded scared and desperate.

"I don't have any safe houses Tiea, but maybe we can raise enough money through my church to send you both back home."

"Do you really think so?" she asked.

"Yes, I am sure we can raise enough, I'll make some calls now." I pulled my cell phone out of my purse, set the little guy down, and made some calls and waited for a call back to see if we could raise the money.

"I don't understand how guys can be so brutal and expect return dates do you Molly?"

"No but those kind of animals have been around right from the get go. I remember some pretty bad guys when I was forced to do things I never agreed to when we entered into the agreement." I chuckled to myself.

"Really, what did you do?"

"Well, I wasn't laughing at the time, I was scared speechless and one time I really thought the guy was going to shoot me." I shuddered thinking about it.

"Gawd, what happened Molly?"

We settled back waiting for the response to my request for funds to pay their flights to Alberta and I started to tell her about some of my dates.

My memories were vivid, the words and places played back in my head as I remembered.

"Molly, you've got a date in half an hour, are you ready?" Bud reminded me over the telephone.

"Yes, Mark is outside ready to take me to the hotel. What do you know about this guy? I have had some bad dates over the past couple of months and I'm still a little gun-shy." Little did I know how those words would come back to haunt me, sooner rather than later.

"He checks out pretty good. He looks clean and speaks well, so I think it should be an easy one for you. Same deal—if things get out of hand call me."

"Yeah, we know how easy that is to do and I know things get out of hand in a heartbeat." I quipped sarcastically. I have to figure my own way out and it usually means hard stuff for me. I don't want any trouble. Know what I mean, Bud? I've had it with rubes that think they can do anything to and with me. The bitch of it is they know they can get away with it because I can't go to the cops."

"Relax, Molly! It's been quite a while since you had trouble. This guy looks good."

"Quite a while works out to one month, in my time zone," I snapped. "I have to go, Bud. I'll call you when I'm done and maybe you and I can catch some dinner later. I haven't been out with you for too long. How about it?"

"Sounds okay. I'll call you." He smiled and walked away.

"Yeah, when hell freezes over! C'mon, Mark, we have to go or I'm going to be late." "Call me when you're finished, Molly. You have two hours on the clock. I'll return in an hour and a half and wait in the parking spot out front."

"Right, Mark. Come on up if I'm more than ten minutes after my time. We're in room 478, right?" I stepped out of the car, straightened my skirt, moistened my fingers and fluffed my hair.

I liked this inn. It was in a lovely spot on the waterfront. It was a long, rambling building. The siding was blue and white and it seemed to shimmer in the sunlight. The grounds were immaculate. It reminded me of a southern mansion in the years before the Civil War. In the evening, it was backlit with bright spotlights that enhanced its elegance.

"That's right, Molly. I'll catch up with you later." He waved as he drove away.

I felt jittery about this date, I didn't know why. Maybe it was because I felt vulnerable being here alone. I tried to pacify myself. I knew that meeting these guys was always a little unnerving. I tamped down my fears and knocked on the door of Room 478.

"Hi! I'm Molly from the agency. Are you Jordan?"

"Yes, come on in." He stepped back and opened the door for me.

"Wow! Nice digs you have here." I slipped off my coat and handed it to him.

I found the lovely sage color of the walls and the charming pictures of soft floras enchanting. The pink and green bedcover blended beautifully with the decor. The chairs were a dusty-rose and the lamps were white with color-coordinated beads that decorated the shades.

My date looked harmless and clean cut. He was blond with green eyes and a mop of hair that curled over his shirt collar. He spoke with a drawl and I wondered if he was from the southern states or Europe. He was really quite cute and I noticed his fingernails were clean and short. He had on gray flannel strides and a long white jacket. He seemed no older than nineteen or twenty. I wondered why he needed to hire the likes of me to get a date?

"Sit down, take off your shoes and anything else you want. Make yourself comfortable while I fix a little drink for us." He hung up my coat and walked over to a table that had bottles and glasses on it.

"Just soda water for me, thanks. I don't like to imbibe before a job. Maybe after our session I'll join you but you go ahead while I slip into the bathroom and get ready."

"Oh sure, okay. You go ahead." He stumbled over his words.

It seemed obvious to me that he had not had a lot of experience with this kind of date. I smiled to myself and shut the bathroom door. I'm going to try and make this special for this young man, I thought to myself.

"Jeez! You look good enough to eat," he said when I came out of the bathroom. His eyes roved over every part of my skimpy revealing underwear.

I had on a pink beaded bra, a pink sheer g-string, a white garter belt with black net stockings and high heels.

"Stefan! Come on out and see the package I got for us!" He called to someone in the other room.

"Oh, ddddon't you jjjust take my bbbwwbreath away!" Stefan stuttered when he came in.

"Uh, wait a minute, guys! The contract is for one person only. What's going on here?" I asked nervously, backing up toward the safety of the bathroom.

"Nuthin' babe. You just come right over here and sit on the bed with us and we'll all get to know each other real well," Jordan said, taking my hand and leading me to the bed.

"No way! This isn't the deal. I'm going to get dressed and leave. You guys can make a new arrangement with my agent. You've got the number." I pulled away from Jordan and started for the bathroom to get my street clothes.

"Not so fast, sugar. Stefan, you know what to do. Do it now!"

Stefan went into the other bedroom and Jordan jerked me around the waist and yanked me into his arms. I kicked and squirmed and then I slumped in Jordan's arms and stared at Stefan horrified. Duncan's face flashed across my eyes.

"Who the hell are you guys?" I choked out. My mouth was dry as parchment and I gaped at the huge gun Stefan was holding. My brain had freeze-dried, caught in memories of Moose Jaw. I wanted Duncan here now! He would know what to do. I was frozen in time. I could hear Duncan's words the last time I was with him. I finally found my voice and peeped.

"Oh gawd, Oh gawd! Get that gun away from me, please! Please, please take it away!"

"Molly, get down on your knees," Jordan ordered.

"On your damn knees! Now!"

I jerked at his staccato voice and knelt on very shaky knees. I silently prayed for help.

"What're you going to do? I'll do anything you want. Ppplease ddon't hurt me!" I stuttered. I was terrified he was going to shoot me.

Jordan took the gun from Stefan and placed the barrel of the gun against my forehead. He was standing not two feet away.

"No one's going to get hurt. You just need to agree to do us both. We paid for two hours and I want my two hours. You're going to spend a half hour with Stefan, half an hour with me and one with both of us. You understand, Molly? Now listen up. Stefan has problems talking, so be gentle with him and he'll be gentle with you, but if you get impatient, he may not be so gentle. He's a little volatile but I can control him pretty good. Do as I say and everyone goes away happy. Got all that, Molly?" Jordan rattled off his instructions, machine gun rapid. He never moved the gun off my forehead. He stood absolutely still.

"I've got it. Whatever you want, just please don't hurt me, okay?" I recoiled in fear and my tongue was heavy in my arid mouth. I was afraid I was going to pitch face forward and end up with a bullet in my head. I couldn't think of what to do. I was like a doe, caught in headlights, unable to move. I was sweating profusely and shaking like a leaf in a windstorm.

He shoved me toward Stefan.

It was a reality check for me. My mind was racing with gut-wrenching fear. I was panicked, but I realized I was on my own and whatever chance I had of getting out of there alive was up to me. I hadn't been physically incapacitated. I convinced myself I could do what they wanted. The only important thought for me was to get out in one piece, so I followed their instructions. I was humiliated and disgusted with both of them and their demands.

But they stayed true to their word and no one got hurt. Those two hours seemed like an eternity, but when they were finally over, I was ushered out the door to safety. I looked to the driveway and I nearly fainted with relief when I saw Mark sitting in the car waiting for me. I thought I was going to puke before I reached the car. I was close to being hysterical. I almost fell against the door of the car. My hands were so slippery with sweat; I could scarcely grip the handle to open the door.

"Is everything okay? Was there a problem?" Mark asked as I fell into the car.

I started to cry hysterically, babbling like a toddler who had just learned to talk. I was not much more coherent than that.

"Jeez, Molly, slow down, breathe, you're okay, your safe. What the hell happened in there?"

I took a couple of deep breaths, stopped bawling and told him everything that had happened. Mark called Bud and we drove to a meeting with him and couple of other guys.

"Jeez Molly what happened?" Bud was in a state himself, pacing back and forth.

I told him the gory details leaving nothing out. I was still gasping for air and choking on my own fear.

"My gawd you could've been killed. I shoulda' known when he gave me his name as John Smith, that shoulda' bin my first clue!" he scraped his fingers through his hair and kept pacing. Bud always fell back to his street language when he was upset. He slurred his words together.

"Well they aint gonna get away with this crapola, no way. We gotta teach them a lesson they won't forget. You guys in? Not you Molly, we'll put you in a taxi and you get on home, get Jill to help you clean up and have a coupl'a drinks and just relax."

I left in a taxi and waited with Jill to find out what happened with their confrontation with friendly Jordan and Stefan.

Bud, Mark and three other guys went back to the hotel to deal with those apes but they had checked out. They had checked in under the names of Smith and Jones. Bud had a friend in the police force and gave a description to him, but we never tracked them down nor did we ever hear from them again.

"Wow, you must have been terrified!" Tiea whispered. Jackson had fallen asleep on her lap. She shifted him onto the mattress and we both adjusted our positions to be more comfortable. All three of us sat on it and Tiea and I leaned against the wall for support.

"Yeah, some times it was tough to do what I did, but as you can see I survived. I met some really nice people too Tiea and I am grateful that Jesus kept me safe and brought some kind and loving souls into my life during that time."

I began again to tell her of some of the better times I remembered.

"Over the years I became great friends with Charlie. He was in fact my best friend and confidante through most of my time in the trade. He was gay and the sweetest man I have ever known. We met in a bar one night, just after I had returned from a date.

"Hi, Molly," Jake the bartender greeted me as I sat down at the bar.

"The usual soda water, Molly?"

"Yes, that sounds good." I smiled; flattered he remembered my drink.

"What a coincidence! Next to whiskey, that's my favorite drink too. Hi! Molly. My name's Charlie. I've seen you in here from time to time and I have wanted to meet you, but you don't hang around long enough for me to get up the courage to do that. It looks like tonight is my lucky night. Lo and behold, who takes the stool next to mine? The one and only you!"

I was hesitant to carry on a conversation with him at first. I didn't know what his game was.

"You need to talk to my agent if you want to set up some time with me," I smiled and sipped my drink.

"No, no! You've got me all wrong. I'm not into that stuff. I just like what I have seen when you come in and I really would like to get to know you. I promise I'm not some weirdo and I'm not trying to skirt around your agent to get a free deal. How about it? Are you willing to take a chance? Friends only! Nothing more, I promise."

He was so serious. I laughed and held out my hand.

"Hi Charlie! It is nice to meet you. I have seen you in here before. I wish I had known you wanted to meet me, I would have made it easy for you," I said, still laughing.

Charlie was openly gay and had that relaxed attitude that left no doubt he was comfortable with who he was. He was rail thin with dark curly hair. He looked older than his thirty years and I wondered if it was because he was obviously a sun-worshipper. He was deeply tanned with piercing blue eyes and he always sported a mischievous quirky smile. He was tall, over six feet and had large hands that were warm and enveloped mine completely. I discovered that he had an amazing capacity to love and was intensely loyal. Conversely, he was not a forgiving adversary.

We became fast friends and shared numerous experiences. One day, he came over to my place to share a cup of coffee.

"How would you like to take a little trip with me, Molly?"

"I can't say until I know where this trip will take me." I looked at him over the top of my cup and took a swallow.

"Have you ever heard of a place called Fire Island?" he asked and poured himself a cup of coffee.

"No, never have, where is it?" I set my cup down.

"It's in Southern Suffolk County in New York." He sat down across from my small table.

"New York? What's so great about a vacation in New York? Why not Hawaii, the Caribbean or some other tropical place? Where there's warm sun, white sandy beaches and bright blue skies. That's what I call paradise!" I chuckled.

"You'll love it, I guarantee. Please come with me. We'll only be gone four days; it will do you good to get away." He had a puppy dog look full of hope, I couldn't say no.

"Okay, why not? It might be fun to spend some time in the most vibrant city in North America. When do you want to go?" I asked.

"How about in two weeks. Can you arrange that?" he seemed excited and anxiously awaited my response.

"Sure, I'll let Bud know tonight. I could use a break!" I studied the little boy anticipation he displayed at that moment.

We made all the arrangements. I was surprised and a little disappointed that Bud didn't seem to be distressed about my impending absence. I put that worry out of my head and concentrated on the journey before us.

"Jeepers, Charlie, I don't remember saying I wanted to spend the better part of a day just getting to our destination. Look at this dreary weather and now we have to travel by water taxi to get to Fire Island." I stared out of the side of the water taxi at the lousy weather.

"Relax, Molly. Another couple of hours and we'll be partying and having lots of fun."

"I'm way too tired to do anything but sleep tonight, Charlie. You can go party if you want, but I'm hitting the hay as soon as we get to our hotel. Look at all that rain! How the hell are we supposed to be in a party mood?" I was full of apprehension.

"Listen, sourpuss, there is one little detail I haven't explained," he said and tousled my hair.

"What's that?" I was uneasy with his apologetic look.

"I won't be at the same hotel as you." He moved closer and held me tightly and I felt his body tense, waiting for my reaction.

"Like hell you won't! If you think you're dumping me in some hotel by myself, think again my friend! It ain't gonna happen." I glared at him.

"Okay, okay! I thought you might not appreciate being on your own." He seemed hesitant.

"I have to explain a couple of things to you. I want to stay in an area of the island that is a primarily gay community with lots of parties. It's a great place to meet others who think the same way. It's a gorgeous place called The Maples. I thought you would prefer a place like Miracle Beach, which is a predominantly heterosexual spot. Again, lots of parties and a great place to meet and greet."

"Not on your life! I'll stay in the same place as you, but in a separate room. That way, if you want to entertain privately you can do so. I just want to lay back and enjoy some quiet time without guests. I may join in on a couple of parties. There's no way I'm spending time on this island alone. You had better get me a room in your hotel."

"As a matter of fact, I booked a room for you in both locations in case you wanted to be with me." He was laughing and hugged me to his side.

"Thanks, Charlie," I snorted.

We had mountains of fun in the three days we were on the island. It was a wonderful place to hide away, although it was hopping and crawling with people because it was the Labor Day weekend. Charlie had a remarkable kindness about him and a shocking sense of humor. We laughed until our sides hurt. We swapped some hilarious stories about our escapades and so did many of the others we met while we were there. We did go back another time during the off-season and had just as much fun.

Unfortunately, this was a time before any of us knew about HIV and Charlie contracted the virus. He never knew when or from whom. None of us was very knowledgeable about the disease and the medical profession didn't clue in that quickly. Charlie was one of the casualties of that ignorance. He spent most of his last years caring for friends as they slowly died. He knitted warm socks and scarves for them in exquisite, vibrant colors. His kind and loving nature were always evident, even in his most painful times. I have never known and loved anyone the way I loved him. Ours was a unique and endearing relationship. We enjoyed the most intimate, sad and happy times together. But never once did we cross the line and become sexually involved. We were both comfortable in our skins. He was one of the few courageous souls, willing to come out of the closet and bare his heart to the world around him. I will always cherish the memories we shared and the love I carry in my heart. He was truly a dear friend and comrade."

Tiea and I were both laughing at my recollections. It was good to see her forgetting her troubles, even if it was temporary.

"And then there was Mac, one very sick dude. Bud had met and arranged a date with him for me. He assured me he was a safe trick and that he had screened him very carefully.

Bud introduced Mac to me and explained the plans he had made.

"Molly, I want you to meet Mac. He's going to be your date for the night. I have booked you a room at that great hotel overlooking the harbor. It is on the front side of the hotel with a view of the ocean and city. I'm sure you'll both have a charming evening."

"Hi, Mac! It's a pleasure to meet you," I said extending my hand in friendship.

"Hi, Molly! The pleasure is all mine. I am looking forward to a night that I hope is going to be full of surprises."

"Let's hope they are all good," I smiled.

"I'll leave you two, then, and I will see you in the morning, Molly. Same instructions apply, should you need me before that." Bud picked up the tab and left.

"Should we go and have a look at our room first, Molly? Then we can go for a bite to eat and look around the harbor before turning in," Mac suggested.

"Sure, let's do that. Knowing Bud, I am sure you will be pleased with the room."

We checked out the room, dropped our overnight bags, went down to the restaurant and made a reservation for dinner in three hours. We spent our time wandering along the harbor front and explored that part of the city. It was a beautiful spot; the harbor had a lit walkway all around with small restaurants lining the way. Motorboats and sailboats of all sizes were moored. Their masters sat on the decks, enjoying the warm breeze, as evening descended. There were numerous floral baskets hanging from the light standards. The pavement was lit with small, subdued light fixtures that gave off a ghostly radiance. Busters, cartoonists, portrait painters and musicians offered their talents for a fee to all who strolled along the causeway. Horse drawn buggies and Kabooki Kabs, along with limousines took tourists and residents to places of interest. The night drew down on us. We decided to go to our room after walking along the causeway for an hour after dinner.

That stunning night soon turned into another one of those weird times.

Mac had a cleanliness fetish and he insisted on scrubbing himself after each sexual encounter. He experienced major difficulty in attaining and maintaining an erection. He blamed his lack of sexual satisfaction because he said he was dirty. As a result, he spent most of the night in the bathroom washing his hands and other parts of his body. He became arrogant afterwards and he would come out of the bathroom, bragging and chanting ridiculous statements.

"I am the world's greatest lover," he chanted and shoved me off the bed onto the floor.

"You are so lucky to have me spend this time with you. Stay down there for awhile, so I can get some sleep. You are nothing but a she-devil, who deserves to rot in the depths of hell. How could you lie to me about who you were? You told me you were an innocent and I believed you. I now see that you are nothing but a harlot going around and destroying the virtues of men of my standing. It is your fault our lovemaking has been this disappointing. I can't keep myself from becoming soiled, every time you touch me." He railed on and on all the time, stopping only to scrub his hands.

"Here we go again," I moaned to myself, *"another momma's boy. He must have been protected and tied to her apron strings and he is still searching for nonsensical excuses for his own shortcomings."* I chuckled to myself at the pun. *He didn't appear able to accept any responsibility for his failures. He had probably always found someone else to blame when things hadn't gone his way.*

"Spare me having to listen to this drivel," I reflected silently.

I curled in a ball in the farthest corner of the room. He screamed at me to come into his bed several times in the night. His rage and incessant chanting nearly drove me insane and I was terrified he was going to do something horrible to me. In his mind his failures were mine and he never acknowledged that he was the one to enter into a contract with me, not the other way around. I wasn't going to bring that little fact to his attention. I just wanted the night to end, so I could get out of there.

I was grateful when the morning finally dawned. We both showered and dressed and our conversation was non-existent. He had little to say to me, he told me, and would appreciate it if I kept quiet. I was elated to see him get on the ferry to the mainland.

"Well, how'd it go?" Bud asked when I called him from home to make a report.

"Don't ask! Please don't hook me up with him again." I went to explain some of Mac's bizarre behavior.

"Wow, I'm really surprised. He seemed like a very nice man," Bud answered.

"I was surprised, too. We had a great time exploring the city, having dinner and walking around the inner harbor. I thoroughly enjoyed his company until we started on the sexual stuff. After that, things went downhill fast. He was really weird. At times, I was scared and other times I thought I had become invisible to him. He seemed to be in his own little world, chanting and washing, but you know, Bud, he is completely convinced that he is truly the world's greatest lover. Just chalk it up to another one of those very interesting dates. Please make certain the word gets out and get him blacklisted."

"What a jerk!" Tiea said.

"You've got that right. But there were other good times.

Martine was one of my regular dates who was always good to me. It wasn't unusual for the two of us to travel to some very interesting and wonderful cities.

"Hi, Molly. How about coming with me to Quebec City, to our little hide-away?" Martine asked in his heavy French accent when I answered his phone call.

"That sounds wonderful. Have you cleared it with Bud and how long do you want to be away?" I was excited thinking about spending time with him.

"I think we should stay for a week. It has been a little while since I saw you last, mais oui ma douce?"

"That works for me, Martine. Have Bud call and confirm when it's all set up."

Martine and I spent a magical week in Quebec. He owned a small walk up there. The rooms were enchanting, none of them was large but it was a very comfortable apartment. The walls were a neutral gray and the three throw cushions were scarlet. The throw over the red sofa was marine blue. The kitchenette was pale blue with a small fridge and stove. The old style wooden table had beautiful lathe-turned legs and claw feet and the table-cloths were checkered. Some were blue and white, some yellow and white, some red and white and some red and blue. We changed it each day to suit our mood. The dishes were a golden yellow and the cutlery was old style silver. We always drank our morning coffee from oversized bright, cobalt cups that sat on huge saucers. They matched the blue of the cups but had a big red poppy with floppy petals painted against the colorful background. It was a fantastic way to start each day. It was a splendid week, with no stress or time constraints. He was my favorite client and I always loved the times we shared. With him, everything was first class.

This was one of the very few positive sides of the trade.

I enjoyed a rather strange friendship with Martine. In our mysterious way, we were very close, but each of us knew the friendship could go no further than that of a professional relationship and it remained confined to the sex trade.

My cell phone rang and I answered it, happy to get off the subject of my escapades.

"Hi Jan, I hope you have good news for me."

"I do Molly, we have agreed to cover the cost of Tiea's trip back to Alberta. She has to agree to stay there for at least a year to ensure the safety of her and her little boy. Will she agree to that?"

"I'll call you back in five, Jan. Thank you, thank you for helping."

I told Tiea what she would have to agree to do if she accepted our help and she readily agreed to do whatever we wanted."

I put her and Jackson on the plane that night and the next time I saw them Jackson was eight years old and still handsome.

I wondered at the wisdom of telling her so much about my own background but never regretted it. In fact, it was nice to be able to share some of those times and at the same time let her know she was not alone.

One day morphed into another and another. I struggled to keep my monsters at bay.

I continued to garner up many memories. Some were superb, others mediocre and still others nightmares best forgotten. The sad part of it was that they must remain my secrets, not to be shared with family and friends. The very fact that prostitution is loathed by most members of our society, dictates the dark corners kept hidden from everyone closest to me. I am certain that Carin would have serious problems connecting that lifestyle to me, her mother. It was a time best tucked away in my heart and mind."

Today I worked in my little garden of plants set out along the front path of my home in various tubs, some wooden, some pottery and some plastic in a variety of shapes and sizes. I love the pansies and other spring flowers I keep in them. Tired and a little sore from the bending and trowling I come inside and make myself a cup of tea and sit in the quiet of my home.

I try not to dwell on my youth and all that I was involved particularly now that I am in my seventies. I cringe to think of some of the things I did during those young and middle years. I know how foolish I was to give up my dream of becoming a surgeon. I do welcome today and all that it has to offer, although I still fear that my sanity is indeed threatened. The happy news is Carin's willingness to consider that it is only a temporary condition. I am confident that while I work with Michael through the unanswered questions that still plague me, it will all be resolved in the near future. I mulled over this and all that had transpired today.

I finished my tea and cleaned up and went out to some shopping. The day was fresh, sunny with skies as blue as a cornflower.

It was close to suppertime when I walked into my house. The dogs as usual greeted me as if I had abandoned them. They jumped and whined and whirled around and around desperately licking every inch of my exposed skin. Their tails thumped against the chairs, the walls, my legs and anything else with which they came in contact.

"You're such a pair of goofs." I laughingly scolded them as I waited for them to settle down. I put them out to do their business and retrieved their leashes and we went for a short walk.

I was amazed of the transformation that had happened to me when I was finally able to walk away from the world I had created for myself.

Life sure has twists and turns in the road we walk along.

It still puzzles me that I became a Christian in the midst of this lifestyle. I was in my early fifties by then. I consider it a miracle and I will always be grateful that He rescued me. Almost immediately I had the strongest calling to start a ministry to sex trade workers. It had been many years since I had worked the trade and I was pretty nervous the first night I went down to where the women worked on the streets. There is always a main area where they make a claim to a specific corner and keep that spot every time they come out to work. It is called the "stroll." I don't think the same structure exists as when I was immersed in it. Although there are still some women that belong to pimps and these pimps refer to their group of women as a "stable." It was pretty easy for me to locate the stroll in Victoria in the early days as it was in a very prominent downtown location inundated with tourists and locals.

I remember the first night I went out and the first woman I approached. I was certain she would tell me to get lost. She actually was very receptive. She told me she was working to pay for her college courses and to care for her little two-year-old daughter. The father of her baby lived in Vancouver and rarely provided money to help with her expenses. I told her we prayed for her and that I was available anytime she wanted to talk or if she needed food for herself or her little girl to please call me day or night. I gave her my first little gift of a few candies and a small spray bottle of body mist. She was very receptive and we hugged one another and from that point on my ministry grew to what it is today.

The location of the stroll has changed as the trade has evolved. Many of the women work inside now. The police have designated the former street corners where they worked as a 'red zone' so if they are caught there they are arrested. The stroll areas are mostly on dark streets out of the main traffic areas. Many of the women are addicted to drugs or alcohol and work mainly to support their addictions. There are few children who remain with their mothers because of the addictions. These women are tragically alone and exist in a dark and foreboding lifestyle with little hope of getting out of it. My prayer for each of them is that they will come to know of the love of Jesus. I love each one I have come to know. Each has a story. Most have been raised in a brutal and loveless home. Some have come from wonderful families and simply chose the wrong path.

I go down to the stroll every week and give out my little gift bags and hugs; I receive bountiful love and hugs in return.

I smiled to myself as I felt a deep gratitude in my heart for the gift of this ministry and my own salvation.

When we got back and had our suppers, the dogs settled for the night and I picked up my book to read I decided I needed a change of scenery. I made up my mind to do something different for the next week. I read my book for a couple of hours, took a long hot shower and climbed into my bed. I enjoyed a great sleep and felt rejuvenated and good to go. I phoned Carin to let her know I was going to be out of town for the rest of the week and if she needed to talk with me she could reach me on my cell phone.

I packed a small suitcase with clean underwear, a couple of t-shirts, an extra pair of jeans, clean sox, toiletries and everything else I would need for myself and my dogs for the next six days. I leashed my dogs, put them in the back of my car and we headed up the island. We didn't stop until we arrived in Comox, a wonderful spot just outside of Courtenay. I was able to rent a motel room that accepted animals and we had a delightful time roaming the trails and walking on the beach. I shopped and found some unique crafts I could use for hostess gifts, birthday treasures for my close friends and some I bought for no particular reason other than I enjoyed how they made me feel.

We came back full of excitement and at peace with the world. I loved to do stuff like this on the spur of the moment. I am thrilled to be free enough to be able to do so whenever I get strong urges to go off on my own. I knew I was more stressed than I was willing to admit to anyone and I needed to get away and just vegetate. I always have my dogs and I enjoy their company almost as much as humans, actually sometimes I enjoy their company more.

I unpacked my car, put the dogs in the house and went to shop for some groceries. I wasn't much for cooking for myself anymore but recognized I needed to have some food in the house. I was a great one for grabbing lunch and sometimes dinner from fast food outlets. Other times I would fill up on healthy stuff like fruits and veggies.

I fell into bed that night after the long drive home and subsequent chores. The next day was another session with Michael.

Chapter 57

I breezed into Michael's waiting room to keep my next appointment.

"Hi Beth! I'm a little early. I had an errand to run and I thought it would be just as easy to come now. I'll read my book while I wait."

"No problem, Molly. Michael isn't in yet but I expect him momentarily. Would you like some coffee, tea, water or anything?"

"No thanks, Beth. I'm all coffeed out."

When Michael arrived, he looked surprised to see me already there.

"Good morning, Beth. Oh! Hi, Molly. I wasn't expecting to see you here yet. Am I late or are you early?"

"I'm early, Michael."

"Good. I hope you don't mind waiting a few minutes while I get organized and answer any urgent calls."

"Not at all. I expected to have to wait until my appointment time."

I opened my book, "Business by the Book" by Sophfronia Scott and stared blankly at the pages. I knew what was ahead and I waited nervously expecting once again to get grilled about my memories.

"Come on in, Molly. Sorry to keep you waiting. I didn't think my call would take so long."

"No problem, Michael."

I took my usual chair and Michael gathered his paper and pen and sat down.

"So, Molly, how are things going? What kind of a week have you had?"

"I went up island for the week and had a wonderful time. I have had a couple of flashbacks, but nothing I can't handle and fortunately, they happened when I was alone so no one else had to know." I tried to get more comfortable in my chair.

"By 'no one else' do you mean Carin? I am sorry things are still not going well with you both."

"You know, Michael, I think things are better than they were. Carin has backed off and she seems willing to admit this is a temporary problem. I truly believe she is convinced we are making good progress. It doesn't stop me from worrying about my future but I am more hopeful than I was. I guess that's the way it will have to be for now. Life goes on, but I do miss not being able to chat with her about things these days. It seems we are both still too tense and up tight to talk about anything that will tip the precarious balance we have achieved."

"Tell me about her young years. Where you close? Where is her father? How did you meet him? Were you still in the Trade? If not, what was it that pulled you out of that lifestyle? We have never talked about that time of your life, Molly. What happened to end the marriage? I want to talk about the room, too, Molly. We have put it off too many times. You need to face up to some of this. You need to quit trying to minimize the effect it had on you."

"Wow, slow down! Why all of a sudden are you interested in my life with her father? I fail to see the connection to my flashbacks!" I was taken aback by the direction he was now trying to take me.

"You know what, Michael, I don't think I want to talk with you today. Maybe when you give some more thought to the things I think are important instead of satisfying your undying curiosity about things that I believe are best left alone, we will do this again. I will come back next week, after you have had some time to think about what you want from me. I need to know that what I think has some value. I hope to get to the bottom of my unreasonable reactions to my daughter and to situations that have resulted in some humiliating experiences for her. Think about all of this, Michael. In the meantime, I will leave you to your thoughts."

I stood up, put on my jacket, turned and left him sitting there. I walked out of his office with not so much as a by your leave to Beth.

I heard her make a remark to Michael and heard his response as I closed the outside door.

"Well, I see that went well again today!" Beth said to Michael when he stepped into the reception room.

"You might say that. I'm going out for a short walk. I'll be back in time for my next appointment." He shut the door a little harder than he intended.

PART 3

Liminal *(lim'l'nal [limmin'l]* belonging to the point of conscious awareness below which something cannot be experienced or felt

I stomped to my car slamming the door as I got in. I could see Michael in my rear view mirror as I turned on the ignition and burned rubber, sending gravel spewing from my tires. I was furious and frustrated by my brief encounter with him. I had hoped my time away would slow down the irrational reaction I had to many topics that I wanted left buried. I drove home and stormed into the house, put the leashes on the dogs and literally dragged them out the door.

The day was partially sunny and well suited for a long walk to settle my nerves and give me space to think clearly.

Chapter 58

It had been a long time since I thought about Caleb, Carin's dad. My heart warmed as I remembered.
My dad had died by this time and Jill and I were still sharing living arrangements. We were the best of friends.

I let my heart open up to the memory of Chick, Carin's father and the love of my life. I remembered his open sweet nature so well and the love we shared. I whispered words, lost to the wind. I wanted to be able to walk with that memory without the ache that was always there when I thought of Chick. That was his nickname. The beauty of that time, so long ago, became as vivid as the path on which I was treading. I recalled our first encounter and still my heart skipped a beat. My own footsteps became lighter and my heart warmed as I recalled that night.

Jill and I were taking a night off and decided to spend some time alone together.
"Where do you want to go after this?" Jill asked when we finished our dinner.
"I haven't given it much thought. Let's go down to our favorite pub and have a couple of beers," I suggested.
"That sounds like fun. I'll get the check for dinner and you can pick up the tab in the pub." Jill put some money down for the waitress.

It only took twenty minutes to get to our pub and, as luck would have it, there were tables available. There were times when there was no way we could expect to walk in and get a table. I remembered how happy we were.

"It sure is nice to relax and just shoot the breeze," I sighed, glancing over to the door. I enjoyed watching people come and go. Whoa! I took a deep breath and watched one of two guys come in and walk up to the bar. They each took a stool that was facing our table, across the small space between us. He was shockingly handsome. His eyes were the color of almonds with a hint of gold. They were protected by long dark feather like lashes. His face had a slight harshness about it. I wondered if he had always had that look. It was as if someone had chiseled any softness from it. His hair was brown with golden blond highlights when the light caught it. He had a hint of a smile where his mouth curled up at one corner. He was a lanky, six feet plus. He appeared self-assured by the way he held himself.

I was more than curious and I wondered at the way I felt drawn to him. Contrary to the requirements of my occupation, I was very shy around men outside of my work environment. I feared rejection more than anything and, as a result, I had never encouraged nor entered into any long term intense personal relationships. Granted Bud and I had a 'thing,' but it was pretty one sided and couldn't be considered a 'relationship.' I certainly had never given any thought to marriage and all the trappings that go with it.

"Pull your eyes back in your head, Molly! You are staring at that guy at the bar. I swear you are devouring him right here, just with your looks. Is he a trick? Do you know him? Are you afraid he will recognize you? C'mon girl, snap out of it! Talk to me!"

Jill snapped her fingers in front of my nose and I was jolted out of my reverie.

"Wow, take a long look at him would you, Jill, is that not a hunk or what? Man! I could really get up close and personal with him," I drooled.

"Yeah, well, the music is on and the dance floor may be small, but there is nothing to say you can't go over there and ask him to dance." She nudged me.

"Are you kidding me? I can't ask him to dance. What if he says no? That would be the most embarrassing moment of my life!"

"Oh, come on, Molly. So what if he says no? I bet you a beer he will take you up on your offer. He hasn't taken his eyes off of you, except to take a drink and talk to his friend. Tell you what! I'll go with you and I will ask his friend for a dance. He's not so hard to look at, either. C'mon, let's do it." Jill grabbed my hand and pulled me over to the bar.

"Hi guys! Do you want to dance?" She directed her question to the hunk's friend.

"Sure!" They spoke in unison.

"Great!" Jill and I reacted to their enthusiasm.

The hunk took my hand and led me to the dance floor. The song, "Too Young" by Nat King Cole was playing. I melted into his arms; my legs felt like jelly.

"I'm Caleb, but my friends call me Chick. What do you answer to?" he asked and leaned his head closer. Up close, those eyes were like bottomless pools and the depth of kindness I saw in them mesmerized me.

He tried again to get my name.

"Hello! Is anyone present in there?"

"Um, oh! I'm sorry! I was caught up listening to the song," I stuttered.

"My name is Molly."

"That's a cute name and it suits you," he responded.

"Jeez! That's the first time anyone has told me that," I answered. I was tongue-tied as usual and at a loss for words. I have zero skills when I try to converse with a guy outside of my comfort zone.

The song ended and we danced over to the jukebox and he put in his quarter and played "Sh-Boom " by The Chords. I was caught up in the moment. All I wanted to do was stay right here and dance all night. I put the next quarter in and played "The Great Pretender" by Johnny Mathis and "Blueberry Hill" by Fats Domino. We walked back to our table where Jill introduced her guy to me. They were having a beer together. He had moved Chick's drink over to our table.

"Molly, this is Rory, Rory this is Molly, my best friend."

"Hi, Molly."

"Hi, Rory."

I introduced Jill and Chick.

"I have to go to work early in the morning, but do you feel comfortable giving me your phone number? I would like to call you sometime, Molly," Chick asked when he stood up from the table.

"Are you kidding me?" I whispered to Jill.

I was shocked that he wanted my phone number.

"Yeah, sure, please do call me. I would be happy to hear from you."

"Oh man! Have you got it bad or what Molly? I've never seen you so moon struck." Jill teased me as we were driving back to our place.

"I know. I sure hope he calls me," I simpered.

"He will, Molly, believe me, he is very interested. My guy was sweet too and a smooth dancer."

I started to sing, "Why do Fools Fall in Love." Soon Jill joined in and we sang the rest of the way home.

Chick and I were really into each other. Over the next few weeks, we spent our days together. I was close mouthed about what my current occupation was. I continued with most of my night life, although I had cut down substantially since the beginning of my relationship with Chick. We were very comfortable with one another. I found myself letting him in to my heart more and more. I had no intention of making him exclusive, because I knew too well that good things like this simply didn't last. Not for me at least and I was not willing to cut all the ties to my night job.

One of the most enjoyable activities we did was hang gliding. If anyone had told me I would be jumping off cliffs with a glider attached to my body, I would have laughed in his face. Well, here I was all alone on top of Mount Maxwell on Salt Spring Island, looking way down and thinking how nuts I was. My heart was beating a mile a minute and I was convinced I would probably die here. I stood and stared at the azure sky and wondered at the beauty of the earth. I questioned my sanity for one brief second and then leapt into nothingness. I soared and soared pushing my bar just far enough to keep me level. It was like heaven. The only sound I heard was the rustle of the fabric of the glider wings as the wind rushed over the top. Without a doubt, it was the most exhilarating thing I had ever done. In retrospect, I wondered if it was a death wish that drove me to challenge life and absorb and relish the wonderful adrenalin rush fed by stark fear.

After a lengthy courtship, Chick asked me to marry him. I was thunder struck and wasn't expecting a marriage proposal now or ever. Chick still didn't know that I was involved in the sex trade in addition to my day job. I held a regular job in the financial industry and that was where we always met after work. We had had some good times together skiing, hiking, hang gliding and scuba diving. We had been on several trips and only recently started talking about getting a place together. Jill and Rory were very friendly and more often than not, he spent the night at our place and I spent the night with Chick at their place. I still had regulars in the trade and I did a great balancing act, keeping my day and night occupations separate. But now this was a real dilemma for me, and I put off answering him by asking him to give me a couple of weeks to think about it.

"What am I going to do?" I cried to Jill, after we have both came off a night with a couple of johns.

"I don't know, Molly. Do you want to get married and settle down?

"I've never given it much thought. I really never thought I would meet anyone with whom I would want to spend my life. I am not a one man person. At least, I don't think I am. I want very much to be with Chick, Jill, but I don't think I am cut out for marriage. I love the freedom I have and I don't want to give up my lifestyle. I do love him, though."

"Only you can make this decision, Molly. Love like this doesn't happen many times, we both know that. Give it time and really think it through before you rush to an answer."

I called Chick the next day.
"Chick, I have an answer for you, but I am not certain you will want to hear it. I would like to take a hiatus for two months. If at the end of the two months, you still feel the same, then we will get married. There is no doubt in my mind that I love you, but you need to know some things about me before we move in that direction. "
"There is nothing you can tell me, Molly, that will change my mind about us. I love you and I want to spend the rest of my life with you." He sounded disappointed.
"I'm coming over, Molly, and we are going to talk about these mysterious things you keep bringing up." He disconnected our call.

I told him all about what I did at night. I left out my young years and nothing of Moose Jaw. He just sat and gawked at me.
"My gawd, Molly! Have you been doing this all the time we have been going together?" He looked astonished.
"Yes. Please don't say anything more, Chick. I have packed up all my stuff from here and I am going to go home. I will wait to hear from you. All I ask is that you give me an answer. Please don't just disappear on me. I will always understand if you change your mind about marrying me." I fought the tears that threatened to fall.
"I don't understand why you would keep doing this and not tell me, after all the times we have spent together, Molly. How many men have you been with?"
"Don't ask me stuff like that, Chick. I am not going to tell you anything more. I don't believe it will serve any positive purpose. You are going to have to trust that what we have is strong enough to endure a life-long relationship, or it is built on ash and dust and isn't meant to be. I have to leave the decision in your hands."
I had become more emotional that I wanted and I was openly struggling to keep back tears.

"I don't expect you to understand, but I am who I am and I can't change what has happened over the last few months. I think I have known I would have to tell you at some point but I honestly, I never really believed you would want an exclusive permanent relationship. I have never given any thought to marriage, Chick. Women like me aren't often given the opportunity. Please just try to understand. That's all I ask. Let's leave it at that."

I gave him a soft kiss on the cheek and left him standing in his front room. I walked through the door and out of his life. It was now up to him to make a decision. He would either accept or reject me. I could do nothing more, other than to wait to hear from him.

Chapter 59

The days went by quickly, but the nights left emptiness and a gaping hole in my heart. Hours became like an eternity. Each night, after I finished with a date, I felt heaviness in my chest. The pain of separation from Chick left a physical pain and a throbbing ache that never stopped. I knew I would have to let him go if that was the decision he made. I didn't often see Jill because she still saw Rory regularly. They stayed at his place on some nights, so I had space to be alone when I was not working.

One night, Jill came in late after a working date. I had only been home myself for a half an hour. I had taken my shower and I was enjoying a quiet cup of tea in the kitchen when she walked in. Her words startled me.

"Hi, Molly! I didn't expect to find you up so late. Don't you have to work in the morning?"

"Yeah, but I'm going in late because I have a mid-morning meeting that will take a bit of preparation before it starts. I want to do the finishing touches on my presentation at home where it is quiet and I can concentrate with no interruptions.

How did your trick go tonight? I don't see too much of you these days."

I stood and poured some hot water into my cup to heat up the tea that had gone cold.

"I had a good time tonight. He is one of my regulars, so it was an easy one. I enjoy my time with this guy. I have been pretty tied up these days, what with keeping a relationship going with Rory and taking care of business. Things seem to be working out okay, though. I am not certain that Rory is completely comfortable with my business, but it is not like I didn't tell him from the get go what I do. How about you and Chick, have you heard from him since you two parted company?"

She poured a cup of tea from my teapot and poured some boiling water from the kettle into it. She pulled out a chair across the table from me and sat.

"No, it has only been six weeks and I asked him to wait for two months. I tell you, it seems like a lifetime since we spoke. I hope I haven't made a mistake here, Jill. There are times when I ache so badly just thinking about him. I know I love him enough to try to make marriage with him work. If only he can let my past go and see me like he did before I told him that I was a call girl. It is wonderful to be in love like this, even if it is complicated and painful. I know one thing for sure, if he decides to end this relationship I will make damn certain I never fall in love again! I will ask you to dump some cold water over my head, should you see me making any moves in that direction."

The tears slipped out of my eyes in spite of my efforts to shut down the pain I felt in my heart. I swiped my hand under my nose to wipe away all the escaping fluids.

"Aw, Molly, I believe he'll come back. Rory says he is just as miserable as you are. That has to mean something. Why don't you call him, get it over with and find out what his decision is? This is nuts, both of you putting yourselves through this kind of torture."

She reached over and touched my sopping hand and gently rubbed her thumb over it.

"I can't, Jill. I have to leave it in his ball park. He is the one with the problem, not me. If he can't forgive me for not telling him at the beginning of our affair, then I can't do anything to change that. It is not like I deliberately kept it from him. I have never tried to hide what I do. I have been doing this for so many years, I don't even think about how others view it. Why would I and why should it make a difference? I can and have always been able to separate my two lifestyles. Anyway, I need to know the truth from him. I would rather find out now so it is still an easy out. He just has to walk away and not look back. Imagine the mess we would be in if I accepted his proposal, assuming he knew, only to find out later he didn't and he couldn't accept it? It is better this way. It won't be the first time my heart has been broken. I can do this if I have to, Jill. Mark my words, I will survive without him. It's late and I've got that meeting in the morning. I'm going to bed. Thanks for listening. Have a good sleep."

I dumped the rest of my tea in the sink, rinsed my mug and set it in the drainer. I gently patted the top of Jill's head as I passed by.

"I will, Molly. I'm going to have a quick shower and hit the bed myself. Will I see you sometime tomorrow? How about you and me meeting up for dinner after you have finished at the office? I don't have a date until nine-thirty tomorrow night and I am not seeing Rory, so we can spend some time together, if you like. What is your evening like tomorrow?"

"I have a date from six until seven. After that, I am free until ten. I'd love to meet you for dinner, say about seven-thirty?" I lingered in the doorway, waiting for her response. I felt a tightening in my chest as I watched her. She was my dearest friend and I was grateful to have her in my life. We had no secrets and we shared our pain. We were there for one another.

"That'll work. I'll make a reservation at Gray's for seven-thirty and I'll meet you there. Do you want me to order a drink if I am there ahead of you?" She rinsed her mug and set it in the sink.

"Perfect! And if I get there first, I'll order up a drink for you. See you tomorrow, good night."

I felt much better as I walked to my room. My footsteps felt a little lighter than they had for a long time.

"Looking forward to it, Molly, good night." Jill turned out the kitchen light and walked to the bathroom.

Chapter 60

"Whoosh, what a day I have had!" I told Jill as I plunked myself in the seat opposite her. "I can sure use this drink, thanks for ordering. I'm sorry I'm a little late, but my date wanted to talk and talk and talk. You know how it goes. I swear I get more tired from a talking session than from any other. I don't think I will ever understand why some dates just want to talk about stuff when they make an appointment for an hour. Surely they can talk to a shrink for less money and hassle. Mmm! This sure is hitting the spot. I love a scotch over rocks after a long day. How did your day go?"

I sat back and visibly relaxed. I glanced around the restaurant out of habit, looking to see if Chick might be here. This was one of the restaurants we often frequented when we were together. I knew it was one of his favorite places to eat.

"My day went great. I had four appointments; three were unexpected, so I made some big money today. I don't mind johns that aren't interested in doing anything other than talking about stuff that is bothering them. Sometimes though, they creep me out when the topic makes them emotional. I worry they might take their anger or frustration out on me. I really don't get off on being a punching bag for those weirdoes. You look pretty exhausted, tough meeting this morning?" Jill raised her glass in a silent toast. She took a long swallow then sat back, sinking into the soft sofa-like seats.

We chatted, ate our dinner and we were just starting on our second drink when my cell phone rang.

I looked at my call display and saw Chick's cell phone number. I took a deep, shuddering breath and told Jill who was calling and answered my phone.

"Hi, Chick! It's good to hear from you. How have you been? Where are you?" I babbled on, running my sentences together. I was ecstatic to hear his voice.

"I'm at our favorite pub. Are you busy right now, do you have you time to talk?"

"Yes, I am just finishing dinner with Jill." I smiled like a Cheshire cat and Jill laughed at my exuberance..

"How about meeting me here as soon as you are free? I'd like to see you, Molly." He sounded pretty laid back. I didn't know how to read him and I felt apprehensive. I experienced a familiar sinking feeling in my stomach and imagined how devastated I would be if this was goodbye. I knew I wanted to be with him more than anything I had ever wanted in my entire life.

"I can do that. It's eight forty-five now. I can be there in fifteen minutes, but I have to leave by nine forty-five. I have an appointment at ten. Will that work for you?" I closed my eyes and waited for his response.

"Nah, how about meeting me at my place after your appointment? Rory is going to call Jill and see if he can spend the night at your place. I really want to see you. I don't suppose you can cancel your appointments for tonight?"

"I will see what I can do. It's a bit late for me to do that, but I will try." I shrugged my shoulders at Jill in a helpless but hopeful gesture.

"I didn't mean for that to sound sarcastic, Molly, but I really find it hard, knowing what your appointment is about." His voice was quiet. I could sense the hurt in his tone.

"Okay, Chick. I will call you right back."

"What's all that about?" Jill asked.

"He wants to meet with me and wants me to cancel the rest of my appointments for the night. He says Rory is going to call and ask if he can spend the night with you at our place. I don't know if this is our final goodbye or if he has decided to try and accept this part of my life and carry on with our affair. I wish I could read him better over the phone." I dialed the number for my appointment and sighed with relief when it was answered on the second ring.

"Hi Matt, it's Molly. Something very important has come up and I am hoping you will let me off the hook tonight if I promise to make it up to you tomorrow afternoon?" I hastily made my request, trying to keep the anxiety out of my voice.

"Oohh, that sounds intriguing! I guess I can wait until tomorrow, but I will insist you make it up with something very special, if you get my drift?" His voice had a sugary, sweet tone that sent chills down my spine. There were times when I hated what I did and this was one of those times. I liked Matt, but he was one of those johns that made me feel like a sleaze when I was with him.

"Yeah, I get your drift, and I promise you won't be sorry. I will come to your apartment at four forty-five and I will give you an hour of fun and games," I answered.

"You ain't givin' me anything! Let's remember whose payin' here. I am going to be so ready for you. I'll see you then. Bye, Sugar and Spice." I heard the click when he disconnected.

I felt defeated and powerless.

"Crap! I hate being in this position, but I want to find out what Chick wants," I told Jill and I dialed Chick's number.

"Okay, Chick. I'll leave here in ten minutes, so I should be there within the next half an hour. I have cleared the night, so we will have lots of time to talk." I squeezed my eyes and crossed the fingers of my left hand and I looked at Jill. I wanted her approval.

"Thanks, Molly. I'll be waiting for you." He hung up and I explained to Jill what my plans were. In the meantime, her call had come from Rory and the two of them were going to hook up at midnight after all her calls were done. Chick and I would have his place to ourselves for the night.

It was with great trepidation that I walked into the pub. My heart raced when I saw Chick. He really did a number on me. Just seeing him gave my heart an enormous kick-start.

This pub was especially cool. It was like a real Irish pub and was located in an authentic British part of Victoria. The atmosphere was always upbeat, with Celtic music playing in the background. The seats were upholstered in a Kelly green with black and grey patterns all over. The seats and back were padded and very comfortable. The wood around the booths and throughout was a rich mahogany color. The hanging light fixture gave off a soft glow and in the middle of them was a lovely chandelier. The individual attached lights were the shape of tear drops, with a shamrock emblazoned on each one. The bar was well stocked and the bar tenders and wait staff were all dressed in black and white, with a shamrock on the back of their shirts. It was small and cozy with subdued lighting. It was alive with chatter and music. The ambiance was great.

I watched Chick for a brief minute and yearned to know his decision. I knew he was the man I wanted to spend the rest of my life with and I hoped with all of my heart that he felt the same. He was sitting with his feet stretched out in front of him under the booth. He was fiddling with something when he suddenly looked up and caught my eye. The look he gave me was one I will forever cherish. Our eyes locked and emotions smoldered in that one look. I started across the floor and he met me halfway. We embraced and I wanted to kiss the life out of him. I believed he felt the same, because of what he whispered in my ear.

"Let's get out of here. Come home with me right now. We can talk and make love, talk and make love all night. I just want to be with you." I saw the sheen of tears in his eyes.

"I'm with you. I have missed you so much," I said. We joined hands and walked out the door.

"I will follow in my car," I told him. We kissed again and I got into my car and followed him.

After an intense couple of hours of getting reacquainted and enjoying the best face-to-face contact I had ever known, we dragged ourselves out of bed. We went into the living room to talk after making some fresh coffee.

"Gawd, I have missed you, Molly! I want to spend the rest of my life with you. Is there any way we can make it work?"

"I sure hope so. What assurances do you need from me, Chick?" I picked up my coffee and wrapped my hands around the hot mug. I enjoyed the heat that radiated from it. I was cold and frightened and wondered how this was going to play out.

"Well, the main roadblock for me is your night work. Will you consider giving it up completely?" He took a great gulp of his coffee. His eyes darkened to almost black and they filled with warmth and love, I wanted the moment to last. I vacillated, not wanting to break that connection.

"I don't know, Chick. You must have figured out that I have many regular clients that I have been with for a number of years. I can't just stop. Will you give me a few months to let them know I am quitting?"

"Why do you need a few months? Can't you just call each of them and tell them over the phone? I tell you the truth, Molly; I am so damned uncomfortable with this whole thing. I can't handle the thought of you getting it off with other guys. I don't care that there is no emotional connection as you put it. I don't want you with anyone else as long as you and I are together. Jeez, it's not like this is a regular job with regular hours and a boss to whom you have to give some kind of notice. Just bloody quit, if you really want to marry me. You have to do this for me! It makes me crazy just thinking of you in the same room as those jokers." He was up and pacing and getting more and more riled.

"Take it easy! I will do what I can to end each of my connections. How about we set a date for the wedding and I promise I will be through with the trade completely at the end of that time? You don't need to know any more than that. As long as we are together, I promise I will never contact another client after that. I love you more than words can say, Chick. Give me this time to get my life in order." I pulled him down next to me, put my arms around his neck and leaned my forehead on his.

"Okay, Molly. Two months from now we get married after that, this part of your life is finished. I promise I will never bring it up again and I won't ask any questions between now and then. Do what you have to do, but do it within the next two months. No delays. I can't live like this." He kissed me. He barely brushed my lips, but then our kisses deepened until there were no holds barred.

Chapter 61

Our wedding was small and intimate. Neither of us had family close by and we made the decision not to send out invitations to those friends who lived out of town. We wanted to spare them the expense of making the trip. We postponed our honeymoon until after Christmas.

Life took on a normalcy that seemed foreign to me. I was adjusting to it. My only jobs now were with a financial institution and being a good wife.

"Molly, Chick is on line three for you." Nancy, my receptionist at the securities office buzzed me through my intercom.

"Thanks, Nancy. Hi Chick what's up?" I fiddled with my pen while I tried to sort through a bunch of circulars.

"Hi, honey. Nothing in particular, I miss you. How about we dine out tonight and take in a movie after, "Psycho" sounds pretty good?" He sounded a little breathless. Something was going on with him. Don't ask me how I knew. I just did.

"That's a great idea. I'll meet you at our Pub around six fifteen. Will you make the reservations? You know how busy it gets on Friday night. I have to run, Chick. I have a ton of reading to get through and I want to be familiar with it by Monday. I have some big investors coming in and there are some important changes."

Our times together continued to be wonderful.

Chapter 62

Our first trip as husband and wife was a group dive trip to the Virgin Islands. Our destination was a small island called Tortola. It was a quaint little island similar to the one that inspired Robert Louis Stevenson's "Treasure Island." The pink stone buildings in the port were picturesque and unique to this paradise. They were the first objects I saw when we came off the ferry to the island. It was a blistering hot day. We caught a cab to Road Harbor where our sailboat, a beautiful three-hulled boat, was moored. We had hired a crew to work on the sailboat that we had rented for the next month. There were eight of us in the group and we were from all over Canada. We spent the next fifteen days on board this sixty-foot sailboat. This was its maiden voyage. Its blue and white paint glistened in the sun. The sails were pristine white with a beautiful red spinnaker. Even the dishes were color coordinated in blue, white and red. The tabletop was blue and the covering on the seats was red and blue. The teak deck and trim were spotless. It had one main hull and two smaller outrigger hulls. It was very roomy and the bunks were quite comfortable, which surprised me. The quilt on our bed was a gorgeous blue with white dolphins frolicking against a brilliant blue sky with scattered lighter blue cloud. The kitchen area was particularly large. Our cook was only nineteen and lovely to look at. The men in our group were very happy about that little bonus. She was a very good cook and the meals were great.

The boat was fast and smooth and rode the seas with ease. Our captain knew the area around the British Virgin Islands like the back of his hand and he took us into some challenging places. One of the most beautiful was the Baths of Virgin Gorda. Great Harbor was a difficult port to get into, thank heavens for a very capable Captain who was an amazing sailor. We visited many unusual and inaccessible ports, if the Captain had not been very familiar with these waters we would not have been able to dock and explore them. He gave us the opportunity to take over the helm on the open seas, but didn't hesitate to reprimand us if we did not pay attention to his instructions. The weather was marvelous. The Trade Winds were warm and gentle. The seas were an exquisite cerulean and at times seemed a deep indigo. It took a while for us to get used to the sun setting at exactly six o'clock. It was pitch black with zero visibility, so we developed a strict routine of early to bed and early to rise.

We averaged three dives a day and saw some of the most spectacular scenery, both above and below the ocean. Sea Turtles, sharks, coral, and stingrays were just a sample of the abundant sea life.

We got pregnant with Carin on that trip, so the next few years were filled with a different kind of adventure but one we both enjoyed. Carin was a joy in our lives. Chick was a great dad and we spent every weekend together as a family. We hiked, we fished, we skied, and we even managed to go to Hawaii twice and learned to surf. We shared laughter, tears, joy and sadness during those years

Chapter 63

I tried to be open with Carin as she grew and developed, but I never told her anything about my horrible time in Moose Jaw as a young child. I skipped over the bitter teen memories and concentrated on the normal things that I had experienced. I was into track in high school and was a talented sprinter. I represented my school in the track and field competitions four of the years I was there. In the mid nineteen fifties all high schools in greater Vancouver and North Vancouver competed at a large track meet every summer. I was always out to win points for my school. I was a cheerleader for the football team and was a good student and graduated with honors. Those were the times about which we talked and shared, it was enough for me. The B.C. Lions football team came to play in the Canadian Football League in 1954 and many of us who had been cheerleaders in high school hoped to become a cheerleader for the Lions. I lamented on that dream and told of my disappointment in failing to fulfill it. We often discussed my career in the financial industry and left it at that. Chick and I had many disagreements about that. He felt that I should tell her about my years in the trade, but I would not be swayed. I still do not believe Carin needs to know any more about my past than what I have told her. I have not openly lied to her. By the time she was in her teens, our marriage was beginning to crack.

We spent the next five years in a reasonable relationship, but both Chick and I understood we needed to do something to rev things up if we were going to continue on.

If anyone were to ask me when and where things started to go wrong, I would not be able to come up with a definitive response. I didn't blame Chick, because most of the dissatisfaction was mine. I didn't believe that he accepted who I was and I was always seeking assurances from him. He was content with our marriage, with me and with our little family. As I look back, I believe Chick must have found it very difficult to continually try to provide all the love I needed just to survive from day to day, let alone over long years. The energy he must have expended doing so, probably drained him.

We had many arguments over my neediness. I always wanted reassurance that I was a worthwhile person and that he still loved me even after we fought. There were many silent times when I would withdraw and not speak for days. The end came slowly and only after he had given all the time, love and effort he could. Finally, we sat down together and he told me I was too damaged. He said he had nothing more to give and he needed to walk away before he became mired in his aloneness. He had finally come to recognize that there was no way he could continue to answer all my needs. I knew it was over long before he admitted it to himself.

I learned some beautiful lessons from Chick throughout our marriage. One was that I had never known before what it was like to enjoy an intimate, sexual relationship with a man in which my needs or desires were considered. Most johns are like rutting animals that are there solely to satisfy their fantasies. I remember one john telling me that he owned me for the two hours he had paid for my services. From Chick I learned the difference between having sex and making love. He was considerate and I knew he treasured me as a woman, a friend and a companion. He looked after all our needs. I was a stay-at-home mom for Carin's young years and a part of me loved that life. But a part of me yearned for the excitement of being free to go and do what I wanted when I wanted. I wish now I had been more centered and comfortable in my own skin. Hindsight can be a bitter lesson, burgeoned in the throes of regrets and wishes.

I had kept in contact with some of my regular clients, but I never crossed the line and had sex with them. I often met three of them at different times over the years. We talked over coffee or an occasional beer. It was natural for me to turn to my old friends after my marriage failed. I reconnected and stayed on the fringe of the trade and I enjoyed the friendship of many of my old clients. The pleasure I received from those friendships was energizing for me. It was a bonus that they expected nothing but friendship from me and I in turn, expected nothing from them. The majority of my time and energy went to my job in the financial industry. I worked very hard to advance my position. It didn't take me long to work my way to management.

Chapter 64

My biggest shock came after a couple of years had passed. Chick called one day to ask if I would meet him for lunch. We agreed to meet at our favorite pub. I couldn't believe the catch in my throat or how my heartbeat thundered when I spotted him coming in. He had called ahead and ordered a burger, chips and my favorite drink: Scotch on the rocks. Everything seemed perfect and I was flattered that he had remembered.

"Wow! Chick, this is so sweet. I can't believe you haven't forgotten my favorite choice of the menu. You even remembered how I like it prepared. I would have thought the little things like this would have been long forgotten." I reached over and squeezed his hand.

He tentatively pulled it away and patted the back of my hand as it slipped onto the table.

'There is a lot you and I don't know about one another anymore, Molly. The last couple of years have changed who we were together." He took a swallow of his beer and looked away.

"What's up Chick? What is so important we need to meet here? Why couldn't we have this talk on the phone? Why do you want to see me?" I nervously talked and took a gulp of my drink. I was grateful for the way it moistened my dry mouth.

"Why don't we eat first, Molly?" He chewed on a fry he had taken off of my plate. He was still averting any eye contact with me.

"Jeez, I don't think I can eat a thing right now. I have a feeling what you have to say to me is going to hurt like blazes," I whispered. I resisted the urge to cry and chastised myself for being so emotional whenever I was around him.

"I don't know how to say this so it won't be such a shock. I am just going to come right out and say it. I am getting married Molly, and I didn't want you to hear it from anyone other than me." For the first time, he looked into my eyes and I saw the pain and regret reflected back at me.

"Oh Gawd! Oh gawd! Oh my gawd!" I gasped. "I can't breathe, Chick!" I jumped up and ran out onto the patio. I gripped the railing and stared out at the city that I loved so much. The pain I felt was bone deep. I hiccoughed and attempted to stop the sobs that racked my body. He pulled me to him and I jerked away.

"Don't, don't touch me!" I was bereft and traumatized.

"C'mon, Molly! Come here. I need to hold you. You know I can't stand to see you cry. It's worse knowing I am the reason for your anger."

"Anger?" I sputter. "I'm not angry. I'm hurt, grief stricken! Why don't you just pierce my heart with a knife?" I fell against him and wept against his chest.

"You must have known this day would come, Molly. You know how I need someone in my life. Please be happy for me. Don't let anger and sorrow come between us. You and I will always have the memory of the years of love we shared. That will always be with us. I want to move on. We both know we can never recapture what we had. It's been over for us for a long time." He caressed my hair and fondly patted my back. He pulled my head up and leaned his forehead on mine.

"Let's always be friends. Let's remember us and what we had. Can we do that? Will you be happy for me?" he whispered. His warm breath brushed against my cheek.

"Oh, Chick! I will be happy for you, but not today. I know I have no right to cling to you, but I will never be whole again. Give me time to digest this news. Have you told Carin?" I took the hanky he offered, blew my nose and wiped my tears. I was still gasping for air and desperate to gain control of my emotions.

"Yes, she's met Wendy and they both seem to get along fine. Wendy knows they won't be close like you and Carin but we just want her to accept the marriage and be comfortable enough to come and spend time with us. Maybe even take a trip with us some day. We'll see how it all works out. Right now, I only want you both to understand this doesn't change my feelings for you. I love Wendy and I believe we will have a great marriage. We are quite compatible and she is happy and has confidence in herself. She's independent but we have shared some good times together. Her ex-husband is fine, but like you, he too wants time to absorb it all. She has four children. They have all accepted me and made me feel a part of their family." He smiled at me, clasped my hand and led me back into the pub.

"I prepaid the bill, Molly. Will you be okay?" He looked concerned.

"I'll be fine. You know me. I'm a survivor." I smiled weakly.

"I'll walk you back to your car."

"Thanks, Chick."

We kissed each other lightly and said our good byes, and then each of us walked in opposite directions.

Chapter 65

That night, I called Jill and it was like old times. She was happy to hear from me. She was still seeing Rory and considered him to be her significant other. They had kept their relationship humming, as she put it. The years had been good to us both.

"Can we meet for coffee tonight, Jill? I would love to see you." I fiddled anxiously with the zipper on my jacket and hoped she would agree.

"I can't meet with you tonight, Molly. Rory and I have a standing date for dinner and a movie each Friday, but how about tomorrow night? I only have one appointment at five o'clock. Will that work for you?"

Hiding the disappointment in my voice, I replied, "Yeah, that's okay for me. I have no appointments, Jill. I will see you at Gray's, our favorite place. Should I make reservations for six thirty?"

"That'll work. I'll see you then. Looking forward to it, Molly. Gotta run. I see Rory coming in." She quickly hung up.

As it turned out, I had to work late to get some last minute reports ready for an important meeting the next week. The night passed quickly and I fell into an exhausted sleep when I got home.

"Whoa, Jill! You look great! It is so good to see you!" I stood up and clung to her.

"Back atcha, Molly!" she said, hugging me back. She sat across from me.

"So, tell me what went wrong between you and Chick? I always figured the two of you would get back together." She took a sip of the drink I had ordered for her.

"I guess it was a lot of things. You know me and commitment! I can't stick it. I get too scared that I will let friends down and not live up to their expectations." I ran my finger along the rim of my glass, tears filling my eyes.

"You know, Jill, I thought we had it made after the first ten years, but I am not built to hold things together with another person. I miss Chick more than I can say, but he is too bruised in his heart, and I know I am responsible for hurting him. I feel black and blue myself. I need to be alone at times and be able to recoup, even when I am working and meeting with my friends. I won't allow myself to get so attached that I need to see them. I can't explain how it is with me, Jill. I know I am not cut out for any kind of intimate relationship. Lord knows, I tried. And Chick is the one that knows how deeply I failed to meet his needs. He did everything he could to make it work between us. Somehow though, I thought we might get together again and start over." I took a long swallow of my drink and enjoyed the feel of the cold as it soothed my parched, aching throat.

"How is Carin handling it all?" She picked up the menu and glanced through it.

"She seems okay. She still spends time with Chick, but is pretty wrapped up in her studies right now. They have always had a close father daughter relationship. She and he are the best of friends and I know that will always be.

"That's good, Molly. Do you think there is any way you and Chick will be able to remain friends?" She had always had that that dared me to try and dance around her question.

"Absolutely! I will cherish his friendship forever, I hope. Carin had told me he was seeing someone and that they both seemed quite happy together. I had no idea how far along the affair was between them, so I was incredibly shocked and upset when he informed me of their impending marriage plans. But you know, Jill, as long as he and I can remain friends for Carin's sake, I can't ask any more than that from him.

Let's order now, and you can tell me what you have been up to over the past few months. I am sorry I cut myself off from everybody, but

I was determined to further my career and I have achieved that. I am proud of what I have accomplished. After Chick and I separated, I was afraid I might fall back into my old ways and become an escort again. I needed the time to do some soul searching and some healing. I hope you didn't take it as a personal affront?" I smiled and reached over to touch her arm.

"Not at all, Molly. I know you well enough to know you have to go off by yourself to lick your wounds. I am very sorry that things can never work out between you and Chick, but I think I understand what you are saying. You have always had such an inferiority complex and have never felt completely at ease with anyone other than Chick. I can't say I know what you are feeling and how hard the past couple of years have been for you. I can't, because I am not built the same as you. I don't need to prove anything to anyone. I believe I have some good things to offer and I know Rory is very happy to be with me. We have a great time together and I think we will stay together till death parts us. I love him to pieces and he makes no demands on me, except to insist we spend most nights and at least four days of the week together. We bought a great little house outside of town and he understands my need to be independent. I have kept my little apartment for work and I understand and am willing to meet him and make allowances to meet his needs." She squeezed my hand.

"Molly, I'm going to have a big steak with all the trimmings and a black coffee. I am off for the night, so you and I can go for a long walk along the Inner Harbor and you can vent your sorrow and tell me about your plans for the future." She finished her drink and waited expectantly for me to make the next move.

"I'd really like that, Jill. I'll get the check."

After we had eaten our dinner, I picked up the check, dropped the tip onto the table and we both left.

"It is such a warm and blissful night. I love walking along the Inner Harbor when the sun is settling. There are always people drifting along the causeway and I never feel alone when I am here. I am very sad these days. Oh, Jill! I adored Chick. I don't know if I can face the fact that we can only be friends. We had some amazing times together. He was a great guy and I am truly sorry I couldn't be a better wife to him. I am grateful to have known real love, Jill. We were like one. My heart was connected to his. I will always miss him. You and Rory seem to have a great thing going. Are you as happy as you seem?" I asked wistfully, wishing in my heart I was walking and talking with Chick.

Chapter 66

"I am fantastically happy, Molly! The world seems right to me and I believe it is spinning on its axis, just as it should. For me, everything is right where it should be. I'm sorry! That sounds so self-centered, doesn't it? I don't mean it to be, but things have been right for me for a very long time. Rory and I have found the perfect way for our lives to work in sync. He is a great guy too, Molly. He is a good friend to Chick and walked with him over the last couple of years. You know, it has been hard for him too. I am glad he is starting a new chapter in his life, and I know that probably hurts you, but I like him too. I hated to see him so sad and alone. You are a lot stronger than me. I could never have let him go." She held my hand and we swung our arms together as we walked along.

"I am not strong in the way you think. I couldn't handle watching him drift away from me knowing, I couldn't change things. I had no option but to walk away from our marriage. Carin was very angry with me for a while, but over the last few years she now seems to understand. She and Chick will always remain close. Don't think I don't envy her that privilege, but I am glad she is not like me. I will always have a tendency to shut down. I get too scared that I will be rejected and hurt." We talked and walked for a couple of hours.

"We should turn around and go home. I can't think of the future tonight. I need to go home to bed as I have an early appointment in the morning. Thank you so much for tonight, Jill! You are a good friend. I hope you will remember if you ever need me, I will be happy to reciprocate."

Jill spent that night with me and listened to my wracking sobs as I came to terms with the wrenching pain in my heart. I wept all my hurts and moaned aloud until I was drained. I will never forget that long night of talking, walking and weeping in the arms of my dearest friend.

Chapter 67

I couldn't stop the tears that welled up in my eyes as I walked along the trail. It was a sweet time, but it became also full of pain for me. I was not so blind that I didn't remember the times I hated Chick. I hated him for accepting me and always being so understanding. He was always content with the status quo. I will never understand why I took such a chance and married him. Stupid! Stupid! Stupid! I had to acknowledge to myself that I could not relate to anyone long term, because I simply didn't know how. I don't think I have changed that much since then. I have always protected my heart, always been afraid someone would stomp on it. I don't remember ever trusting anyone for any length of time when I was growing up. I was always brought back down to earth when I let myself open my heart up to someone whom I thought I could trust. They never let me forget that I wasn't worth the time or energy needed to make a relationship work. It was no wonder my marriage failed. I needed it to end so I could prove myself right again, to reassert that I was worthless.

Those were long ago years and painful memories mixed in with some fabulous times, shared with my one true love. Chick has been dead for six years now, but I still feel that ache when I think of him. I pray his second marriage gave him the happiness and love he deserved.

Those were my thoughts as I walked my dogs.

"Why am I putting myself through this?" I asked my dogs.

"Get real, Molly, and quit feeling sorry for yourself again! You are the author of your destiny," I chastised myself.

"C'mon, you two, let's go home and get some dinner. I want to sit and vegetate in front of the television tonight. There are a couple of good shows on." I talked aloud to my dogs.

On the following visit with Michael I would tell him all of what happened over the years I was with Chick and the subsequent breakup and how I had moved on. I would explain to him that I had to shoulder most of the blame for our failed marriage. I wasn't ready nor did I have any idea of what an average family looked like from the inside and that I had been too self-centered to be a good wife.

I continued on home preparing in my mind all that I would say to Michael.

Chapter 68

The light was blinking on my answer machine. I listened to a message from Carin and I was to call her back. There was another one from Michael. He wanted me to book an appointment the day after tomorrow. It was too late for me to call his office, so I would try to remember to do so the next morning. I felt a twinge of remorse and some embarrassment by my rude behavior at our last session. He was, after all, a very kind and good friend. I picked up the phone to dial Carin's number.

"Hi Mom! Where have you been? Michael called me hours ago and he seemed a little upset. What's going on now? Are you having problems again?" She rattled on, running her sentences together. "What do you mean, Michael called you? Did he tell you anything? What business is it of yours what happens in my sessions with him? He has no right to call you about anything to do with me." I spat the words out, furious that he had taken this kind of liberty. "Take it easy, Mom. He didn't tell me anything. He is worried, that is all. Good Lord! You are over-reacting just a little, don't you think? Did something happen today to upset you? Did you say something to him that caused him to be concerned enough to call me? For crying out loud, Mom, can't you see we are all just trying to help? You seemed to be settling down and making progress over the past weeks. Please don't be upset with him or me. I thought you were back to your normal self. It is impossible to get a straight answer out of you when you jump to the wrong conclusion. No one has been discussing you. Certainly not Michael and I! You are scaring me again, Mom! I don't want to make any threats, but please calm down and tell me what this outburst is all about. You know he would never betray your confidence. Call me back when we can have a reasonable conversation."

I heard the click in my ear as she hung up the phone.

"Well! I never! Who does she think she is talking to?" I bleat to the dogs.

"I have had all I am going to take"

I slammed down the phone, switched on the television and slumped down in my chair. I had lost my appetite and I sat and glared at the screen, not seeing or hearing anything. I was enraged by Carin's outburst and rude behavior. I sat trying to think of what I could do to smooth things over. I didn't want to get myself into a tizzy that would send me off the deep end again. She knew how hard I had been working with Michael to get through this difficult time. I needed more time to get over the glitch that was stopping me from moving forward. I was too restless to do anything. I put on my coat, snapped the leashes on my dogs, grabbed a flashlight and left, slamming the door behind me. I was infuriated. I stomped down the road and on to the path that leads to the field. I didn't care that it was dark.

I knew I would be able to get myself back on an even keel and Carin would stop her worrying over me, if only I could just figure out how to stop the flood of memories. Gawd! I was scared of having to sell my house and pack up my things. The thought of moving in with a bunch of old people gave me the creeps. I determined not to let that happen.

Chapter 69

I remembered how easily I could talk with Duncan and how he would walk with me and listen to my whining. He always had some words of wisdom for me to cling to and he gave me the tools to work through the problem. I used those tools over the years to come to terms with many issues that seemed gigantic at the time, but which in hindsight became small, insignificant concerns. I remembered one of those lessons.

***

"Duncan! Duncan! I'm so glad you came today. You just came to visit me didn't you? You aren't here to take me to the room are you?" I asked my questions breathlessly, hoping against hope that he was here to take me for a walk as he often did.

"Hold on, Molly! I am here to see your mother for a few minutes, and then I have a couple of hours before I have to tend to some other business. If you can manage to wait ten minutes, I will take you for a walk and we can try to figure out what is so urgent that it can't wait for another time. Is that okay with you, missy? You are hopping around like a jack-in-the-box! Has someone hurt you? Are you in trouble with your mother again?" He put his hands on my shoulders and looked right into my eyes.

"No, I'm not really in trouble, but I have to talk with you. You have to take me away from here so I can ask you stuff. It's real important, Duncan." I held his hand and clung to it.

"Okay, Molly, as soon as I have finished talking with your mother, I will take you out. You can get your things together and wait outside

for me. In the meantime, take it easy. Whatever's bothering you won't end the world, so calm down." He hugged me to his side.
"Thanks, Duncan! I love you so much," I whispered into his tummy.
"I know you do, Molly and I love you just as much." He eased me away and walked down the hall to the kitchen to look for my mother.

I hopped from foot to foot waiting for him to finish his business with her.
"Okay, little grasshopper, let's go for that walk and see if we can solve this crisis." He ran down the porch stairs, took my hand, turned me to him and swung me into his arms.
"You are like a Mexican jumping bean!" he said laughing. He put me down and we walked hand in hand down the road.
"You have to promise not to tell anyone, Duncan. Will you promise please?" I looked up at him pleadingly.
"You know you can tell me anything, Molly and it will stay behind my lips forever, I promise. What's happened to upset you like this?" He looked at me with a worried expression.
"Well, there's this man who my mommy really likes and they do stuff in the basement room that is really bad. My daddy will be very mad when he finds out and he might shoot my mommy when he comes home from the war and finds out how bad she has been. I don't want him mad at me too, so I want to tell him, and then he will know that I don't like what she does, and he will like me and won't hurt me. I know what she does is bad because she shook me really hard when she saw me peeking in and watching them. She told me if I ever told anyone, she would tan my bottom so hard that I wouldn't be able to sit down for a week. I am scared, Duncan. I don't know what I should do. I don't like the man she is with so much. I am afraid of him too. He looked real mad at me when she was shaking me. She slapped me hard on my face and called me a nosy little bitch and said I was always making trouble. I don't make trouble, Duncan. I try to be as quiet as I can when I am near her and I scrunch to make myself small. I want to make myself be invisible

so she can't see me. I know she doesn't like me and sometimes I don't like her either. I want my daddy to like me when he comes home, and I want him to know how bad she is." I rushed through my speech, glancing up at him when I bothered to stop and take a breath. I was relieved to see he was listening intently.

"Well, Molly, I guess you have a pretty hard decision to make here. I remember a similar problem we discussed a while ago." He led me to a bench, sheltered by the trees.

"What do you mean, Duncan?"

"Let's sit down on this bench, Molly."

For the first time, I looked around and noticed we were in the park in a really pretty spot. We seemed to be alone, except for the birds darting from branch to branch and tree to tree. I noticed a black squirrel scamper across the grass and run up a tree.

"We should have brung a picnic, Duncan." I laughed at the squirrel.

"Well, first we need to put to rest this very serious problem of yours, don't you agree?" He helped me up onto the bench and sat next to me. He put his arms over my shoulders affectionately.

"I guess so." My shoulders slumped with the weight of my problem.

"Okay, Molly. Let's go over both the hurdles you are facing. There are two questions here. Do you tell your dad about your mothers' bad behavior, or do you keep it a secret and let your them sort out any problems that come up, once he returns home from the war? So now, ask yourself this question. What good will come of my telling my dad?" He looked at me and waited for my answer.

"He will know I want him to like me and I want him to know how bad she is." I didn't hesitate for a second with my response.

"Okay, that's a fair answer. My other question is, if you keep it a secret, will it cause you any hurt and will it hurt anyone else?" Again he waited for my response.

This time I hesitated as I thought about the question.

"No, not really, I guess. But what if my daddy finds out, and then he finds out I knew and didn't tell him?" I was agitated, thinking about such big issues.

"What if he does, Molly? Do you think he will blame you for your mommy being bad?"

"No, I guess not." I squirmed and looked up at him.

"What do you think is really behind this?" He chucked me under my chin and pulled my face up so he could see my eyes.

"What do you mean, Duncan?"

"Do you think maybe you just want to get your mother into trouble so your daddy will choose you over her?"

I wiggled my dangling feet and shuffled on the bench and turned my face down and stared at my hands.

"I dunno," I whispered.

"I think you do, Molly, and it's okay for you to feel this way. You want your daddy to love you and there's nothing wrong with that. Every little girl wants that. I don't believe you want to get that love by doing something you might regret one day. Maybe he will be very angry with you and hurt, that you would betray your mother. You need to think this through, Molly, really carefully. You don't want it to backfire on you, so you end up being the one he doesn't like. Does this make sense to you, sweetie?" He again pulled my chin up. We sat and looked at each other for what seemed a long time.

"I guess so." I started to cry.

"I don't want to be mean, Duncan, but she is so mean to me." I wailed into his side. I was inconsolable with frustration and hurt.

"I know, I do know what it's like for you, pumpkin and I wish it was different, but you want to be better than that, Molly. You want to be kind and wait for the good things that will come. Trust me." He pulled me onto his lap, held me close to him and lovingly ran his hand down the back of my head.

"Problems like this will solve themselves, Molly. You are too young to understand that now, but one day you will. And you know what?"

"What?" I asked my voice muffled as I leaned into his chest.

"One day this will seem like such a small thing. Problems tend to lose their bigness with time. You mark my words, little one. Do you

want to see if we can find a store near here that sells ice cream or popsicles or maybe even a candy bar?" He wiped my nose with his hanky, kissed my eyes and set me down.
We went in search of a store that sold treats.

***

Chapter 70

That memory was vivid in my mind's eye. How true his words proved to be! Things that seem catastrophic in the moment tend to diminish dramatically with time. Maybe all I needed to do was to take a breath and let time do its thing. I wondered if Michael and Carin would let time deal with all of this turmoil? Were they going to leap in and take over again? Carin might even begin to think about having me sell my house and put me in a home for the elderly? I was babbling to myself.

I started to panic and I felt my heart starting to race.

I carried on a conversation in my mind, and I could hear my words echo in my head.

"Get a grip on yourself! They can't just come and take over your life. They have to have a good reason for that. Oh right! Like that is based on what, Your experience? Think back and remember how many rights you had growing up! Zilch! Nada! None! Yeah, but I was a kid. Kids don't have any say in the way their parents want to treat them. At least, back then they didn't. It was do as I say or else!"

I really could use a friend right now, particularly one who knows all about me and could help me work my way through my fears. Duncan always knew what to say and was always willing to listen and advise me. I have this gaping hole in my heart that has been with me since he went away.

Enough! He is not here, so you better come up with your own way out of this mess.

I snapped the leashes on the dogs. I felt uneasy.

It was pitch black now, but I didn't want to go home in case they were waiting for me. There were still people walking their dogs in the field so I was not frightened of being hurt.

What if Carin and Michael were waiting for me, what could they do? I wished I had thought to bring the phone number of a lawyer I could call for advice. I was starting to freak myself out.

"What was that? Is someone calling my name? Nah! The dogs would bark if someone were that close. Wait! I hear it again. They are calling my name I hear them."

I yanked the leashes and started to run in the opposite direction of the voice. I was heading right into the deep bush. This wasn't right. Who could be after me? I stopped, hidden by the trees and listened for footsteps or voices. I didn't know who would chase me. Surely if I knew them, they would have identified themselves, rather than run after me.

"Good grief! What if it is Carin and Michael and they have the police with them. Maybe they really believe I can't look after myself because of my last outburst. How childish of them! I am entitled to get angry just like anyone else. What of Carin's behavior? I don't ever remember hanging the phone up in her ear without a by your leave, good-bye or anything else. That was extremely rude and out of control. Maybe I should report her! What about Michael? I should report him for contacting Carin without my permission! I am certain that is a breach of my right to privacy! Damn! I wish I had thought about a phone number for a lawyer."

My dog whined and pulled on her leash.

"Hush, Christine. We'll start back in a minute. I have to make certain we are not being followed." I listened but heard nothing except my own breathing and that of my dogs shuffling and snuffling.

"Okay, let's get back on the trail so we can go home." My voice sounded gruff.

The gravel crunched beneath my feet. I felt incredibly vulnerable out here on my own. We kept on the trail, but I was still on my guard in case anyone tried to jump me.

"Hush! Stop!" I snapped at my dogs in a garbled voice.

"Did you hear that? Is that someone coming down the trail?" I peered into the dark, pointing my flashlight straight ahead, trying to discern if someone was approaching. I couldn't see anything and I didn't hear anything. We inched forward once again, but then I pulled up short.

"There it is again, someone is calling my name! Can't you hear it? Of course you can, but you can't tell me, because you are dogs. Lord I am losing it! I truly don't expect you two to answer me. Let's get out of here!"

"If Duncan were here, I know what he would do right now. He would tell me to stand tall and face down my fears."

"Wait! There it is! That same noise again! Someone is on the trail." I heard a chatter of voices and they were calling out to me.

"Christine and Pippa, stay close now!"

I stood still.

"Both Carin and Michael know about this field. They know I come here whenever I need to be alone. If it is them, why can't I see them? Why would they scare me like this? They want to put me in a home, that's why! That way, I won't be causing either of them any more trouble! Both you dogs need to protect me! I don't care if you bite them. Do whatever you have to do to keep them away from me. Don't let them take me away. You hear me? Answer me!" I was caught up in my own nightmare. I was frantic with fear.

Chapter 71

The air felt thick. I gasped, trying to gather my wits, but terror spewed out of me. I could no longer stand. My legs were numb. They refused to hold me and I sank to the ground. My arms were like lead. My mind was riddled with flashing lights. The world around me was spinning. I was caught in a whirlpool tearing at my consciousness. I could not keep my eyes focused. My heartbeat was like a loud rumbling in my ears, adrenaline was blasting through my veins. I could no longer struggle against the vacuum. I wrapped my arms around my chest and curled my knees to meet them. Darkness engulfed me.

"Duncan?" I whispered the words, but they were lost on the breeze and silence was my answer. Memories and wishes pummeled my mind. Light and darkness, soft music and then the harsh notes of violence crashed around me. The air whirled and sucked me into a vortex of darkness and complete silence. Peace at last! That thought, like lightning, passed and was overtaken by chaos and turmoil that thrashed in the depths of the darkness. I reached for the silence, but it escaped my grasp . . . . .

Chapter 72

Far in the distance, words slipped in and out like whispers on the wind.

"Is she Okay?" "What happened?" The voices were far off and strange to my ears.

I struggled to pull into the light, but the weight of the air in my lungs was too heavy. I gasped like a fish out of water and I tried to open my eyes. My eyelids were weighted down with something and I couldn't lift them. I tried to move my arms, but they were too heavy and they remained locked around me. Finally, I released my mind to the darkness and the silence shut out the world.

"Where am I?" This was my next coherent thought. I looked around the strange room and I was immediately panicked.

"What is happening to me? Have I slipped into a time warp?" My last memory was when I was walking in the field. I was now in a bed and I have restraints on my wrists and ankles.

"Help me, somebody please help me!" I screamed as loud as I could. I had obviously been kidnapped and brought here for heaven only knew what.

A strange woman came into my room.

"Be quiet, Molly. You're okay. Michael will be in shortly to see you."

"What do you mean, I am okay? Take these cuffs off of me! Why have you tied me down like this? How long have I been here?" I was thoroughly rattled and combative. I wrestled against the restraints. "Who the hell are you?" I demanded.

"Whoa, hold on, Molly! Settle down!" Michael came into the room. He sat down on the bed and held my hand.

"You're alright, Molly. You have had a severe breakdown, caused by all the stress you have been under." He had a stillness about him that should have helped me feel calm.

"What are you talking about? I am perfectly fine, Michael. What have you done? How long have I freaking been here?"

I was strung as tight as a drum. I thrashed about, trying my damndest to break free of my bindings.

"You're too volatile right now, Molly. I have asked the nurse to give you something to calm you. I'll come back in the morning and answer your questions. In the meantime, try to relax and gather your thoughts. You're safe here. I'll call Carin and let her know that you've come around. She has been here several times. She is very upset." He seemed too laid back, which was infuriating.

"I'll see you in the morning, Molly." Just like that he turned and walked away.

"What's your fricking problem, Michael? Have you lost your bloody mind? What do you bloody well mean, 'the nurse will give me a shot?' What kind of nightmare have you created for me? Don't you walk away from me! Come back here! What's going to happen to me? I want to talk to another doctor. You are no longer my doctor! Do you hear me?" I stopped my tirade when I saw that same woman standing over me with a needle in her hands.

"Get away from me, you stupid hag! You're not sticking that in me!" I yanked on the straps. I even tried gnawing on them. To no avail.

"Take it easy, Molly. You'll feel better once this medicine takes effect. My name is Terry and I'm here to help you. I know you don't believe that right now, but you soon will, dear. Now, take a deep breath. You can't free yourself, so please stop fighting against me. This will hurt more if you keep struggling." She injected me with the drug and then sat on the chair at the side of my bed.

I started to feel the effects of the drug. The blood in my veins felt like sludge. It was as if I could hear it crawling along. My heartbeat was a faint throb and my body felt like it had sunk into the mattress. I pitched and heaved and tossed my head from side to side, desperate to escape the cataleptic shadow trying to overtake me. Black was encroaching on the light. Slowly, slowly I lapsed into obscurity. My voice screamed silent protests.

I began to drift back to the edge of awareness. There was movement in my peripheral vision. I peeked through my half closed eyes and saw a nurse with a food tray.

"Good morning, Molly. It's a little cool out today, but there's a nice blue sky to lift your spirit. How are you feeling, dear?" Honey dripped from her every word and I was tempted to puke all over the bed. She bounced around the room, straightening this and that, shifting some half dead flowers off my bed table and cheerfully set the tray onto it.

"First and foremost, I am not your dear. Secondly, I don't give a rat's ass what color the sky is. Thirdly, I am not eating anything from this God forsaken place. Lastly, you can dance your way right out of here and leave me alone. Before you go, tell me where Michael is. I want a second opinion on why he has imprisoned me here." I turned my face into the pillow and hoped she would remove the tray and herself from my presence.

Helpless rage enveloped me. I started to hyperventilate and searched for a soft place to land. I listened to her take the tray and leave my room. My thoughts were muddled, my mind sluggish and I was unable to think clearly.

"How did this happen? Why can't I make them all realize I am okay? They need to stop filling my veins with those drugs."

I closed my eyes and searched the fog for clarity.

***

I drifted off and my thoughts morphed to a day when Carin, Chick and I went on a day trip. We caught the Blackball Ferry from Victoria to Port Angelus in Washington State. We drove along the Washington coast until we came to Ruby Beach, a favorite haunt of ours where we often dug for razor clams. It was one of those phenomenal days that is seared into my heart. The sky was cobalt blue with the sea to match. The vibrant green of the massive Douglas Firs against the backdrop of the sky was breathtaking. Blue Spruce joined the parade of colors. The mountains hung in the background, regal in their snow-dappled elegance. The tide was far out and it was akin to doing a three-mile hike to reach the ocean. The surf lapped at our ankles, while the three of us gazed across the open water, each of us lost to our own private thoughts.

Carin suddenly jumped and squealed with delight when a clam squirted water onto her leg. We all giggled, knelt on the wet sand and dug feverously to try and catch it. We spent the day catching clams, swimming in the cold salt chuck and lazing in the sun. We put the clams on ice in our ice chest and caught the Anacortes Ferry back home.

I made a pot of fresh New England clam chowder for supper. I always used thick cream with lots of clams, potatoes and onion. It was delicious and, of course, loaded with calories. We heated buns, lathered with butter and enjoyed the sin of lining our arteries with plaque. It was a fabulous day. I had been introduced to clam chowder long ago. I languished in my mind and easily slipped into another time.

***

Duncan had brought a tin of clams over on one of his ordinary visits. We were in the kitchen in the house in Moose Jaw. He was explaining what he was doing and I sat completely enthralled by what he was telling me. I was perched on the edge of the kitchen table, my legs swinging back and forth. My socks hung haphazardly on my ankles, the elastic had long disappeared with too many washings. He and I were alone. I couldn't remember where everyone else was. They were off on an errand, I guess, or simply elsewhere in the house. Duncan was chopping the clams into small pieces and putting them into a pot with water. He was cooking them to make them tender. He continued to explain, and I hung on his every word. He told me the water would become the nectar full of flavor for the chowder. He chopped the potatoes and onions and added them to the tenderized clams. He finished by adding milk and a little more water and let it all simmer slowly. We, of course, couldn't use cream because it was so scarce during the war years. That night, my family, Duncan and I sat down to a dinner of sizzling hot New England clam chowder, hot buttered toast and corn syrup for dessert. It was a night emblazoned in my mind and I have loved clam chowder since that very special day.

***

I hovered on the edge of consciousness, but I could hear a voice somewhere in the confusion that was fogging my brain.
"Molly, can you hear me? Time to wake up! I hear you've been giving Terry a hard time." I recognized Michael's voice as it invaded my space.
I opened my eyes and felt the tears caught on the back of my eyes and felt the dampness on my cheeks. Memories, lost to time, left pain and yet I resented Michael's intrusive words.
"Leave me alone! I just want to lay here until you are ready to release these shackles and let me go home."
"I am going to remove the straps now, Molly and I want you to go with Terry and have a shower. She will bring you to an interview room when you are ready to sit down and talk. The choice is yours. We can do it today or next week, whenever you are ready to cooperate."

"Me willing to cooperate! Who was the one who brought me here and put these freaking restraints on? I am not the one who created this mess. You, my so-called friend and no doubt my daughter, have me trapped here. I am not here by choice. I will have a shower and I will come and talk with you after, but I want you to cease and desist using those mind blurring drugs on me." I sputtered the words, totally humiliated by his scathing comments.

"Good! I'll see you in about a half an hour." He smiled.

"I am in heaven! The shower feels awesome," I told Terry, who was standing just outside the shower stall. I stood and let the water cascade over my body and head. I reveled in the warmth and the heavenly clean smell of the soap. My brutalized brain fought for clarity and lost. Finally I had to get out although I would have stayed under that safe canopy for much longer.

"Hi, Molly! You look a lot better. How do you feel?" Michael was his usual laid-back self.

"Jeez, Michael, how do you think I feel? I am confused, angry and hurt. What about Carin? Am I in jeopardy of being committed here for a long time? What about my dogs? Who's looking after them?"

"Carin and Meagan are looking after them and your house. You don't need to worry about anything right now. Let's just concentrate on getting you better. I want you to talk to me about the house in Moose Jaw. I believe it is critical to my helping you to get well." He picked up his notepaper and pen.

"What about the drugs, will you stop them please? I can't think clearly with that crap in my system."

"We'll reduce the dosage and see how you do. You have been very disoriented and combative since you were admitted, and that makes it dangerous for both you and the nursing staff."

"Okay, thanks, Michael. I'm sorry I've been so much trouble," I mumbled.

"Not to worry, Molly. It's understandable, considering the circumstances under which you were admitted. What do you remember about that night? What caused you to black out and become so traumatized? I believe it is important for you to try and connect to that if you are able?" He jotted down something on his notepaper.

"I will try, Michael, but my thoughts are in chaos. I feel as if I am in some kind of thick fog. My brain seems numb and slothful. I don't remember coming here. I try to grasp at coherent thoughts but they elude me. The more I try to focus, the muddier it gets." I attempted to relate how I was feeling, hoping he would understand it was the drugs that were to blame and not me.

"Tell me about the room, Molly. Remember in our last session you said you couldn't recall much? I want you to go back there today and tell me more about it. I am convinced it holds some significant memories that tie into the flashbacks. What about Duncan? Your mixed feelings about him are bringing some turbulent emotions to the surface."

"Why do you insist on going back to that time?" I snapped at him, squirming in my chair and wringing my hands.

"What is it about that room that makes you so uncomfortable, Molly? I am trying to get to the bottom of your outbursts, so we can put to rest any thoughts that Carin or anyone else might have about your mental stability. The panic attack that put you here was severe. What is so frightening? I can't help you if I don't have all the information. I can't do much when I only get part of your memory. I need the whole picture. The sooner you remember and are willing to share those thoughts, the sooner you will be on the mend."

He leant and took my hands in an effort to comfort me.

"Then accept the fact that I don't want to remember that room and all that happened there. Duncan was my friend and the only one who really cared for me during those years in Moose Jaw. Why can't we just leave it there, why do you have to be so relentless? Do you get some sort of perverted pleasure from hearing about things like that?

"You know me better than that, Molly. I won't take offense to that remark this time, but I hope you think before you speak next time you have such thoughts. Maybe you should consider that's what Carin has been trying to tell you. You tend to blurt out things without giving any thought to the consequences to yourself, or the hurt you might be inflicting with your words."

"Oh, really, if that's what you think then maybe it is time for these sessions to end."

"You really are having problems with me today! Maybe we should back up and look at the reasons for your discomfort." He leant back in his chair.

"Give it up? It seems to me you are the one with the problem. You have tunnel vision and insist on going to places I refuse to take you. I keep telling you, I don't need to go back there! There is no good reason to dig up that crap." I stood and then started to pace.

"Why do you think that, Molly? What is it about those memories that keep you stuck where you are? Help me to understand."

"There is nothing worth remembering. I promised I would never tell and I will keep that promise, Michael."

"Who did you promise?" He looked startled by my words.

"That's none of your business! It's a vow I intend to keep."

"Did you promise Duncan or was it Sadie?"

"What the hell difference does it make who it was? Why can't you just leave it alone?" I was almost hyperventilating.

"Take it easy, Molly! It matters because of the hold it has on you."

"What happened to cause you to change your lifestyle so drastically after so many years?"

"You know the answer to that question! I got married! What is wrong with you today? You seem bent on riling me, so I can't think anymore." My voice was rising.

"Tell me Molly, what happened to change your direction? Once your divorce was final, what kept you from going all the way back to what gave you the security and love you sought and received in that lifestyle?"

"Shut the hell up! I'm out of here, and I doubt I will be back, Michael. Or maybe you can call me when you feel a little more like helping me, rather than churning my insides outside?" I was yelling as I stomped out of the room and through the reception area.

"Find me a new doctor, one that will help and not hinder me. I want out of here now!" I shrieked at an alarmed stranger in the hall.

I heard Michael speak to a Nurse.

"Get Carin on the phone for me."

"Carin's on line one," the voice related to Michael when he pushed the answer button on his intercom.

I crept back to the doorway of his interview room to listen.

"Hello Carin. It's Michael Wilson. Do you have a few minutes to talk with me right now? That's great, Carin, I will see you tomorrow."

I don't know what Carin said to him, but he sounded pleased." I headed back to my room, trying to figure out what the two of them were planning.

The next morning, Terry came in to take me to the interview room.

"Let's go, Molly. Michael wants to see you."

"What for?" I asked sullenly.

"I have no idea, but I am sure his intention is to help you."

"Okay, I'll go this time, but if I have anymore trouble with him, I am going to insist you discharge me from this place."

I was blown away when I walked into the room and saw Carin sitting there. She and Michael were talking with each other.

She had on a blue sweater and navy slacks. She was wearing boots with a two-inch heel. Her curls were loose and bouncing around her face. She has a tendency to bounce her head and wave her hands when she talks.

I glanced down at my attire and was mortified with my dreary green gown, loosely tied over my hospital nightshirt. My slippers were thin-soled pieces of paper that slapped against the floor with each step. My hair was limp from the drugs. My eyes, I felt certain, were dull and lifeless. I dragged myself into the room and sat down in a chair next to Carin and opposite Michael.

"Good morning, Molly," Michael greeted me.

"Hi, Mom. How are you feeling today? It's great to see you up and looking like your old self." Carin smiled and hugged me.

"I'm as good as I can be, considering. What are you doing here?" I asked suspiciously.

"I asked her to come in. I want you both to help one another get over the wall you have erected. It's not doing anyone any good and, in fact, it is making things much more difficult. Carin, why don't you start and explain to your mother what it has been like for you the past few months?" Michael leant back in his chair and put down his pen and paper, waiting for Carin to begin her response.

"Thank you. Michael. I appreciate your inviting me here. Mom, you know I love you and I will do anything to help you, but you need to understand how worried I am for you. I haven't been able to make sense of your behavior lately. I am not sure that putting you in the hospital was the right thing to do."

"Well, I can agree with you on that point," I interrupted with a snide remark.

"Molly, let Carin finish. You'll get an opportunity to tell your side then."

"Mom, we haven't had a reasonable conversation for months. It seems every time I try to talk to you about anything personal, you freak out. I am beside myself trying to figure out what I can do. I believe I have a right to know. After all, you are my mother and we have been open and loving with one another for as long as I can remember. I know you were hurt by that man who beat you up, but your erratic behavior has me at a loss to know how I can help you. I am not your enemy. Your episodes have embarrassed both Meagan and me. You know that it's difficult enough to be a teenager, without having a grandmother creating havoc in public places. Won't you please try to see my side?" Carin jabbered on, barely taking a breath.

Michael interrupted her.

"Slow down, Carin. I understand how you feel. We are doing our best to find some answers for you. I don't have any right now, but I am concerned that Molly is becoming more agitated and I need your help. Molly, can you understand how concerned she is and why?" Michael leaned forward in his chair and directed his question at me.

"Yes, but you continue to talk to me with threats," I replied as calmly as I could. "I am scared to death you are going to put me in a home. Look how easy it was for you to put me here. It is as if I have no rights. I don't even know how I got here and why. I know my behavior hasn't been typical for me, but I am experiencing some memories with which I can't cope. I asked you weeks ago to back off and let me deal with things my way. I thought things were going better, and then, all of a sudden, here I am being treated like a prisoner or a mental patient. How do you think I feel, Carin? Have I ever caused you harm or been a burden to you? I just want you to have some confidence in me. I can't tell you about my flashbacks. They are too difficult for me to discuss. I don't want you to be hurt by knowing more than is necessary. My brain is so muddled with the drugs right now, it is difficult for me to put words together and make sense. Please, dear, let's try to get through this without any more hurt. Give me some time to get back on my feet. I love you very much and I know you love me. We have to trust each other. I can't begin to function as long as your threats are hanging over me." I was twisting a tissue to shreds as I made my plea to my daughter.

"Oh Mom, let's not do this anymore! I will let you and Michael work through things here and we will go from there once he believes you are well enough to be discharged. I won't bring up anything about you moving or making any other changes until we see how you fare." Carin stood up, wiped the tears from her face and leant over to hug me.

Carin turned to Michael, "Of course, I will do anything to help. Just tell me what to do."

"I think you've been very helpful today. Maybe you and your mom can talk about some of your young years. That might help. What do you think, Molly?

"I really don't care to discuss any of that right now, Michael. It has nothing to do with you, Carin, but I feel a deep sadness whenever I remember our times with your dad."

"That's okay, Mom. I agree with you. I want to leave things as they are. You and Michael can work on dealing with whatever it is that is troubling you. I don't want to alienate you anymore. Now, if you don't need me any longer, I would like to go home. I have some work I need to catch up on. I am going to paint the hall and I want to finish with the prep work."

"No problem, Carin. I will talk with you soon. I love you, dear."

Michael shook Carin's hand and walked her to the door.

"Maybe you're right, Carin. I had no idea things were this difficult with you and I am sorry. My intention was not to make things more strained between you and your mother. I will be in touch. Take care!"

He turned to me with that winning smile of his.

"How do you feel, Molly? Was it helpful to have things out in the open between you and Carin? Do you feel more at ease now?"

"Yes, I guess so. At least, I don't need to worry that she might be selling my house while I stay stuck in here."

"I don't believe she ever intended to sell your house out from under you. You do have legal rights. Nothing has changed in that regard. You are here because you had some sort of seizure in the flats when you were walking. Some people called 911. I was brought in when the emergency personnel found my card in your pocket. Thank you for carrying that with you, as per my instructions. You were in and out of consciousness for a few days. When you did come around, you were too disturbed to talk sensibly and we had to restrain you for your own protection. I want you to continue with the reduced drug dose, at least for the next couple of weeks."

"Couple of weeks! How long do you plan on keeping me here?"

"That depends on you, Molly. I think we have done enough today. I am proud of both you and Carin. I am very hopeful things will progress fairly quickly from this point on. Let's not worry about how long it will take. You don't need to be apprehensive about it. Trust me when I tell you I don't believe it will be that long before you are home again. Can you do that?"

"I guess I don't have much choice do I? I will stick it out for a couple more days, but after that I will call a lawyer and find out what my rights are. I do trust you, Michael, but I have to look out for me." I stood up and left.

Back in my room, I began to feel the walls closing in and I started to feel panic creeping up my spine.

"Why do I let them fool me like this? Why don't I have the backbone to stand up to them and demand they let me out of here? I hate being confined like this. I think I might take a little trip. This whole therapy thing is getting way too intense. I don't need to put myself through this nonsense." I love that I can carry on a conversation with myself. No one argues with me. I have control and no one can challenge me. It is too cool! I knew the next session with him would be very difficult. On and on the little voice whispered to me.

"It is hard to go back to a time that I believe is best forgotten. After all, why should I be made to dredge up all that past dirt in front of anyone to see and pull apart? I have all the answers I have ever needed and I don't appreciate Michael or anyone telling me what to do and how to live my life. Oh pshaw! What do you know about it all? I have made up my mind I am going to take a trip and leave all this behind.

"What a grand idea and where might we go and for how long? And oh, by the way, what about Carin and her family? Do you think they might deserve some consideration and maybe even be allowed to offer their opinion on a snap decision such as this?" "Don't you get it? I need to get away and think things through myself and do a little inner cleansing and soul searching. Give me a break! I have made up my mind I am going to go away for a while. Maybe I'll go for six months or even a year. There's this lovely little place in the British Virgin Islands where I spent a few weeks with Chick, my ex-husband. We rented a sailboat and explored all the little islands in the area. We did tons of scuba dives. We swam in the clearest blue water I have ever seen. At six every night, the sun would go down and the stars would light up the blue black sky. It was a time of sheer bliss and I loved every moment of it. I want to go back there to relax and get my life back together."

"I'm with you, babe! If that's what you have decided, then let's get on with it."

Chapter 73

Max, my nurse for this shift, called to take me to the reception area in preparation for my next session with Michael.

"Hi, Molly. How are you doing today? Michael will be along shortly."

"I wonder where Beth is?"

"I'm good, and you?"

"Fine. I love this time of the year. Early fall, when all the colors are vibrant and still full of life, just marking time until that time of cold and rain and rest. The earth absorbing everything until it is time for renewal and the cycle begins again. I love it. Sorry, Molly. I tend to get carried away with my answers sometimes."

"No problem. I enjoy the different seasons too."

"Hi, Molly. Go on in. I will be right with you. I just want to make a cup of tea. May I get you one?"

"Not on your life! I don't know how you can drink tea with canned milk. That is just wrong, Michael! I don't need anything to drink right now, but thanks for the offer."

I turned my nose up at his particular taste in tea.

Chapter 74

"What has your time been like since our last session, Molly?"

"Same old same old, boring and I still feel like a caged animal, doped so it is hard for me to think clearly. How has your time been, Michael?"

"I have a busy week ahead, but to date all is well with me and my time has been very productive. But then, we are here to talk about you and not me." He smiled.

I replied sarcastically, "Right! How foolish of me to think we could just chat over a cup of tea! It's my dime, remember."

He smiled. "I remember! But it's my time."

"Tell me about Duncan, Molly. What is it about him that endears him to you, in light of all the abuse you suffered at his hands?"

"There was no mean spiritedness about Duncan. He was kind in a way most people could not understand. Those who knew him as a man who preferred to engage in sex with children, assumed he was a pervert. As do you. Am I right? He wasn't like my dad. He always apologized when he hurt me and he treated me with gentleness after he was finished with me. He truly loved me, Michael. There is no doubt in my mind about that."

"I don't think he knew the true meaning of love, Molly. He was wrapped up in his own needs and certainly gave no thought to you. He couldn't have cared what damage he was inflicting on you. Not just the physical, but also the emotional trauma it has left in its wake. Surely you see how he has left you with some very deep-rooted confused feelings?

"You don't understand, Michael, you never met him! Have you ever had anyone love you so much, they are willing to die rather than continue to hurt you?" Tears were stinging my eyes.

"I don't believe most of us ever have to make that kind of decision or choice. Did Duncan ever participate in the goings-on in the room in the basement?"

"Yes, at times, but then most of my mother's clients were invited into that place." "Why would they want someone as young as you to know what was going on down there?"

"Because she got big bucks for me and the people there enjoyed watching the interaction between clients. It was a room where sexual acts and ritualistic orgies took place. Most of them had to pay a premium price to be invited into that room. The entrance fee was based on the list of options available to them. Duncan always ensured I was with him when he was given the invitation. I always knew I would be safe with him and that I would even be shielded from watching some of the other participants."

"What a terrible experience for you to endure, Molly! I can understand why you would feel an emotional connection to Duncan, but do you really believe he was acting in your best interest?"

"I don't know. I never gave any of that a thought at the time. I was grateful it was him I was with and not one of the others. Many of them behaved more like rutting animals. Most of them had no feelings for their partner. It was chaotic and the noise was deafening at times. I hated and still do hate that room. I hate all memories attached to it."

"I'm sorry, Molly. I don't mean to put you in a position where you feel cornered. I am just trying to understand your mixed feelings about the room and, above all, Duncan's role in it. It makes me angry to know he would involve you in any way."

"Duncan's only role was that he was a paying customer. He was one of few who had a conscience, and because of the years I spent living in that house, I did become attached to him. I loved him in a different way from the way I loved Chick, but in my childish way, I adored him. Maybe it seems like an unhealthy relationship from your perspective, but you weren't there nor can you offer an opinion how you would have behaved if you had been there. You have no right to sit in judgment of Duncan or me or anyone else for that matter. There was a war on. Men and women took advantage of any kind of emotional outlet available to them. Remember, a number of the clients of the house were in the armed forces and many died and never came back. Emotions ran high and people behaved in ways that probably were not normal for them. I know some of the ones I had to service were brutal and cruel, others were gentle and kind and out of them all, Duncan was the most caring. He taught me many things, Michael, including the value of human companionship in the midst of utter loneliness. He taught me how to speak words out loud so they didn't hurt so much when I thought them silently. He taught me that in the midst of chaos one could find an island of peace and order if one simply remembered a time that was better. He taught me to reach out and hold on to good memories that were strong enough to block out what was taking place in the present. Without him, I don't believe I would have survived those years. So, yes, I did and do still love him and the memory of him."

"You and I share some history, Molly. You came to me to help you through your divorce. I hope you trust me to know I only want to help you now. Many years have gone by since then, but I am still your friend. You must know I won't do anything that will cause you harm. I am not curious about that time of your life for my own perverse pleasure. I want you to see the relationship for what it really was, and not for what you remember it to be. I believe your memory won't allow you to look at the reality of it, because it will mean that even Duncan betrayed you. In fact, he did deceive you more than anyone else, other than your parents."

"How can you sit there and say that? Have you not heard one whit of what I have said? Are you listening at all? Or have you drawn your own conclusions, based on what you believe of deviant behavior? Hear me, and hear me good, Michael! He was kind to me, he loved me more than anyone else in my life and I loved him and let's just leave it at that!" I was distraught at the injustice he was piling on Duncan.

"Okay, Molly. Let's leave it alone right now. Tell me why you stayed out of the sex trade after so many years? If I remember correctly, you told me you had a few regulars that enjoyed your company and you loved to spend time with them. I know you never fully went back to the trade, but you did spend time and you even had a long term relationship with one of them. You held a responsible position in a legitimate occupation and you were well respected in your field. You were single, your daughter was grown and was raising her own family. It seems it was a lifestyle that worked well for you."

"It did, it really did. I met a woman in my place of work who was a Christian and she didn't appreciate my use of profanity and the Lord's name in the same context. She hounded me to death, insisting I cease doing it. Out of respect for her religious beliefs, I stopped and every time I slipped up, she would admonish me. Once we got that behavior straightened out to her satisfaction, she then kept inviting me to her church or some church function. Sometimes, she would give me a book to read, describing the Christian way of life. I became desperate for her to leave me alone. One day, when she was prattling on and on about how I would enjoy this particular function and how it could change my life, I told her I would go to this one church function with her if she promised to stop harassing me. That evening, she and I went to a big church rally and I found myself spellbound by the simple message. The priest's main message was on how we should all love one another and reach out to help those in less fortunate circumstances than ourselves. The rest is history. I became a believer and I eventually gave up all immoral behavior. That included ending my relationship with my male friend. We were living together outside of marriage, and I knew I had to honor my beliefs. Oh, don't get me wrong. I still do many things and say many things of which I am not proud. But I love my church and I love my Christian family who is always there in a crisis, in my every day walk and in the sad and happy times. No matter where I go in the world, I know if I need to I have only to call a church and ask for help, or simply go for fellowship and sustenance. It is a wonderful place in which to be, and I am most grateful to my friend for her persistence. I love and believe in Jesus Christ in the very depths of my soul."

"I agree, Molly. Our love for Jesus is something we share. It is amazing to me how you did a complete one eighty reversal of your life. Have you ever contacted any of the women with whom you worked? How about the men? Your deep connection to some of them lasted over several years. Do you know where any of them are?" Michael settled back to get more comfortable in his chair.

"Oh, my! Yes! I have kept in touch with Martine and we remain good friends. I haven't seen him for many years, but when I go back and visit with my friend Rachelle who lives back east now, I call Martine and we laugh and cry over the many happy and sad memories the years have bequeathed us. One time, when I went back, he and I went to spend a day in Montreal. We visited his lovely little walk-up in which we shared so many nights. It was like turning the clock back when we walked into the front room. I remember the good times very well. I know how that must sound, considering what I did in order to come to know men like Martine, but it was both a wonderful time as well as a horrible time in my life. Martine was unique and he was quite charming as well as handsome, caring and loving in a very special way. I cherish the memories and I cherish him and his friendship."

I continued, "My friend Samantha has been ill for many years, and has aged with great difficulty. She is thin and fragile, I weep each time I visit with her and see how she is wasting away. She married a sweet man who cares for her in every way and I am grateful she found true happiness and even though she suffers physically, I know her heart is at peace and she knows how much her Howard loves her. Another gal I worked with in Vancouver for some years is another dear friend with whom I have stayed connected. We don't see a lot of each other, but when we get together, we share laughter and tears. Some of our recollections send us into peals of laughter that border on hysteria! Oh, Michael, some of it was so much fun and some was right out of a horror movie. The early years of my life I would love to forget entirely, but the years between twenty and forty were filled with mixed adventures. My dearest friend, Jill, died a few years ago and her significant other, Rory has passed as well. So, in answer to your question, I do know where several of my peers are and, of course, many are dead and gone. I never repeated a bad date and I will always be grateful to Bud for his careful scrutiny of my clients. Granted some nastiness slipped through the cracks, but he did well and never did he make the same mistake twice. It was a different world, and a different time with some truly interesting people making up the canvas. The colors, vibrant at times, sometimes soft and glorious and others, just plain ugly, but together they make the whole, and I am who I am today because of where my journey took me.

I now have a ministry where I work with sex trade workers both on the streets and in escort agencies, and I love what I do. I have met some amazing women and seen many of them turn their lives around and are today living and honoring Christian values. I have kept in touch with all of them and I enjoy watching their lives go forward in such positive ways. It makes my heart sing with the joy of it. I know I would not be able to do this work if it was not for my own past. I know what it is like to endure deep and lasting emotional and physical pain at the hands of others. I pray I never forget that no matter what life hands us, we can overcome and we can be good citizens. I value my independence and freedom. I want to be able to come and go as I please. Is that so wrong?" My agitation was beginning to show.

Chapter 75

"There's nothing wrong with those thoughts at all, but I think it would be a good idea to sort out the feelings that overtake your logical thinking. Those are the ones that cause you to over-react to situations and things people say and do. Don't you agree?" Michael responded.

"Of course, it is just that I don't understand why we can't get off of this merry-go-round we are on. You wanting to delve into the intricacies of my past but I just want to get on with my life. Can we at least come to a meeting of the minds in this regard?"

"We absolutely can do that, Molly. I will accept and do all I can to help you to get on with your life, but first I need you to explain to me in detail, why you are so protective and willing to defend Duncan. Logically, it makes no sense for you to take this stand."

"I do so because, as I have told you over and over again, he loved me as no other in my life at a time when I really needed someone to be there for me. He helped me, time and again, to work through the bad things that were happening."

"Tell me, Molly, did you ever find out what happened to Sadie? Did you ever contact her or locate her after you left Moose Jaw?"

"No, I never did. I have no idea what happened to her. The last I remember was her going down to the basement and I never saw her come out. I know when I was taken downstairs about fifteen minutes after I saw her go down, there was a lot of noise and confusion in the room when they took me in. Some of them were crying and wailing, others were scurrying around trying to get dressed and out of there. Others were cleaning the table and the floor area around the table.

I have never really been able to figure out what was going on, and I was always too scared to think of anyone or anything whenever I was taken to that room. I can't remember the details of that night. I only know I never heard from her, nor did I ever see her again. No one was willing to talk about her that much from that day forward, and no one else seemed any wiser than I. For all I knew, she had quit and gone back to her home or wherever she came from. I don't remember her ever telling me much about her life before she came to work for my mother. As an adult, I shudder to think what might have taken place in that room."

"Do you think she may have died that night?"

"I don't honestly know. If she did, I don't know what they did with her or how they got her out of the house. I never saw anything that would make me think she was bodily removed in any way. I always wondered why she never said good-bye, but then, she could have been fired and kicked out by my mother. I don't know the answers to any of your questions about that night, and I am not prepared to make any guesses so many years later. Most, if not all, of the people involved at that time are dead and buried, so it doesn't matter one way or another."

"It does though, Molly. What of her family and friends? Don't you think they deserve to know what happened to her?"

"For crying out loud!" I yelled, "Don't you ever hear what I say to you? I don't know that she didn't go home. I don't know what happened to her!"

"You're right! There really is no way of finding out anything about that night. I am very concerned, though, that something terrible might have happened to her."

"We don't know, Michael, and we will never know, because there is no way to find out. She, like the others, just appeared one day to apply for a position in my mother's house. I don't recall any of them talking of the time before they came. Sad as it is, we will never know the truth."

"Do you remember if Duncan was there that night? Why were you taken to the room? I understood you to tell me you were only taken there when a client wanted to meet with you there and that it cost quite a bit more for that kind of service?"

"It was very expensive for anyone to be allowed into that room and almost three times as much for my dates to take place in there. I abhorred that room and would beg my mother not to make me go there. They were all perverted and there was too much booze, swearing and raw sex happening there. I was always sick to my stomach when I went in there. Duncan was there that night and so was Roger. I don't remember who I was with, but I remember Duncan was different after that night."

"In what way was he different?"

"I don't know if I can explain. He seemed sadder and quieter. He didn't seem to enjoy the company of anyone else, except for me. After that, he rarely came early and had a drink with his other friends in the house. He never joked or played around with me like he used to. He just wanted to go to my special room and we would talk about the war and how it changed people in very bad ways sometimes. He would whisper warnings to me to never let down my guard and always make sure I was never alone in the basement room. I told him there were always some people there when I was taken there and I reiterated that I wished no one else was there because I was always so embarrassed and ashamed of the things I was expected to do. He became almost hysterical and grabbed my arm and made me promise I would always make sure one of the women from the house went with me into the room, even if it meant my making a big scene. I was to always remember and keep my promise to him."

"What did you do or say?" Michael asked.

"Of course, I promised him what he asked and I was glad to do it. It was such a freaky place."

"Where is Duncan now? Have you ever seen him or heard from him over the years?"

"Of course not! I don't believe in ghosts do you?" I snickered.

"No, I don't, but that's not what I asked. Do you know for certain that he is dead and if so, then you must have had some contact with him over the years."

"Michael, he died those many years ago, before I left Moose Jaw."

"What?" Michael's jaw dropped in total awe and confusion as he struggled with this information.

I sat back in my chair and fiddled with my fingernails, thinking I should get them filed and polished soon, certainly before I went on my trip.

"Molly, you never told me he died long ago! What happened? Was he killed in battle? How did you find out and why have we never talked of this before today? He was a major player in your life and you casually throw that out today! Why?" Michael shot his questions in rapid fire.

"You never asked, for crying out loud! You have been so busy putting him down and insinuating he was no good and that his treatment of me was abhorrent, I didn't think it would make any difference one way or another. I assumed you would be happy he was dead and I didn't want to make you happy with that news. It is just one more memory that I want to keep buried."

"I can't believe we have never uncovered this information! Tell me about it what happened and how did you find out?"

"I was there. I did it."

"What!" he gasped?

"I said, 'I was there and I did it.'"

"I heard what you said, but what happened? I thought you loved him and he loved you? Those are your words, Molly, and not mine, nor do I believe for one moment that they have a ring of truth, if all that you have told me about Duncan is true." He was almost falling off his chair.

"For the love of God," he continued, "tell me what happened!"

"Jeez! Michael, this happened years ago! Why are you getting so bent out of shape now?"

"Just tell me what happened, will you?"

Tears were stinging my eyes as I whispered, "I don't know if I can."

The reality and impact of that memory was unbearable.

"I did love him, Michael. And he loved me, more than you can know. I am afraid to tell you what happened that day."

Tears streamed down my face and I slapped angrily at them. Here I was again, annoyed that I couldn't control my emotions and I couldn't keep my mouth shut. I believe that some memories should not be shared and this was one of them. I wanted it lost to everyone but me.

"I won't judge you. Whatever happened that day is important to your getting better, Molly. It must have been a traumatic and soul-wrenching experience for you." He wrapped his hand around my clenched fist.

"Take your time, close your eyes and try to picture that day and what led to his death." He was more composed.

"Oh, sure! I'll just relax here, while I tell you about the worst day of my life!" My words dripped with sarcasm.

"Help me here, Molly, I am incredibly upset with what you are saying. Please continue." He wiped the sweat off his forehead. Maybe he was not quite as unruffled as I thought.

"It was an ordinary day. My mother had told me Duncan was coming for me and I was to be ready for him. I was to get prepared in the usual way, you know, bath, hair braiding put on the clothes he had specified to her when he called. I was of mixed feelings, knowing what was ahead. I was excited at the prospect of seeing him and talking with him once we were finished the date part. He seemed very sad when he took me up to the room. I can see it all so clearly and I can hear his words and see the sadness in his eyes." I began to sob, recalling and repeating the conversation between Duncan and me.

***

Chapter 76

"Come here, Molly. I've missed you the last couple of weeks. How have you been? Has there been any excitement in the house lately?" Duncan was sitting on the edge of the bed.

"Not really. Sadie is still gone and no one knows where she went. Do you, Duncan?"

"No, I don't. Maybe she wanted a change and moved to some other place to make a new start." He stared at his hands that were folded in his lap.

"I miss her and wish she would write or something," I sighed.

"Let's not talk about Sadie. Come here and sit next to me and let me look at you for a while before we get down to business. You look so sweet in that frilly dress and you are growing like a weed. We'll soon need to buy you a bigger dress again. I wish little girls didn't grow up so quickly."

"It takes a long time to grow up, Duncan. I can hardly wait to be big and I won't have to have anyone look after me and I won't have to do what anyone says, because I will look after myself. I'm still little, but I'm going to be smart when I grow up, and I am never going to do anything I don't want to ever again."

"Ah! But growing up comes so quickly. Life slips by and the years will have passed before you know it, Molly. Remember to fill every day with something good. Enjoy your life when you get older, live each day like it is your last. You're still too young to appreciate the freedom to choose and to dream big dreams, but when that day comes, I hope you will live out each of your dreams.

"I have dreams now, Duncan. I am going to be a really good surgeon. I will make a lot of money and I will be very famous."

"You've earned it, my pet! Now come over here and sit on my lap. Let's take this pretty little dress off you."

By this time, he was crying uncontrollably.

"What's wrong, Duncan? Why are you crying? I don't want you to be sad. Are you sad because I am going away and we won't see each other here again? Maybe you will be moved to Mossbank too. That would be good, wouldn't it?"

"It's okay, baby, it's not you that is making me feel sad. C'mon up on my lap. I want to hold you close to me. Have you ever seen a gun, Molly?"

"I don't think so. Not a real one, in person. I have seen pictures of them in comic books. Why?"

"This is a gun, Molly. I don't want you to be afraid today, but don't ever pick up a real gun, unless you intend to use it. Before you do that, make sure you know how to use it. Be sure and take some lessons and once you have mastered it, always keep up with your target practice at gun ranges. Promise me you will always remember the things I'm telling you today."

"I promise, Duncan, but why have you brought a gun here? Are you going to teach me how to use it, because we don't have anywhere where we can practice? Mommy will be really mad if you shoot in her house. We might break something or the noise will scare her. Don't you think?"

"I know. Now I don't want you to worry about any of that. I would like you to do as I say. Do you know I love you?"

"Yes, I know and I love you too." He was getting upset.

"Always remember how much I love you. I love you too much to keep doing bad things to you. I know you are going away, but there will be other children and I know I can't stop, so we have to do this today. It's not your fault, Molly. You are an innocent, please remember that. I wish I could watch you grow into a young woman. I hope you'll remember all the good things we shared and forget the bad ones. Do you think you can do that?"

"Sure! But where are you going?" I was distraught and scared by his conversation.

"I don't know for sure, but I hope it's a place like heaven." He was weeping, taking great gulps of air.

"Duncan! You're scaring me! Why are you doing this? I don't like the gun. Can you put it away, please and maybe you should lie down so you don't feel so bad."

"I'm sorry, Molly. I don't mean to scare you." He lifted and turned me to face him on his lap.

"See how I hold the gun, Molly? I have my finger on this bar which is called the 'trigger.' When I squeeze it, the gun fires a bullet out of the front of the barrel. Remember this, always. No one will ever love you as much as I." Duncan was shaking and blubbering, and I was mystified and terrified.

***

Chapter 77

I looked around the room and Michael was sitting in front of me. I realized I had been remembering each moment of that day and I felt the terror of the memory so close in my head.

"Michael, I can't do this! I can't go back over it!" I was clutching at my throat and gasping for breath.

"You're doing fine! Tell me the rest of it." Michael reached over and took my shaking hand in his.

"I'm cold. I don't want to do this." My whole body was shaking.

"You're okay, Molly. You're safe here. You can't stop now. Tell me the rest of it. I know you can do it. Take a couple of deep breaths." Michael's voice was calm and reassuring. I heard the tremor and terror in my own voice as I continued to tell him what happened.

"He put the barrel in his mouth and we pulled the trigger. The noise was deafening, my ears were ringing and I screamed and screamed. I fell on top of him when he fell back onto the bed. Blood was everywhere. It was warm and sticky. I was covered in it.

"I can see it, Michael. It is all over me!"

I screamed frantically, trying to rub the blood off of me.

"The smell permeated around me! It was a sweet, metallic smell, mixed with a harsh sharp one. The whole top of his head seemed to be gone. There was tissue and bone spread on the walls and bed and his blood was everywhere. It was my fault. I remember all the chaos that followed. My mother and the other people in the house were screaming and crying. The emergency vehicles arrived with sirens wailing. Strangers, medical people, police rushed into the house. It was like looking through a window somewhere else. It blurred into a reality I couldn't bear to feel."

"I let out a prolonged high-pitched cry of pain. I was lost to reality. I needed him to be alive so he could tell me what to do with the agonizing pain that now ripped at my heart. No one else could soothe my aches the way Duncan could. I couldn't let him be dead."

I collapsed under the horror of relating the story. I writhed and scraped at my skin.
I moaned and gasped and screamed! I am suffocating, Michael! Help me please, dear God help me! I can't feel my bones anymore!"
Liquid was pouring out of every orifice on my face. My body, too, was drenched in perspiration with the emotional upheaval of the relived trauma. I couldn't bear to feel the horrific memories tied to it.

Michael held me tightly, as the deep wrenching sobs released all of my pent-up feelings.
"Let it all out, Molly," he whispered, tears streaming down his own face.
I didn't see him push a button to summon a nurse. She came in with an injection that took me out of my agony. Sleep, soothing nothingness captured my soul and silenced my grief-filled cries.

I could not stop the anguish of what I had done. I cried inconsolably between drug-induced waking and sleeping. I could find no comfort in the light of day. I surrendered to the darkness of sleep. I heard in the distance Michael's and Carin's soft, caring words. Their gentle touch was like a burn to my skin, so raw with the torture of memory. I refused to stay in the present and continued to seek the past in an attempt to erase the memory of the loss of my dearest friend. In that darkness, I searched for reason and answers but of course, there were none. He chose death and made me a partner with his deep sorrow and inability to face his demons.

I finally came to realize it was a time of horror and undeniable suffering. It was a time when there was no reason. It was a time, perhaps, that Duncan knew was coming to an end, and he had fallen into a hell of his own making and could not go forward.

I awoke one morning and embraced the sunlight as it poured through my window. I was ready to walk in the truth of who I was now. I knew I could survive. I knew I was strong enough to face the world I had created for myself.

Chapter78

"Molly is doing well these days, don't you agree, Michael?" Terry asked, as she was straightening my bed.

She had been my main nurse throughout my stay.

"Yes, I will be releasing her in the next couple of days." Michael looked up from writing his notes in a patient chart.

"What happened to put her in such a tailspin? She's been consumed by sorrow for the past four days. I swear she could hear and see sometimes. I tried to speak to her, but she refused to even acknowledge I was there. I could hear her mumble to herself through the tears. I was honestly afraid, and was beginning to wonder if she would ever come back to us." Terry sat down and engaged Michael in an earnest conversation, sincerely wanting to get some answers.

I lay in my bed, feigning sleep, listening to their conversation. I remembered Duncan once told me it was not good to listen, but if I did accidentally hear something that I wasn't supposed to, I was to keep what I heard a secret.

"It is a simple case of PTS. When she was assaulted, her history of abuse reared its ugly head and spun her back to her early childhood days. I knew if I could make her relive the one memory that seemed to have her stuck in her past, it would open the floodgates and bring it all into the fore-front. I prayed that would allow her to move forward and get on with her life. The mind is a most powerful thing and it is crucial we understand how fragile the balance is.

"Yeah, you've got that right! You know, she's talking about taking some trip for a year? Go figure! She's seventy four years old, for crying out loud!" Terry chuckled and left.

A couple of days later, Michael told me he was discharging me.

Max, another of my nurses, brought Carin into my room.

"Carin is here, Molly. Are you ready to go? Are you sure you have packed everything?"

"I'm ready, Max. Thanks for everything you did for me and thanks for your kindness. Say goodbye to those who are off today, and give them my regards"

I hugged him, tears stinging my eyes. I knew I would probably never see him again. In a way, I knew I would miss the sanctuary of this place and the protective shelter it had provided. My dear friends from my knitting group were standing with me.

Betsy smiled and whispered, "Tea at my place tomorrow at 2:00PM. Be there and don't be late. Hi Carin we were just leaving, we are all very happy you and Molly have come through this."

"Isn't it wonderful how these old friends have stayed together and supported each other for so many years. I envy them and hope when I am their age I have some dear friends like them." Carin smiled and directed her comments to Max.

"Let's go, Mom." Carin put her arms around my shoulders and we walked out together, leaving Bill to pick up my belongings. Max followed us to the front door and stood on the steps waving as we drove away.

With mixed emotions, I turned back, smiled and waved to him from the car.

Epilogue

I lie on the deck of the sailboat as we slip along the glass smooth sea. The sun blazes, caught in a clear blue sky that stretches as far as my eyes can see. We are looking for a passage into a small inlet that leads to a beautiful little island with sand as white and clean as new fallen snow. I remember it all so well. Chick and I had spent two months here many years ago, exploring every nook and cranny around Tortola. I plan to spend at least a year here. The first six months I will rest . . . *and remember . . . .*